Let No One Deceive You

Confronting the Critics of Revival

Other Books by Michael L. Brown

From Holy Laughter to Holy Fire:
America on the Edge of Revival

Israel's Divine Healer
(Studies in Old Testament Biblical Theology)

It's Time to Rock the Boat:
A Call to God's People to Rise Up and
Preach a Confrontational Gospel

Our Hands Are Stained With Blood:
The Tragic Story of the "Church" and the Jewish People

Whatever Happened to the Power of God:
Is the Charismatic Church Slain in the Spirit
or Down for the Count?

How Saved Are We?

The End of the American Gospel Enterprise

Compassionate Father or Consuming Fire?
Who Is the God of the Old Testament?

For information on ICN Ministries, or for a listing of other books and tapes by Michael L. Brown, write to:

ICN Ministries
8594 Hwy 98W
Pensacola, FL 32506
Phone: 904-458-6424
FAX: 904-458-1828
E-mail: RevivalNow@msn.com

Let No One Deceive You

Confronting the Critics of Revival

Michael L. Brown

Revival Press

An Imprint of
Destiny Image® **Publishers, Inc.**
P.O. Box 310
Shippensburg, PA 17257-0310

ISBN 1-56043-693-X

For Worldwide Distribution
Printed in the U.S.A.

This book and all other Destiny Image, Revival Press,
and Treasure House books are available
at Christian bookstores and distributors worldwide.

For a U.S. bookstore nearest you, call **1-800-722-6774**.
For more information on foreign distributors, call **717-532-3040**.
Or reach us on the Internet: **http://www.reapernet.com**

Check out the Brownsville website:
http://www.brownsville-revival.org

Dedication

*To everyone who serves so faithfully
and sacrificially in the Brownsville Revival,
laboring day and night for the Lord and for the lost;
to every volunteer, staff member,
ministry team member, and leader:*

This is for you!

Contents

Preface

For the last 15 years, the message of repentance and the promise of revival have been the dominant themes of my life and ministry. I have read about revival, written about revival, preached about revival, prayed for revival, fasted for revival, wept for revival, and experienced personal revival. But I have longed to see a real visitation, a bona fide national awakening in our day, a *corporate revival.* After much heart-searching in the 1980's ("Will God send revival to us, or is it too late for our nation?"), I became convinced that He would, indeed, visit us again, and I was encouraged by the growing spiritual hunger among leaders and believers around the world. Instead of strutting and boasting, leaders were falling on their faces and crying out for mercy, even coming together for city-wide prayer meetings and times of repentance and confession. These were wonderful signs!

In 1993, I became convinced that this longed-for visitation could be on the immediate horizon and that there would be two primary roadblocks that would stand in its way: a critical, religious, faultfinding spirit that would oppose revival in our day, just as every past revival had its staunch critics and opposers; and, on the opposite side of the spectrum, a superficial sensationalism that focused on manifestations and experiences instead of focusing on Jesus, holiness of heart, and reaping the harvest. It was to address those issues that I wrote *From Holy Laughter to Holy Fire: America on the Edge of Revival.* (Most of the book was written in 1994, with two new chapters added in 1996.) Anyone reading *Holy Fire* will see how things have played out: As real revival has broken out in churches, college campuses, and homes over these last two years, the critics have come out in force while, on the flip side, others have been content to merely frolic in the river as the world plummets headlong to hell. Having spent years addressing our desperate need for revival in the Church, I feel deeply burdened to address the critics now that revival is beginning to sweep the land, and now that the critics are speaking even more loudly.

But why even bother with those who resist a true move of God? Does the Spirit of God need to be defended? Won't a revival speak for itself? And anyway, aren't we called to bless those who curse us?

Let me answer these questions briefly. First, true revival does not need to be defended. What God births He will back, and the fruit will speak for itself. So, this book is not defensive. Second, this book is not vindictive. Even if brothers and sisters went so far as to "curse" revival leaders, that would not mean that we should curse them in response. Throughout the pages of this book, I appeal to the critics to come and join us in the harvest fields. On the other hand, the fact that we reach out to the critics does not mean that we should not rebuke them and call them to repentance, answering them decisively when necessary. This book has been written to interact with the critics as well as to answer, refute, and, when necessary, rebuke them. But I want to make it perfectly clear that this book deals with biblical and theological issues, not personalities or groups. I have made efforts to communicate with almost every single critic to whom I refer in *Let No One Deceive You*, and, whenever possible, I have carefully summarized their views, rather than singling them out by name. I did this because I did not want to embarrass them, since I am sure that many will live to regret their harsh criticisms of a true work of the Spirit. Still, the refutation of their erroneous positions had to be clear and emphatic, always going back to the Word. (You will notice far more serious treatment of key Scriptures throughout this book than you will find in a great number of the publications of the revival critics.)

Some people would say that if you respond to the critics you give them credibility and exposure, when, in fact, many of them are unknown outside of an Internet web site (how true this is!) or a small mailing list of a few thousand people. Unfortunately, just like bad news and gossip often spread like cancer, the words of the critics spread, bringing confusion to many. So, even though some of the critics addressed are virtually "ministry nobodies" in their home cities and countries, they have provided a platform for themselves through the Internet or the airwaves, and they need to be refuted. False reports about the current revival have been spread (some unintentionally, some quite intentionally), misleading information has been disseminated, rumors have swirled, misunderstanding has been rife...it's time the truth be told!

Of course, if you concentrate on the attacks of the critics you can become defensive and lose your spiritual focus, you can become polluted and tainted by all the negative things you hear, and you can get drawn into controversy. But, if you don't respond to the critics you seem to have no answer for their charges, you allow innocent believers to become discouraged and misled, and you fail to warn and refute the critics themselves. I trust that, by God's grace, a proper balance has been struck here, and by providing hungry believers and serious readers with an antidote for the critics of revival, we can press in and press on, maximizing these glorious days of visitation.

In this light, some critics might find it interesting to know that, as soon as the Lord called me to become part of the leadership team in the Brownsville Revival in Pensacola, Florida, I began to read books like Charles Finney's *Reflections on Revival* (where, 20 years after the first season of powerful revivals that he experienced, he pointed out faults and shortcomings in present revivals as well as mistakes made in the past) and Iain Murray's *Revivals and Revivalism* (critical of the whole "revivalism" movement). I did this to learn from the mistakes and criticisms of others, seeing that only a fool would make himself impervious to correction and reproof. In fact, my first week visiting Brownsville, my friend Steve Hill, the evangelist whose preaching spearheads the revival, took me aside and asked, "Do you have any concerns or corrections or criticisms?" To this day, when a letter is sent to the leaders that seems to raise a valid concern, we circulate it among ourselves and, when necessary, discuss it. And as seasoned leaders visit the revival, we are careful to ask them, time permitting, for any thoughts they may have for us, always willing to prayerfully consider their input. I still await such constructive, substantive input from the critics! To date, I have been sadly disappointed by the lack of substance in most of their attacks, and—this is truly pathetic—by the venom in *some* of their words. (Thank God for those who can disagree without being disagreeable, on both sides of the fence!)

Again, I make an appeal to all critics of the current revival and to all those who have been influenced by the critics: Read this book carefully and prayerfully (with Bible in hand!), and be open to the possibility that revival really is here, and that God is more than ready to use *you* to help further and promote this wonderful work.

Two last words of clarification: 1) Whenever I refer to "the revival" or "the current revival" throughout this book, I am referring to the repentance-based, evangelistically driven, holiness-stressing revival similar in emphasis to the Brownsville Revival, but certainly not limited to Brownsville. A similar move of the Spirit has been taking place for several years now, and it has impacted both Baptists and Pentecostals, colleges and churches, Americans and believers from many nations. As for Brownsville itself, revival fires are spreading from here throughout the world, but there are many different ways that revival will come, many of them *very* different in style from Brownsville. 2) I cannot speak about other recent renewal movements, since I have not been personally involved with either the movements themselves or the leaders of those movements. (This is not to be critical; rather it is to say that that this is not what this book is about, nor am I qualified to address those issues because of lack of firsthand participation.) However, where the criticisms of a recent renewal movement also apply to the current revival, I have sought to answer the questions and respond to the charges. In that way, I pray that this book will be profitable to all those who have been touched by the Lord in Heaven-sent renewal and revival in recent years, as well as to those who have been injured or confused through so-called renewal and revival during this time.

Although the ideas for this book germinated in my heart for the last six months of 1996, the release to write did not come fully until January 31st of 1997 (see Chapter Two for the background), and so, virtually the entire book was written from February to May, all the while laboring in the revival itself for about 40 hours each week. The endnotes merely hint at the scholarship that undergirds the book itself, which has intentionally been written with simplicity and clarity. If the endnotes are a distraction to you, read the chapters through and check out the notes later; others can utilize the full arsenal of information as they read. The reason for the special appendix is stated in the first endnote to the appendix.

When I wrote the final words to Chapter Fourteen at 3:30 a.m. on May 14th, suddenly, I began to cry. At last, after writing about the *coming* revival for years, I was writing about the *current* revival. The Lord knows that this is the hour so many of us have been longing for, for so many years. (How this applies to my dear wife Nancy, who has shed buckets of tears for revival and the glory of God.) Now that revival has begun, I urge you with all my heart: Don't miss out! This is *your* hour of visitation.

A penny biography of Mr. Moody sold widely in the London streets that spring [of 1875]. Everything that could be done to counteract his influence and prejudice the public against him was attempted by certain papers. Londoners were told that, "judged by the low standard of an American ranter, Mr. Moody is a third-rate star." His reading of Scripture was severely blamed. "Mr. Moody, with a jocular familiarity which painfully jarred on our sense of the reverential, translated freely passages of the Bible into the American vernacular. The grand, simple stories of Holy Writ were thus parodied and burlesqued." But in spite of all the hostility of the press, it soon became manifest, not only that the "common people heard him gladly," but that society itself was moved and deeply impressed by his preaching. One of the first to attend the meetings was Lord Cairns, then Lord Chancellor in Mr. Disraeli's government. He occupied a prominent seat in the Agricultural Hall, Islington. Very soon nearly all the leaders of society had followed his example. The epithets "pernicious humbugs," "crack-brained Yankee evangelists," "pestilential vermin," "abbots of unreason," with which the anti-Christian press pelted the preachers, gave way to much more polite language when the highest in the land were numbered among their hearers.

William R. Moody, *The Life of Dwight L. Moody*

"This [meeting] is contrary to [an] Act of Parliament....and besides, your preaching is frightening people out of their wits." "Sir, did you ever hear me preach?" "No." "How then can you judge of what you never heard?" "Sir, by common report." "Common report is not enough. Give me leave to ask, Sir, is not your name Nash?" "My name is Nash." "Sir, I dare not judge of you by common report. I think it not enough to judge by." Here he paused awhile, and, having recovered himself, said, "I desire to know what this people comes here for:" On which one replied, "Sir, leave him to me: Let an old woman answer him. You, Mr. Nash, take care of your body; we take care of our souls; and for the food of our souls we come here." He replied not a word, but walked away.

John Wesley, *Journal*, June 5, 1739

It is only at the tree loaded with fruit that men throw stones.

Charles H. Spurgeon

Chapter One

Who Is Deceiving Whom?

I want you to try an experiment. Take out the yellow pages of your local phone book and go to the section labeled "Churches." Beneath that listing you'll find all kinds of "Christian" denominations and groups, some of them with pretty weird (and long!) names. Now keep looking. See if you can find a listing for a denomination called "The Church of Partial Truth." Can't find it? How about "The Counterfeit Church of Christ"? Is it listed? Well, maybe you can spot a flashy ad that says something like this: "Come visit our service this week! We preach the *limited gospel* every Sunday." No luck?

What about looking up "The Congregation of the Deceived" or "The Assembly of the Misled"? Have they paid for space in the yellow pages? Not on your life. Such groups don't even exist, let alone advertise. Why? Because no one is knowingly deceived. No one is willingly duped. *Deception is very deceiving.* So be careful. Everyone thinks that it is "the other guy" who is off track.

Just because you warn people about deception does not mean that you are not deceived. Just because you call yourself a spokesman for the Lord does not mean you really are. Just because you are sure you are right does not make you right. Just because you claim to stand for the truth—"the whole truth, and nothing but the truth, so help you God"— doesn't mean you haven't bought into a lie. To repeat: Deception is deceiving! You may be in for a surprise. You may think you are the last of the undeceived of this generation, a lonely and loyal voice in these deluded and dangerous times, exposing the counterfeit while everyone else is getting duped; when in reality you are like the false teachers of old, deceived and therefore deceiving. I ask you in the sight of Almighty God: *What makes you right?*

One author recently wrote a short book attacking one contemporary "renewal" movement. (The general rightness or wrongness of the movement he attacks is not the issue here at all. It is the spirit and attitude of the author that I want to highlight.) This apparently earnest Christian explains:

> I wrote [this book] with all sincerity of heart to warn God's people of this deceptive movement and would not have proceeded to write even one page if there was a one percent chance of this move being of God. [It] is christian spiritual apostasy and deception on an unprecedented scale. False doctrines, like leaven, corrupt the Whole Body of Christ.[1]

Well, at least he puts his cards on the table! There is not even "a one percent chance" that this so-called movement is anything less than "christian spiritual apostasy and deception on an unprecedented scale." That's pretty forthright (not to mention bold!). But it is his next line that is the killer: "We, who are not deceived, need to come forward and make a stand for the Truth and for the sake of what's left of Christ's Body."[2] Did you catch that? Yes, "we, who are not deceived"—we who alone have remained faithful, we who are the true remnant—*we* must stand for the truth.

Of course, "we" are not deceived. "We" are never deceived—at least, "we" don't think we are. That's the whole principle of deception!

But it would be useless to argue with this author. Why? *He has been appointed by God.* As he writes in his acknowledgments:

> The fruit of this research is the result of a burden and calling not of man but of the Lord. May the honour of God's Word be restored in all His churches and may all glory always be to the Father, Son, and Holy Spirit, without whom this work would not be possible....[3]

So that settles it. He writes out of *God's* burden. His calling is not from man but *from the Lord*, and the work was only made possible *by the Holy Spirit*. Simple. He must be correct. He couldn't possibly be deceived. He wrote his book for the glory of God! Therefore he is right. Right? Maybe not! Deception is very deceiving. Could it be that those who caution us most strongly about being deceived by the devil are the ones who have been duped? *Who is deceiving whom?*

This is something to think about. Sometimes the ones who warn us most loudly lead us most woefully. Sometimes the teachers need to be taught and the "spokesmen" need to be spoken to. Careful, dear critic!

A self-proclaimed "revival historian" living in a faraway land recently attacked a prominent, strongly evangelistic, repentance-based outpouring—without ever attending any of the meetings—and challenged the many leaders who have endorsed this movement as a modern-day revival. He asked: "What do you think God will do to you Christian leaders if you are wrong and you have led His precious flock into open deception?"[4] Apparently, this author, who brands the outpouring as demonic and fleshly has failed to ask himself that question: What if *he* is leading God's people into open deception? (By the way, what is the meaning of "open deception"? Is it different than "hidden deception"? Does it announce loudly and clearly, "I'm coming to deceive you in broad daylight," as opposed to deceiving you in secret?)

How interesting! Without any firsthand knowledge, he plainly states that a mighty spiritual move is "from the devil," claiming that those who have embraced it are deceived. Could it be that his rejection of the Spirit is just another form of deception? Isn't it just as dangerous (if not even more dangerous) to reject a God-sent visitation as it is to embrace a counterfeit visitation? (Which is worse: to follow a false spirit or to reject the true Spirit?) Isn't it just as bad for a leader to lead God's precious flock *away* from living water as it is to lead them *to* poisonous streams? Critics, take care! You had better ask yourself again: What makes you right?

If you say, "I base myself on the Word of God and prayer," then I say in response, "So do I!" If you say, "I live a holy life," then I say in response, "So do I!" If you say, "I am a student of Church history," then I say in response, "So am I!" What makes you right? Give me biblical and spiritual *proof*—not speculation and opinion and inference and innuendo—that this current Christ-centered revival is *not* of

God. I will give you proof—no, proofs, by the multiplied thousands—
that the work *is* of God. Dear friend, do you *really want to know the
truth?*

After his attacks on this current revival were seriously challenged, this authority-from-afar wrote:

> I believe that the warnings I have given on this subject have not
> been overstated, but rather have provided a reasonable and
> timely reminder that the possibility for deception exists EVERY-
> WHERE, not just in the cults or the New Age movement. Just
> how alert are we Christians in these last days—the days in
> which deception will abound?[5]

Yes, he argues "that the possibility for deception exists EVERY-
WHERE"—just not in his own backyard. Apparently, he meant to
say, "the possibility for deception exists ALMOST everywhere." In
other words, "Everyone else may be deceived; I am not."

He questions "just how alert" we Christians are "in these last
days—the days in which deception will abound"—apparently dis-
counting the possibility that *he* could be slumbering in the light. Mr.
Critic, how is your vigilance any better than mine?

Of course, he could turn around and say to me, "OK, big shot.
How do you know that *you* are not deceived? Is there no possibility
of deception in your position?" Of course there is the possibility of
deception: if I claim to be always and only right; if I make judgments from a distance, especially based on second and thirdhand information; if I ignore the concrete testimony of transformed lives; if
the Scriptures are not my starting point as well as ultimate guide; if
I isolate myself from the Body and am not submitted to other (non-
isolated!) leaders; if I highly esteem my own position and despise
the position of others; if there is moral compromise in my private
life; if I am not walking in conformity to biblical holiness; etc. If I
am guilty of any of these things, I have no business claiming to be a
spiritual authority, or watchman on the wall, announcing my position for all the Church to hear. (Just the issue of holy living might
disqualify many contemporary critics!)

The fact is, I often ask myself, "What makes you so sure about your views?" This is the way I have lived for years. I grill myself, I examine the arguments of those who differ with me, I read the writings of people who see things differently than I do, I try to challenge the validity of my position based on the Scriptures, I attempt to see things from the vantage point of those who disagree with me, I am even open to receiving correction and input from strangers, and then, having done all that, I say, "Father, I'm totally dependent on You! What do I know?" The words of Paul in 1 Corinthians 3:18 are very meaningful to me: "Do not deceive yourselves. If any one of you thinks he is wise by the standards of this age, he should become a 'fool' so that he may become wise."[6]

But there is good news: We don't have to be deceived! If we don't claim to be the holy heroes of the hour, the mini-saviors of the moment, the enlightened leaders of the Critical Intelligentsia Association (CIA), the elite members of the Faultfinding Brotherhood International (FBI), if we are quick to hear and slow to speak, recognizing that God is raising up a large and varied army, the Lord can keep us safe from delusion. But we must take heed and search our hearts on a personal, deep, and even uncomfortable level.

What is one of the roots of spiritual deception? Pride. "*I* have special revelation; *I* am right; *I know*." And this reveals one of the strongholds of the destructive, critical spirit: Truth doesn't matter. Evidence doesn't count. "I have an opinion!" That's what really matters. "After all, I am a critic. I am rational and reasonable. How dare you question me?"

This kind of attitude is all too common among many of the contemporary critics of revival. You've probably seen it dozens of times. For example, the so-called revival historian who claimed that the outpouring he was attacking was an "alien mixture" stated that real revival would be marked by strong repentance preaching resulting in deep conviction of sin and genuine conversion of the lost—which are the very hallmarks of the revival he maligns. He could not have given a better description of that glorious moving of the Spirit. (This, of course, is something he would not know, since he never attended a single service.)

Of course, many believers (myself included) informed this brother that, in fact, the repentance preaching every night in the revival is confrontational and cutting, the conviction of sin in the meetings absolutely intense, and the conversions indisputably genuine, proven out by multiplied thousands of lives. What was the response?

Well, his response came six months later and basically stated this: "It is true that there is strong repentance preaching, and I'm sure there have been genuine conversions, but I still stand behind what I wrote before. This is a deadly form of mixture, the evangelist is operating under an alien spirit, and more and more churches are being taken in by this great deception."[7] What blindness! This critic claimed that true revival would be characterized by certain essential elements, but when he was informed that these very elements characterized the movement he had attacked, he responded, "Maybe so, but I still state the revival is spurious." Do you see how the critic is *still* right in his own eyes despite truthful interaction which should have caused him to alter— or, at least, seriously reconsider— his position?

There is a famous anecdote about the German philosopher Hegel. As the story goes, one of his students, after hearing him present his unique theories, said to him, "But Professor Hegel, the facts of history are against your theory!" To which Hegel is said to have replied, "So much for history!" Yes, so much for history— or facts or truth. "I have a theory!" And the critic has a viewpoint that seems etched in stone.

Yes, all too often, the real issue is not truth, facts, and evidence, but rather *the critic's opinion*—and the attitude behind that opinion can be blinding. It is frequently self-anointed, generally self-appointed, and virtually always right. How can the critic possibly see clearly?

The critic is often more influenced by what he thinks and "discerns" than by what the evidence, the clear and powerful evidence, says. "I still believe I'm right"—no matter what you say, no matter what scriptural proof you provide, no matter what other proven leaders believe. As Judith Crist once remarked with reference to art and literary critics, "To be a critic, you have to have maybe three percent education, five percent intelligence, two percent style, and ninety percent gall and egomania in equal parts."[8] This applies to some spiritual critics too!

Just think: Thousands of godly Christian leaders from around the world have attended meetings in one particular revival that began in the United States (and I speak as an eyewitness to this). Many of these leaders have been highly respected in their homelands, known as men and women of integrity, people of the Word, leaders who lead by example, ministers with excellent track records over many years. Some of them have sacrificed greatly for the faith, even being stoned, attacked, or beaten because of their loyalty to Jesus. Others have wept and prayed for revival for years, longing for a true visitation that would shake their land. They came to the revival and were mightily touched by the Lord, often testifying with tears, "This is the real thing! This is it!" And many of them, upon returning to their countries, witnessed exceptional movings of the Spirit, marked particularly by deep brokenness, holy conviction, and glorious conversions. They raise their voices in one accord to affirm that this is the beginning of the revival for which they have yearned for years. Yet critics who have never even bothered to make the effort to attend one week of meetings take it on themselves to denounce the revival as a satanic mixture and counterfeit. *Who is deceiving whom?*

Can any of you— especially those of you in leadership—imagine yourself claiming that another minister was operating under an *alien spirit*, was *deceived by the devil*, and was involved in *a deadly form of mixture* (these are no light charges!), publishing your opinions through book, tape, or the Internet, naming names and being specific, rarely (if ever) attempting to dialogue with those whom you accuse, hardly (if ever) attempting to ask them a clarifying question, but broadcasting your views for the world to hear just because you believe you are right? Let's take this a step further: What if you never even heard this supposedly deceived minister in person or by tape or printed page? And what if thousands of respected leaders who did know him firsthand vouched for the man and his message? What kind of arrogance would it take to publicly say that he was operating under a satanic spirit? Where is the fear of God?

The critic might say, "You've got it all wrong. It's *because* I fear God that I must write these things." Hardly! If you really feared God you would take pains to get your facts in order, to investigate carefully, to learn the particulars firsthand, before daring to attack those whom God Himself supports. Careful, dear critic! Do you *really* want to know the truth, or have you merely painted yourself into a corner from which you cannot escape—unless you humble yourself and see your error? Is your identity found in glorifying Jesus, or is it found in criticizing and attacking and being "right"? If you really wanted to know the truth, you would go and find it out for yourself (with an open heart and mind).

After I taught one day on the characteristics of a critical spirit, someone handed me a copy of a statement from Herbert Spencer, quoted in an Alcoholics Anonymous manual: "There is a principle which is a bar against all arguments and which cannot fail to keep a man in everlasting ignorance—that principle is contempt prior to investigation." This may hurt, but it certainly hits home. Once the critic has arrived at his conclusion there is no discussing the matter. (Thank God for the rare exceptions to this rule.) *If every allegation the critic raised proved to be untrue, he would still attempt to hold to his views.* After all, they are his views! Why investigate any further?

But it doesn't stop there. Once the critic has made up his mind, he seeks out confirmation to prove that his negative suspicions are true. In fact, he will give more credence to one negative report that agrees with his position than 1,000 that contradict and refute it. You might say to me, "That's hard to believe! How could anyone be so closed-minded?" But that is the blinding deception of a critical spirit. (For more on this, see Chapter Three, "Noble Bereans or Negative Brethren?")

When D.L. Moody ministered in England, his biographer noted that:

> Curious reports of Mr. Moody's provincial tour went before him to London. "The World" said: "In many large English towns they (the evangelists) had the satisfaction of throwing females into convulsions, and have been lucky enough to consign

several harmless idiots to neighboring lunatic asylums." Those who attended the meetings bore testimony that this element of violent excitement was totally absent from them.[9]

Yet the critics howled and mocked and repeated the stories that they heard one from the other. Anything to confirm their negative suspicions, true or not.

Yes, there is a cozy cocoon of criticism that feeds on itself and draws strength from its rumormongering. May God's light penetrate this darkness, and His truth pierce these lies! This kind of junk—repeating libelous falsehoods about our brothers and maligning faithful servants of the Lord—is as far from constructive correction and godly rebuke as Death Valley is from the Arctic Circle. It not only misses the mark, but instead of shooting at the enemy's target, it fires at its own side.

Consider these entries from the journal of John Wesley:

> Tuesday I rode to Bradford, five miles from Bath, where I had long been invited to come. I visited the minister and asked permission to preach in his church. He said it was not usual to preach on the weekdays, but if I could come there on a Sunday, I could assist him. Then I went to a gentleman in the town, who had been present when I preached at Bath. There, with the strongest marks of sincerity and affection, he had wished me good luck in the name of the Lord. Now it was all changed and I found him quite cold. He began disputing on several points. At last he told me plainly that one from my own college had informed him I was always considered a little crack-brained at Oxford....[10]

There you have it. "Wesley, I've heard it from someone who heard it somewhere that you were always a little weird. Therefore, regardless of the purity of your doctrine, regardless of the undeniable fruit, I'm going to hold to my opinion." Blind guide!

> The last Monday in August, I took up my cross by arguing for two hours with a zealous man, laboring to convince him that I was not an enemy of the Church of England. He admitted I taught no other doctrines than those of the church, but could not forgive me for teaching outside church buildings. Indeed, the

reports now current in Bristol was that I was a Roman Catholic, if not a Jesuit. Some added that I was born and bred at Rome, which many wholly believed.[11]

Yes, John Wesley was a Roman Catholic, a Jesuit, born and bred at Rome—"which many wholly believed"! Yet Wesley's opponent admitted that Wesley "taught no other doctrines than those of the church." What then was the problem? He "could not forgive me for teaching outside church buildings"![12] "Mr. Wesley, you just don't do it our way. Therefore you must be wrong ."

This "zealous man" (as Wesley called him) would have done far better to ask himself if *he*—and not Wesley—was wrong. Instead, because Wesley violated the dead orthodoxy of the day, even though no one could genuinely point a finger at him, rumors were repeated and slander spread to discredit this holy man of God.

Thank the Lord, over the course of time, the only ones discredited were the destructive critics. (It has rightly been said, in the context of the arts, that "a statue has never been set up in honor of a critic."[13] It's true!) Most believers would be hard pressed to name the chief critic of the Great Awakening, or the leading opponents of the ministry of Charles Finney, or the main antagonist of the Welsh Revival. These names have faded into infamy, while the names of those whom they ridiculed and reviled are now revered.

How do you want to be remembered? On which side do you want to be? On the side of the critics, who freely air their opinions for the world to hear— even when confronted with truth— or on the side of those who are bearing much fruit for the Kingdom of God to the glory of the Son of God? On whose side do you want to be when the Lord stands to sort things out?

If you want to be on the right side then, you had better be there now. Are you?

We should be afraid of censuring the devotion of others though it may not agree with our sentiments because for aught that we know the heart might be upright in it and who are we that we should despise those whom God has accepted? If we can prove ourselves to God in all we do in religion and do it as before the Lord, we need not value the censures and reproaches of men.

Matthew Henry, to 2 Samuel 6

*In the spiritual domain, criticism is love turned sour…If criticism becomes a habit it will destroy the moral energy of the life and paralyse the spiritual force….*Criticism is deadly in its effect because it divides a man's powers and prevents his being a force for anything….Whenever you are in a critical temper, it is impossible to enter into communion with God. Criticism makes you hard and vindictive and cruel, and leaves you with the flattering unction that you are a superior person. It is impossible to develop the characteristics of a saint and maintain a critical attitude.

Oswald Chambers, selected from his writings

But we might pause humbly, rather than proceed hastily, in evaluating all of this. When a bush catches fire, or tongues of flame fill a room and people speak in strange languages, it might be wise to take off your shoes and listen for God's voice and even wiser to steer clear of leveling charges of drunkenness.

Jack Hayford, from his message,
"Stanced Before Almightiness"

But how fearful should they be of loading any with reproaches now whom their common Judge shall hereafter commend.

Matthew Henry, to 1 Corinthians 4

Chapter Two

Scorning the Sacred: When Critics Enter the Danger Zone

Blasphemy of the Spirit: It is a terrifying sin, a horrible sin, a sin of disastrous consequences. It is the only sin specifically described in the Bible as unforgivable. Just the thought of it is enough to send spiritual chills down your spine.

What makes this sin so severe? Listen to Jesus:

"I tell you the truth, all the sins and blasphemies of men will be forgiven them. But whoever blasphemes against the Holy Spirit will never be forgiven; he is guilty of an eternal sin." He said this because they were saying, "He has an evil spirit." (Mark 3:28-30)

To blaspheme the Spirit is to knowingly attribute to the devil Jesus' work done in the power of the Holy Spirit. It is the ultimate offense. And it is something from which we must flee. Why tamper with a sin which can lead to eternal judgment? *There is nothing more dangerous than blasphemy of the Spirit.*

Jesus could not have stated it more plainly, and we dare not take His words lightly, especially in the day and age in which we live. When revival fire is falling, when the Holy Spirit is moving in power, we do well to examine this portion of the Word afresh. And though it is true that there is debate among Bible scholars as to the exact nature of the sin of blaspheming the Spirit, there is no debate as to its eternal consequences![1]

But first I want to make something perfectly clear: *I am not saying for a moment that the Christian brothers and sisters who attack the current outpouring are guilty of blaspheming the Spirit.* I am not saying that those believers who attribute the whole revival to the devil are guilty of this sin. I do not entertain such a thought for even a moment. I know full well that godly leaders in the past attributed the modern Pentecostal outpouring to the devil, and that there are committed believers today— blood-washed, Spirit-indwelt saints—who still believe that speaking in tongues is from below, not above.[2]

God is great in mercy and often overlooks our ignorance. He knows that the way we are raised spiritually can color our thinking and cause us to reject something He sends. He recognizes that we may hear bogus reports about our brothers and misleading talk about other churches, denominations, and ministries, leading us to form wrong conclusions and make incorrect judgments. He is also aware of the fact that many extreme, unusual, and even bizarre things can be done in the name of the Holy Spirit, making it hard to see the holy forest because of some unholy trees. And He understands that we sometimes struggle with anything that is new and different, even if it is totally scriptural, not to mention the many times we foolishly elevate our traditions and customs above the clear teaching of the Word—in the name of faithful adherence to the Word! Yes, God understands our folly. But that doesn't mean that He is pleased with it, and there are times when the Spirit says, "Enough."

You see, it is possible to scorn the sacred and despise the divine until the Lord Himself raises His voice in rebuke. I fear that some critics are nearing that place of danger, and this chapter is written to warn them and help pull them back.

"But wait one second," you say. "You just made it perfectly clear that you don't believe that the critics of the current revival are guilty of blaspheming the Spirit or even *in danger* of blaspheming the Spirit. So what kind of 'danger zone' are they entering?"

The answer is very simple: When we rightly understand what blasphemy of the Spirit is and why it is so serious in God's sight, we flee from anything that resembles it, just like a former adulterer distances himself from anything that is sexually suggestive and a former drunkard keeps far from bars. When you understand that murder is a direct assault on man, who is made in God's image, you realize that even hating and mocking those whom our Maker made is also ugly in His eyes. So, when Jesus warned us so sternly about the eternal danger of knowingly attributing His works, which were done in the power of the Spirit, to the devil, we had better be sure we know *exactly* what we are talking about when we attribute a contemporary outpouring of the Spirit to Satan. Since it is especially grievous to sin against the Spirit, we should be especially careful about the possibility of speaking against Him and His work.

Is this too much to ask? Is there anything extreme in this position? Isn't it entirely reasonable in light of the whole counsel of the Word of God?

"But what about testing the spirits?" you ask. "What about the many warnings in the Word about not believing every message and not listening to every voice, even when those messages and voices come in the name of Jesus?"

That's another good question. In fact, several chapters in this book are devoted to examining the New Testament's warnings about deception.[3] For now, let me say this: There is quite a difference between identifying the demonic nature of a spirit that says that Jesus Christ did not come in the flesh (see 1 John 4:1-6) and classifying as demonic the Spirit behind tens of thousands of conversions to Jesus Christ. There is quite a difference between testing the spirits and grieving the Spirit!

It is one thing to have honest questions and concerns about a particular movement, to make cautionary comments, to check the nature of the waters carefully before diving in. It even makes good spiritual sense to do this.[4] *But it is another thing entirely to glibly scorn the testimonies of scores of hundreds of godly Christian leaders whose lives have been dramatically transformed through today's revival, to ridicule the reports of parents, educators, and law enforcement agents who can attest to a radical work of the Spirit among the young people, to mockingly reject the words of hungry children of God who have experienced the love, mercy, grace, power, and holy awe of the Savior like never before.* It is dangerous to scorn the sacred!

When Aaron and Miriam freely spoke against Moses they were in for a surprise. The Lord Himself chastised them, questioning their judgment:

> Miriam and Aaron began to talk against Moses because of his Cushite wife, for he had married a Cushite. "Has the LORD spoken only through Moses?" they asked. "Hasn't He also spoken through us?" And the LORD heard this. (Now Moses was a very humble man, more humble than anyone else on the face of the earth.) At once the LORD said to Moses, Aaron and Miriam, "Come out to the Tent of Meeting, all three of you." So the three of them came out. Then the LORD came down in a pillar of cloud; He stood at the entrance to the Tent and summoned Aaron and Miriam. When both of them stepped forward, He said, "Listen to My words: When a prophet of the LORD is among you, I reveal Myself to him in visions, I speak to him in dreams. But this is not true of My servant Moses; he is faithful in all My house. With him I speak face to face, clearly and not in riddles; he sees the form of the LORD. Why then were you not afraid to speak against My servant Moses?" The anger of the LORD burned against them, and He left them. (Num. 12:1-9)

Did you notice those key words? "Why then were you not afraid to speak against My servant Moses?" Moses had a special walk with the Lord, a special intimacy, a special calling. God had chosen to reveal Himself to His faithful servant Moses in an unusual and distinct way, speaking with him "face to face, clearly and not in riddles." Therefore Aaron and Miriam should have known better than to rashly speak against their brother Moses. God had singled him out, and he should have been treated with the utmost respect. That's why the Lord's anger burned against them. And that's why His anger may soon burn against some of the critics. They have been rashly speaking against things that God Himself is doing.[5]

Of course, I am aware that through the years many leaders have abused these verses in Numbers, as if anyone who would dare question their authority was guilty of high treason, as if they alone were the Lord's anointed and, as such, stood above criticism and accountability. That too is a dangerous position to take. No leader is above correction, no leader is unapproachable, and no leader is so special that the rest of the Body of Christ is reckoned to be of no account.

But the fact that some have misused this portion of Scripture does not mean that there is no application for us. The lesson is crystal clear: When God's hand is on someone in a distinct and definite way, when the Lord has singled out a church, group, or individual for special favor and blessing, when the Spirit is working powerfully through that person or assembly, you had better tread carefully with your criticism. To approach the Spirit's sacred work with a cavalier attitude is to seriously dishonor the Lord. And if there is anyone you don't want to dishonor, it is Him!

On Friday night, January 31, 1997, I returned from a service at the Brownsville Revival at 1:30 in the morning, and I was moved to write the following words.[6] They were written with an unusual urgency and intensity. No doubt, you will sense it as you read:

> I want to share my heart honestly with you, holding nothing back. I want to make myself totally vulnerable. The fact is, I *must*.
>
> I have just come from the beautiful presence of the Lord, from a night of glorious baptismal testimonies and incredible stories of wonderfully changed lives, a night of sovereign visitation, a night of deep, sweeping repentance, of radical encounters with the living God, of public acts of repentance—from young people throwing their drugs and needles into the garbage to old people discarding their cigarettes— a night of weeping under conviction and rejoicing in newfound freedom, a night when the Spirit fell upon the children in a side room until their intercession and wailing permeated the sanctuary, a night when Jesus was exalted in the midst of His Church. Yes, I have come from the holy presence of the Lord in the Brownsville Revival on January 31st, 1997. The Spirit moved, the tears flowed, the Lord touched, the demons fled. This is what happens when revival is in the land!
>
> At the end of the night, amidst shouts of joy and victory, amidst the sound of the newly redeemed enjoying their first moments free from captivity, I turned to my dear friend, Evangelist Steve

Hill and said, "We don't have to quote from the history books about revival. It's here! We're seeing it before our eyes."

Who can describe a night like this? Who can describe what it is like to be so caught up with God that heaven is virtually here and you can almost sense the sound of the Judge knocking at the door? What can you say when young men come to the platform and begin to throw away their earrings, and another wants counsel because he doesn't know how to remove his *eyebrow* ring, and another tosses out his condoms, while still another throws his knife into the trash? What can you say?

What can you say when a thousand people respond to the altar call and stay there for two hours getting right with God? What can you say when the prayers you have prayed for your nation, prayers for the real thing, for genuine visitation, for bona fide outpouring—not hype, not sensationalism, not a superficial show, but an awakening of historic proportions—when those prayers are being answered before your eyes and you know that you know that your country will be *shaken*? What can you say?

What can you say when all you want is Jesus, when pleasing Him is your total delight, when you just have to tell everyone about God's great salvation, when sin's sweetest temptation is utterly repulsive to you, when you just can't find the words to express to the Lord how utterly wonderful He is, how He really is your all in all? What can you say at a sacred time like this? It is too precious to fully describe, too intimate to wholly communicate with mere human speech.

Truly, my heart is blessed beyond measure. But it is also burdened. Around the country—no, around the world—people are spewing forth gossip and garbage, spreading baseless accusations and sharing biased opinions, telling all who will hear that this glorious revival is not of God. How tragic! How pitiful! How sad! Really, it hurts just to think about it. Is there nothing sacred to the critic? I hurt for these poor, blind guides who think they are such heroes of the faith, and even more for the innocent saints whose hopes were finally beginning to rise until a critical voice assured them that this outpouring was nothing more than emotionalism at best or demonic deception at worst. I hurt for these souls!

Does it mean nothing to the critic that the angels in heaven are rejoicing because of the thousands who are being saved every month? Is the critic more selective than the heavenly host? Are his standards higher than theirs? Is it something to be scorned when, on any given night, scores of teens from one of our local schools can be radically converted and return to their school on fire, when in only six months, one particular high school with 2,100 students has seen 300 converts? Is something which is highly significant to the Church, the community, and the Kingdom insignificant to the critic? Is there no reverence for repentance and no respect for renewal? Is nothing sacred to the faultfinder? *God Himself* is moved by the gut-wrenching cries of the six- and seven-year-olds, by the tears of the little ones pouring out their hearts to Him for the salvation of their friends and unsaved loved ones. Yes, the heavenly Father is deeply moved, but the critic is not moved at all. It really is perverse!

Do our detractors really know the truth about that which they speak against and denounce? Do they really understand what is happening? It would be far better for them to put their hands over their mouths and put their swords back into their sheaths until they see for themselves the reality of the Spirit's mighty move here, rather than to continue to oppose Jesus Himself. And what holds true for the current revival holds true for revivals around the world. They are not to be lightly discarded! The very attitude behind that scorn reveals a heart that knows very little of the holy presence of the King.

Yes, it's a good thing He is so patient and understanding. But I warn you, dear reader, there is a limit to His forbearance. Soon the Lord may say to some who erroneously claim to speak for Him, "Silence! Your empty words of ignorance are befouling the pure and hallowed atmosphere. You dishonor Me and deny My work. Do you think I will tolerate this for long? Here I am building My Church, responding to the fasting and prayer of My people, and all you can do is tear down what I build and criticize what I do. I rebuke you for speaking falsely in My name. Repent while there is still time. My kindness toward you is running thin." That is a word for some of you![7]

Are you totally and absolutely sure that you are right in attacking the current revival? Are you willing to wager your salvation on the fact that you are correct?[8] If not, how in the world can you dare risk the possibility that your zeal is misguided and that you are opposing God Himself? Is there no holy fear in you, no sense of the greatness of the Lord, no awe of His mighty works, no recognition that it is far better to tread carefully in your public judgments than to speak rashly about matters in which you are not, in fact, expert? Will you risk reviling the very One you claim to represent? I hear the Spirit saying once more, "Careful!" Are you *sure* I'm wrong?

Friends, it's time we stop throwing around empty opinions—as if God even cared about what *we* thought about *His* work—and instead fall on our faces and repent for speaking so quickly and rashly about things of which we are ignorant. Please listen, my quick-to-criticize and eager-to-be-opinionated brother and sister. May I speak with you candidly?

I can fill a football field with men and women who were hardened adulterers before the current revival but are now serving God with unadulterated hearts. I can present you with a mile-long line of freed fornicators, delivered drunkards, sanctified Satanists, purified perverts, converted criminals, liberated lesbians, and homosexuals who have been made holy. I can introduce you to thousands of transformed teens and countless committed kids. I can show you videos stacked as high as a New York City apartment building chronicling every service of the revival, letting you hear the simple, biblical, Christ-exalting, sin-exposing message that is preached night after night. But you don't like the style of worship, or the occasional snaking bothers you, or perhaps the altar calls are not to your fancy, so you say to as many as will hear your voice, "This is not of God!" What a pathetic, foolish, and dangerous stand to take.

Really, it makes me wonder. How could anyone walk closely to Jesus and cleave to His holy Word, yet be so quick to speak about something so sacred to so many of God's people? How could anyone be so hasty in dealing with the holy?

"But," you say, "I'm not sure if it really is holy." Then by all means, be quiet until you *are* sure! Do you want to be remembered as one who ignorantly slandered the Spirit? There *is* a time to hold one's peace.

Think back to the dramatic conversion of Saul of Tarsus. He thought he was on a divinely appointed mission. He thought he was doing God's will when he persecuted the followers of Jesus. But then he had his divine encounter on the road to Damascus, and he received the shock of his life: The One he was persecuting was the Lord of all! Yes, God had mercy on him because he "acted in ignorance and unbelief" (1 Tim. 1:13), but the Lord was not pleased with Saul's actions: "Saul, Saul, why do you persecute Me? *It is hard for you to kick against the goads*" (Acts 26:14b). Is the Spirit saying this to you? Why follow Saul of Tarsus' pre-conversion pattern of acting in ignorance and unbelief? Is there nothing to learn from his experience?[9]

I am convinced that some of you reading these words are under conviction of the Spirit even now. You know better than to speak the way you do. You are too mature to be guilty of such vile talk. You have met with the Lord too many times in the secret place to fall into such crass judgmentalism. And deep down, when you received reports about the revival, when you heard about the multitudes of changed lives, when you were told that God had answered the prayers of His people, you *knew* that the work was from Heaven, that revival was at hand. What happened?

Maybe it was pride that got in the way ("Why didn't the revival start with my group or ministry?"), or maybe it was the fear of man ("How can I go against those who are telling me that this is a bogus revival?"). Maybe it was just foolish talk ("Everyone wants to know my opinion, so I need to say something that sounds spiritual!"), or maybe it was simply the result of being around too much garbage for too long, the fruit of listening to the wrong people saying the wrong things about a topic about which they know next to nothing. Whatever the cause, you now find yourself to be guilty of criticizing Christ, of scorning the sacred Spirit, of mocking His mercy and vilifying His visitation. You find yourself to be "kicking against the goads."

If that is you, follow the example of Saul of Tarsus. Fall to your face, repent of your sin, and pray that the Lord will visit *you*. Then ask Him, "What will You have me to do?" Don't be surprised if He says, "Prepare for revival!"

It's time.

One may be as straight as a gun barrel theologically and as empty as a gun barrel spiritually. In fact, it may be that in their very opposition to evil men and false teachers these Ephesian saints [in Rev. 2:1-7] had left their first love....so often it turns out that fundamental and orthodox Christians become so severe in condemning false doctrine, gnashing their teeth at every sniff of heresy, that they end up without love. One may do a right thing in a wrong way. The same Paul who wrote, "...though we, or an angel from heaven, preach any other gospel...let him be accursed," also wrote the love chapter to the Corinthians. Unless we can get that combination we shall be theological Hawshawks and doctrinal detectives, religious bloodhounds looking for heretics but with hot heads and cold hearts.

Moreover, Ephesus proves that religious activity without love calls for repentance. I have wondered what would be left nowadays if we eliminated from our church work all that is not the spontaneous expression of our heart's love for Christ.

Vance Havner, *Messages on Revival*

I left London early Monday morning. The next evening I reached Bristol and preached to a large congregation. Howel Harris called on me an hour or two later. He said he had been much dissuaded from either hearing me or seeing me by many who said all manner of evil of me. "But as soon as I heard you preach," he stated, "I quickly found of what spirit you were. Before you were done, I was so overpowered with joy and love that I had much trouble walking home."

John Wesley, *Journal*, June 18, 1739

Christ's ministers must not think it strange if they be censured and quarrelled with, not only by their professed enemies, but by their professing friends; not only for their follies and infirmities, but for their good actions seasonably and well done; but, if we have proved our own work, we may have rejoicing in ourselves...whatever reflections we may have had from our brethren. Those that are zealous and courageous in the service of Christ must expect to be censured by those who, under pretense of being cautious, are cold and indifferent. Those who are of catholic, generous, charitable principles, must expect to be censured by such as are conceited and straitlaced, who say, "Stand by thyself, I am holier than thou."

Matthew Henry, to Acts 11

SERMON NOTES

DATE: _____   SPEAKER: _____

TEXT: _____

TITLE: _____

IMPRESSIONS, THOUGHTS AND IDEAS RECEIVED:

_____
_____
_____
_____
_____
_____
_____
_____
_____
_____
_____
_____
_____
_____
_____
_____
_____
_____
_____
_____
_____
_____
_____
_____

PLEASANT VALLEY CHRISTIAN CENTER
160 East Birch Street
(MAIL: P.O. Box 585)
Coalinga, CA 93210
(209) 935-2944

Chapter Three

Noble Bereans
or Negative Brethren?

Everyone knows that when revival comes, things get hot. Unfortunately, believers get hot too—and I don't just mean on fire for God. Sometimes tempers flare and invective flies. The revival critics call certain movements demonic, and the revival defenders call certain critics devilish. Is all this really merited? As pointed out by one critic, "It would seem that anyone who wishes to discuss [a particular, current 'revival' movement] in the light of the whole counsel of the Word of God has indeed become, at best, a 'Pharisee', and, at worst, the enemy."[1]

In fact, this writer summarizes what one revival defender said about its critics:

He likens us to those who crucified Jesus Christ.

Adjudges us to be:
Scribes and Pharisees
Religious and angry
Attacking and persecuting
In violation of Scripture
Possessed of ungodly attitudes
Issuers of mean spirited commentary
Liars ("deceitful reporting")
Accusers of the brethren
Motivated to tear down churches
Proud, jealous, fearful
Ignorant

Obviously, that is not how the critics see themselves! Rather, they fashion themselves to be like the Bereans of Acts 17. The Word tells us that, in contrast with certain Jews who opposed the message of Paul in Thessalonica (see Acts 17:1-9), "the Bereans were of more noble character than the Thessalonians, for they received the message with great eagerness and examined the Scriptures every day to see if what Paul said was true" (Acts 17:11).

"You see," the critics explain, "we are only following the noble example of the Bereans. We are examining the Scriptures to see if these modern-day claims of revival are really true." But there's something many of these critics have missed. The Bereans not only carefully examined the Word to verify the accuracy of Paul's preaching, but, as translated in the New Revised Standard version, "they welcomed the message very eagerly." In fact, the New Revised Standard version translates the beginning of Acts 17:11 with, "These Jews were *more receptive* than those in Thessalonica."[2] This helps to explain the "therefore" in 17:12: "*Many of them therefore believed*, including not a few Greek women and men of high standing" (NRS). Are the modern critics really Berean in spirit? While I certainly hope that some of them are, almost all of what I have seen, heard, and read has been anything but Berean.

Do the critics receive the contemporary reports of revival with openness and excitement, hoping that this might possibly be the real thing, that perhaps at last, their prayers for revival are being answered (if they're even praying for revival), that the Lord is truly visiting His people; or do they receive such reports with suspicion and skepticism, if not deep-seated cynicism and hostility?

This is the difference between the destructive critics and the hungry believers, both of whom say, "I'm jealous for the real thing." The critics sit on the sidelines, glibly rejecting every effort that falls short of their unattainable ideal (an ideal, of course, which exists in their eyes alone and can only be realized by them, since they are not interested in criticizing themselves). They hardly ever shed a tear for the lost or give themselves to fasting because of the compromised state of the Church, and they almost *hope* that the latest report of the "real thing" turns out to be just another passing fad, since much of their identity is based on finding fault.

In contrast, hungry believers are hopeful (although often doubtful) that the new move will really be "it," and they are profoundly disappointed when, yet again, a trickle is called a river. They hurt inside, since they have been praying, fasting, weeping, and longing for revival. Truly hungry believers will not rest until revival comes; critical believers will not rest when it does come! The sincere are grieved if the exciting reports of revival prove untrue; the cynical are grieved if the reports are true!

The Bereans were hungry for God, willing to receive a man of God with open arms, to give him and his message time, and then to study the issues carefully for themselves. Because of that humble and hopeful attitude, many of them believed! This reminds me of hundreds of leaders who have traveled to some current revival meetings to "check things out," not wanting to get excited just because someone else gave them a glowing report, knowing all too well that much of what has been called revival in our day has been anything but revival. Yet they went, not to mock or attack, but rather to see for themselves, even if they were admittedly skeptical. And when the Lord Himself touched them, when they saw sinners flocking to the altars to repent, when they observed the zeal and commitment of the young people, when they heard for themselves the simplicity and purity of the holiness message, and—best of all— when the Spirit began to move in similar ways in their own churches and ministries after they returned home, they exclaimed with joy: "This is it!"

Truly, these men and women were Berean in spirit. Their attitude was cautious but open, as opposed to closed and obstinate. They were careful but not cynical. There is quite a difference! And they took the time to find things out for themselves.

The same cannot be said for many critics. Some of them are bent on proving their own point, even if it means taking their "opponents" completely out of context, misquoting and misinterpreting their messages and words, and using extreme (and often unrepresentative) examples to "expose" the errors of the movement that they attack. Rather than being honest enough to actually take the time to check things out in detail firsthand, they seek out negative information the way a gossip columnist seeks out dirt. This is not Berean!

Of course, this does not apply to all critics. But it is far too common for comfort, and quite often the "ministry of criticism" is fueled by the exact opposite of the Berean spirit: "And the critics heard the message of revival with antagonism, examining the Scriptures to prove that the claims were false."

The Bereans studied the Scriptures to see if Paul's message could really be true. The critics study the Scriptures to prove that the contemporary reports of revival couldn't possibly be true. Why? Their spirit is wrong. Revival is not their heartbeat. Being "right" is what makes them tick. Keeping the church "pure" is *their* unique and special calling. After all, they are defenders of the faith! Just ask them. They'll tell you. To paraphrase one group: "We alone are examining these spurious spiritual movements in the light of the whole counsel of the Word of God." That's right! I guess the rest of us don't even bother to open our Bibles anymore.

Jesus actually addressed this non-Berean, never-satisfied, religious spirit in Matthew. After praising the life and ministry of John the Baptist, He said:

> To what can I compare this generation? They are like children sitting in the marketplaces and calling out to others: "We played the flute for you, and you did not dance; we sang a dirge, and you did not mourn." For John came neither eating nor drinking, and they say, "He has a demon." The Son of Man came eating and drinking, and they say, "Here is a glutton and a drunkard, a friend of tax collectors and 'sinners.'" But wisdom is proved right by her actions. (Matt. 11:16-19)

How does this apply to the contemporary critics of revival? The dialogue (if it can be called dialogue at all) goes something like this:

"You talk about radical, even violent conversions in the revival, but that's unscriptural."

"What about the conversion of Saul of Tarsus? That's a perfect example of a radical, even violent conversion."

"Yeah, but that was a one-time event."

And I thought you really had an honest, biblical question!

Then there is this scenario:

"If there was real revival in your area, there would be a marked change in the community, evidenced by dropping crime rates."

"But there *are* marked changes in the community, evidenced by dropping crime rates, especially among the young people."

"Well, many different factors can contribute to dropping crime rates! In fact, crime rates are dropping all across the country."

So much for truthful interaction!

Often it sounds like this:

"If there was real revival in your church, there would be lots of conversions."

"Then by your own definition, there *is* real revival in our church, because there have been multiplied thousands of conversions."

"I seriously doubt it! The fact is, whenever a church claims to have lots of conversions, you can be sure that they are superficial at best and spurious at worst."

This is a no-win dialogue!

Or, with a slightly different twist:

"If there was real revival in your church, there would be deep conviction of sin— often with weeping and wailing—just like there was in great revivals of the past."

"But there *is* deep conviction of sin— often with weeping and wailing—just like there was in great revivals of the past."

"Well, all that weeping and wailing stuff is just a lot of emotionalism!"

Thank you, Mr. Critic!

An even uglier version goes like this:

"We've heard about the tens of thousands of alleged converts, but where are they? If they were truly saved, there would be lasting fruit."

"Actually, there is *lots* of lasting fruit: Many local churches have experienced substantial growth; the school systems have been impacted dramatically; some of the converts are now preparing for ministry; thousands of marriages have been restored...I could go on and on with examples of former godless sinners who are now committed followers of Jesus."

"Yeah, but what Jesus are they following? Paul warns us about following another Jesus."

May God help the negative critics! In their eyes, you are wrong if you do ("That's just a lot of flesh!") and wrong if you don't ("Show me the proof!").

One of the most zealous critics on the Internet has received hundreds (if not thousands) of God-honoring, Jesus-exalting testimonies from those who have been powerfully touched to the glory and honor of the Lord Jesus in a particular revival he attacks. Included among those who have e-mailed him are numerous respected ministers of the gospel. Yet he neither responds to the e-mail nor even makes mention of these reports on his "revival" web site. Rather, when he receives a critical note that confirms his claims—to date, never from a Christian leader, but rather from one-time visitors who did not even stay for a whole service, or from people who never even attended a meeting—he posts it for all the world to see.[3]

Other critics actually lift quotes completely out of context— with full knowledge of what they are doing— or use highly selective, unrepresentative material, in order to discredit the particular movement that they attack. Thus they misrepresent or grossly caricature the positions of those whom they assail. Could it be they believe that the more foolish they make their opponents look the better *they* will look to their constituents? Could it be— God alone knows and He is the Judge—that constantly combating "controversy" crowns the critic in the eyes of his followers? And could it also be, again only the Lord knows in full, that by presenting ludicrous examples and ridiculous extremes as the norm the critic appears to be the savior of the hour, helping him bring in big bucks and sell bundles of books? What could be less Berean? The fact is that God despises such misleading, even libelous techniques.

Look at Proverbs 6:16-19:

There are six things the LORD hates, seven that are detestable to Him: haughty eyes, a lying tongue, hands that shed innocent blood, a heart that devises wicked schemes, feet that are quick to rush into evil, a false witness who pours out lies and a man who stirs up dissension among brothers.

God hates those who are false witnesses and those who stir up dissension among brothers. How much more does He abhor those who through their inaccurate witness stir up dissension among brothers? Of course, I pray that He hates only *what* these particular deceitful critics do as opposed to actually hating *them*, but the Word makes it clear that His displeasure is great. *It is earthly, immature, and even demonic to look for a bad report about the ministry of a colleague (not competitor!) so as to confirm one's suspicions— and thus elevate oneself.*[4]

You may ask, "But isn't it right to warn the Church about aberrant groups and abnormal doctrines even if it undermines the apparent unity of the believers?" Of course it is. It is right to sound the alarm when heresy is being introduced in the name of Jesus and to expose false teachers who seek to lead people after themselves. That is correct and valid, godly and necessary. Biblical unity can only be built on truth, and the Church can only be as strong as it is pure.

But such warnings have *nothing whatsoever* to do with the current, repentance-based, Christ-centered revival that is sweeping the land. Any believer who is truly Berean in spirit would know this within one week spent worshiping with the renewed believers, meeting the regenerated former sinners, and listening carefully to the sermons being delivered. Instead of lambasting the work they would laud it; instead of excoriating it they would embrace it.

To give just one example among many, a highly-respected leader from India whose home church, leadership team, and orphanage children have been praying for revival 24 hours a day for almost three years visited the Brownsville Revival. This is a man who has been stoned for his faith and who would die for Jesus without a moment's hesitation. He carries a deep burden for the compromised, worldly, lazy Church in the West, and he had not been impressed with recent claims of renewal and revival in North America. In fact, after one "renewal" meeting he attended, he was deeply disturbed. Yet, after three nights in Brownsville, he sobbed in my arms like a little baby, repeating over and over, "This is the revival! This is the real revival! This is what we have prayed for all these years!"[5]

Yet almost all of the destructive critics don't even bother to come to the doors of the churches they attack, preferring to gather any negative information they can secondhand, esteeming the opinion of a one-time visitor (whose integrity they cannot even vouch for and whose reliability is unknown to them) to the seasoned judgment of men and women of God who verify the Heaven-sent nature of the revival. How is this Berean? These critics would rather believe an inexperienced, unrecognized—and possibly disgruntled—one-time guest who has something bad to say than a trustworthy, recognized, and widely experienced leader who has something positive to say. Doesn't this say something in and of itself?[6]

Years ago, D.L. Moody made some strong statements about the importance of the Church walking in true love:

> The only way any church can get a blessing is to lay aside all difference, all criticism, all coldness and party feeling, and come to the Lord as one man; and when the church lives in the power of the thirteenth chapter of First Corinthians I am sure that many will be added daily to the flock of God. I would like to have the church read that chapter together on their knees on Thursday and, as you do so, pray God to apply it with power. Of late my earnest prayer to God has been that He would help me to save more, and I cannot tell you how wonderfully He has answered my prayer. It seems as if you were all much nearer and dearer to me than ever. My heart goes out to you, and I long to see you all coming constantly to God for a fresh supply of love.

> I found a verse in 1 Peter 4:8, today. I never saw it before: "Above all things put on love." Think much of that one expression. Put it at the head of the list. Faith is good, but this is above it. Truth is good: it is a beautiful sight to see the church of God study the Word, but what are we if we do not have love? May the dear church get such a flood of love from on high that it will fill all our hearts. The last night Jesus was on earth, before they crucified Him, He said to His disciples: "This is My commandment, that ye love one another as I have loved you." Let us think

on these solemn words, and may the love of Christ draw us all together so we will be as one man.[7]

He did not overstate his case.

In a similar vein, G. Campbell Morgan wrote:

I seldom find men strenuously fighting what they are pleased to call heterodox teaching, and in bitter language denouncing false doctrine, without being more afraid for the men denouncing than for the men denounced. There is an anger against impurity which is impure. There is a zeal for orthodoxy which is most unorthodox. There is a spirit that contends for the faith which is in conflict with the faith…. There have been men who have become so self-centered in a narrowness that they are pleased to designate as holding the truth, that the very principle for which they contend has been excluded from their life and service. All zeal for the Master that is not the outcome of love to Him is worthless.[8]

Paul wrote in 1 Corinthians 13:7, "[Love] believeth all things…" (KJV). We all know what this verse does *not* mean (it's not teaching us to be empty-minded idiots!), but do we know what it *does* mean? It certainly means more than, "love believes everything the Bible says." Just read the surrounding verses as expressed in the classic words of the King James Version:

Charity suffereth long, *and* is kind; charity envieth not; charity vaunteth not itself, is not puffed up, doth not behave itself unseemly, seeketh not her own, is not easily provoked, thinketh no evil; rejoiceth not in iniquity, but rejoiceth in the truth; beareth all things, believeth all things, hopeth all things, endureth all things. Charity never faileth. (1 Cor. 13:4-8a)

Where among the critics is the love that believes the good reports of committed, godly believers? Where is the love that believes the testimonies of former sinners who are now saints? Where is the love that actually asks the one with whom it differs, "Are these concerns and charges accurate and true?" Where is the love that is careful to not take its "opponents" out of context but rather gives the benefit of the doubt when given a perfectly plausible explanation? Where among the critics is this love that "believeth all things"? Where among the critics is this love that "always trusts" (NIV)?[9]

It is one thing to be gullible and believe every positive report that comes down the pike, not even attempting to verify the facts. It is another thing to be predisposed to dismiss the good reports as bogus and accept the bad reports as true! But, again, the negative critics have an answer: "We are only measuring the reports we hear by the clear standard of the Scriptures, and the reports we hear about today fall far short of that sound scriptural standard." There is only one problem: The so-called scriptural standard being used is both *un*scriptural and *un*sound. It is both faulty and fallacious.

How so? I can best illustrate this with a story I once heard about a newly married man who loved hamburgers. Every night his dear wife did her best to cook him the perfect burger, and every night he would say: "It's really good, honey. I appreciate your cooking so much. But it's not like Mama used to make!"

One night, his wife got tied up on the phone while cooking dinner, forgetting all about the burger on the grill. When she finally hung up the phone, she remembered that she had left the burger cooking. It was burned to a crisp! Apologetically, she said to her husband, "I'm so sorry! I totally burned your burger. Give me a few minutes and I'll make you another one. This one is tougher than a hockey puck!" But he replied, "No, honey, that's all right. You're so busy. I'll eat it just as is." She resisted but he insisted, so she put it in the bun and, reluctantly, served it to him.

Somehow, he managed to bite into that charred meat, chewing it gingerly and swallowing it slowly. Then, to his wife's total surprise, he exclaimed: "Mmmm. Just like Mama used to make!"

That's the way some of us are! The ideal—in other words, *our* ideal—by which we judge and criticize everything and everyone else is not only biased, it is bogus. "Your so-called revival is not to my liking!" the critic proclaims. We reply: "Yes, but what you like and what God likes are two totally different things!"

You see, there is a small-minded attitude that stands completely opposed to a true Berean spirit. It fosters doubt instead of faith and pessimism instead of hope, leading to a sterile Christianity that gets in the way rather than leads the way. It wants a thoroughly sanitized, "old-fashioned, historic" revival, which, in fact, never existed except in the imagination of the critic. It is no more credible than the burgers that Mama used to make were edible, and yet it is the standard by which everything else is evaluated: "If there were real revival, it would be the way Grandpa described it to me before he died."

Sorry, friend, but Grandpa's revival in Grandpa's day looked and felt a whole lot different than the way you heard about it when you sat on his lap. He edited out the excesses, forgot about the flesh, disregarded the divisions, and cut out the critics. The revival you heard about never existed. In fact, many of the past revivals in which we all glory had far less national impact— even in their peak—than the current revival that is just beginning to sweep the nation. But for the negative critic, nothing meets his elevated (and ethereal) criteria. Nobody makes those burgers like Mama used to make! Take it from the non-Berean critics. They know what they're talking about.

About this time I can hear someone protest: "You're missing the point again! Following the example of the Bereans means more than emulating their attitude. It also means that we follow their pattern of carefully examining current spiritual phenomena in light of the Word of God."

Actually, I agree with this statement. I only question whether the critics are following it. You see, "carefully examining current spiritual phenomena in light of the Word of God" does not simply mean studying the Scriptures to see if a specific phenomenon taking place today took place in the Bible. (As in, "Show me in the Word of God where people ran to the altar to get saved.") Rather it includes studying the biblical ways God moved and spoke, considering the warnings in the Word against abuses and deception, and welcoming a fresh move of the Spirit that is in keeping with the principles laid out in Scripture. The negative critics rarely even attempt to follow this line of study.

"But where does it say that the Bereans did this? Aren't you simply reading your own ideas into the Word?"

Not at all. You see, if the Bereans followed the method of the modern critics, *they would have rejected Jesus entirely* (for more on this, see Chapter Six, "Was Jesus a False Prophet?"). There were plenty of things Jesus did that were not specifically spoken of in the Word of God. In fact, there were things He did for which there was not any kind of precedent or *hint* of a suggestion in the Old Testament. The Bereans could have said to Paul, "Is it true that the man you call the Messiah did all kinds of things that our Bible never speaks of? Then how could He be the Messiah?"

But that was not their approach. Instead, even though Jesus did things that were without previous biblical precedent, even though His death by crucifixion was unexpected by the Jewish people of His day, even though the Messiah they were awaiting looked much different than the Messiah Paul preached, they received Paul and his message "with great eagerness and examined the Scriptures every day to see if what Paul said was true." If the modern critics followed the spirit and method of the Bereans, they would look at God's written promises to pour out His Spirit in answer to prayer, they would see the scriptural signs of a true moving of God, and they would *recognize by the Word* that the Lord accomplishes His purposes in many diverse and often unusual ways.

For example, they would not dispute the miraculous conversions taking place in Muslim and Hindu lands today, even though there is no example of such conversions in the Word. (To give one case in point, where in the Word did people see a vision of a crucified Jesus suspended in the air over their village and then get saved by the hundreds? But, according to missionary reports, that very thing happened a few years ago in a village in the Hindu city of Kathmandu in Nepal. Was it from the devil?) A Berean spirit would say—in the words of Randy Sprinkle, the director of the Southern Baptist Foreign Mission Board's international prayer strategy office—"We can't tell Him how He can and can't do things. If He chooses to do it in what to our Western minds is an unusual way such as dreams or visions or angels, the Scriptures are full of those examples."[10] Yes, the Scriptures are full of similar *examples*—but not necessarily the exact same things. A Berean spirit recognizes this. A negative critic says, "Show me that in the Word! That is probably a counterfeit conversion. I can document similar phenomena in New Age cults!" Do you see how the non-Berean critic paints himself into a corner?

Take the account of a young Muslim who tore up a Christian tract he received and threatened the Christian worker who gave it to him, only to return the next day and ask for another booklet. Why? "The previous night, he recounted, he had felt two hands shake him awake and heard a voice say, 'You have torn up the truth.' He read the tract and became a believer in Christ."[11] The open-minded but studious Berean hears this report and asks himself, "Is this *contrary* to the Word of God?" The answer is no. He then asks, "Is there any kind of parallel to this?" The answer is yes, the dramatic conversion of Saul of Tarsus. He then inquires as to the lasting fruit: "Is this a genuine conversion? Is this young man now a truly committed Christian?" The answer again is yes. The Berean rejoices!

The non-Berean critic, however, who is both small-minded in his attitude and narrow in his studies, argues, "This Muslim is basing his faith on a dream. He has no empirical evidence for his decision. What happens the next time he has a dream? Will he convert to *another* religion? Plus, the account of Paul's conversion is certainly not the expected norm, and it didn't happen to him when he was asleep but when he was wide awake. Jesus spoke to him directly and told him who He was. There are profound differences here!"

And what about the fact of this Muslim's conversion? "Let's see where he is ten years from now! Anyway, I'm not going to adjust my theology based on the alleged conversion of one individual in a faraway land. I go by the Book!" Do you really?

The truly Berean student of the Word hears the contemporary reports of revival. He listens to the simple, scriptural, and sound message being preached. He sees that Jesus is being exalted and receiving the honor, that man is not taking credit, and he hears the reports of the dramatic impact of the revival on the local community and of the converts of the revival being trained for ministry and missions. He also hears of some people shaking and trembling, of some falling to the ground after prayer— or before prayer— of people sobbing and weeping, and he asks, "Is this from God?" His answer will be emphatically "Yes": The message is biblical; the Jesus of the Word is the center of attention; the converts and ministers pass the "fruit test" with flying colors (see Matt. 7:15-18); and shaking, falling, or weeping neither proves nor disproves the validity of the revival (see Chapter Ten, "All Shook Up Over a Little Shaking"). According to scriptural examples, such things *could* happen when God is moving, but they do not have to happen. Simply stated, they are not the issue.

Soon enough, the modern Bereans are rejoicing: "This is it! This is the revival we have been praying for! Let's dive into the river of God." Yet all the while, as this mighty river rushes on (see, e.g., Ps. 46:4),[12] the negative critic sits back on the dry land looking dour and dusty—but with his Bible in hand—as he watches the Christians joyfully swim by. He scowls at them, shaking his head in despair. "You're so deceived," he cries out. "Get out of the water! It's not of God."

Little does he know that this river of revival flows from the heavenly throne, and, in the words of the ancient prophet, "where the river flows *everything will live*" (Ezek. 47:9). Everything, that is, except the negative critic. He refuses to get in. Meanwhile, his Berean brethren have long since taken the plunge.

I realize how dangerous criticism can be, even when you try to sanctify the term by calling it constructive criticism. It is often tainted with personal feelings and reactions.

Floyd J. Goins

Watch the thing that makes you snort morally....Beware of anything that puts you in the place of the superior person.

Oswald Chambers, selected from his writings

A man is a critic when he cannot be an artist, in the same way that a man becomes an informer when he cannot be a soldier.

Gustave Flaubert, letter, 1846

"Thou shalt see it with thine eyes, but shalt not eat thereof." [2 Kin 7:2] Listen unbelievers! ye have heard this morning your sin; now listen to your doom: "Ye shall see it with your eyes, but shalt not eat thereof." It is so often with God's saints. When they are unbelieving, they see the mercy with their eyes, but do not eat it. Now, here is corn in this land of Egypt; but there are some of God's saints who come here on the Sabbath, and say, "I do not know whether the Lord will be with me or not." Some of them say, "Well, the gospel is preached, but I do not know whether it will be successful." They are always doubting and fearing. Listen to them when they get out of the chapel. "Well, did you get a good meal this morning?" "Nothing for me." Of course not. Ye could see it with your eyes, but did not eat it, because you had no faith. If you had come up with faith, you would have had a morsel. I have found Christians, who have grown so very critical, that if the whole portion of the meat they are to have, in due season, is not cut up exactly into square pieces, and put upon some choice dish of porcelain, they cannot eat it. Then they ought to go without; and they will have to go without, until they are brought to their appetites.

Charles H. Spurgeon, "The Sin of Unbelief"

Chapter Four

Characteristics of a Critical Spirit

In one of his most penetrating passages, Paul confronted those who bragged about their relationship with God and claimed to have a superior knowledge of His will, challenging them point blank with these words: "You, then, who teach others, do you not teach yourself?" (Rom. 2:21a) Yes, you who claim to be specially "instructed by the law," you who "are convinced that you are a guide for the blind, a light for those who are in the dark, an instructor of the foolish, a teacher of infants" (Rom. 2:18-20a)—is it possible that rather than being a guide for the blind you are actually a blind guide?

Jesus reserved some of His strongest words for such leaders:

> ...Every plant that My heavenly Father has not planted will be pulled up by the roots. Leave them; they are blind guides. If a blind man leads a blind man, both will fall into a pit. (Matt. 15:13-14)

> Woe to you, blind guides! ... You blind fools! ... You blind men! ... You blind guides! ... Blind Pharisee! (Matt. 23:16-17,19,24,26)

The Lord actually pronounced *woes* on these sightless leaders. This is serious business!

It is one thing to be blind. It is another to be a blind *guide*. It is one thing to fall into a pit. It is another thing to lead others into that same pit. It is one thing to be misled. It is another thing to mislead others. How dangerous it is to be a blind guide! How dangerous it is to take the lead when you yourself don't even know the way. How dangerous it is to direct others into something you have never experienced yourself. Careful, dear critic. Your sight may be seriously impaired.

> Jesus said, "For judgment I have come into this world, so that the blind will see and those who see will become blind." Some Pharisees who were with Him heard Him say this and asked, "What? Are we blind too?" Jesus said, "If you were blind, you would not be guilty of sin; but now that you claim you can see, your guilt remains." (John 9:39-41)

Now, the religious leaders whom Jesus sternly rebuked did not truly know the Lord. They had religious involvement without relational intimacy. They were strong in hypothetical theory but weak in experiential reality. They were lost sinners who did not recognize their need. In New Testament terms, they would not be part of the Church. But there are blind guides today who are our brothers and sisters, who have a relationship with the Lord, and who will be with us in the Kingdom forever, yet they commit the very same errors as the hypocrites of Jesus' day. They think they see, but their eyes have been blinded. What is it that impairs their sight? *A destructive, critical spirit.* And to the extent that any of us fall prey to this negative, damaging mindset, our vision will also be obscured.

One well-known critic objected strenuously when someone implied that he was a blind guide. Yet, this really is a fair description of anyone who claims to lead the way and expose error while, in fact, he or she does not see clearly. The fact is, if God is moving in revival today (and He is!) and a Christian leader doesn't see it at all, claiming instead that this move of the Holy Spirit is either the work of the flesh or the devil, then as far as revival is concerned, that leader is rightly called a blind guide. I would have no problem at all with someone calling *me* a blind guide if God was working mightily and I didn't see it, causing me to lead many others astray. Yet some critics who are so quick to dish out strong accusations against other leaders are shocked when similar accusations are brought against them: "Me?? I'm on the side of truth!"

Of course, it is absolutely true that there is such a thing as constructive correction (all truthful correction delivered in the right way and at the right time is constructive), and this is good and necessary. It exposes error, warns of coming danger, shores up weak spots, reveals sore spots, and uncovers blind spots. It is motivated by love and is willing to be misunderstood. It is patient and persistent, and it never says, "I told you so!" Its words are right and its spirit is right. It is Christlike in character as well as in content. Constructive correction helps— even if it hurts. It may sting in the short term, but it will soothe in the long term. It gets its hands dirty and serves on the front lines, never engaging in smug spiritual sniping from its snug security zone. Perish the thought. The genuinely constructive critic is a cherished co-worker and friend.

He can come in the form of a fatherly pastor, putting his arm around his young associate and speaking the truth to him in love. Or he can appear as a passionate prophet, pouring out his broken heart to a complacent congregation, urging the people to consider their ways. The bearer of correction can come in the form of a godly wife, warning her well-known husband that he has become professional and cold in his work, lacking his earlier passion and zeal. Or she can appear as a prayerful missionary, challenging her fellow laborers to beware of the Martha syndrome, always working for the Lord and never waiting on the Lord.

Over and over again, the Word exhorts us to heed these life-giving, corrective words, even praising those who are quick to hear and promising them blessing and increase. Here is just a representative sampling:

> The fear of the LORD is the beginning of knowledge, but fools despise wisdom and discipline. Listen, my son, to your father's instruction and do not forsake your mother's teaching. They will be a garland to grace your head and a chain to adorn your neck. (Prov. 1:7-9)

> Do not rebuke a mocker or he will hate you; rebuke a wise man and he will love you. (Prov. 9:8)

> He who listens to a life-giving rebuke will be at home among the wise. (Prov. 15:31)

> A rebuke impresses a man of discernment more than a hundred lashes a fool. (Prov. 17:10)

Flog a mocker, and the simple will learn prudence; rebuke a discerning man, and he will gain knowledge. (Prov. 19:25).

Like an earring of gold or an ornament of fine gold is a wise man's rebuke to a listening ear. (Prov. 25:12)

Better is open rebuke than hidden love. Wounds from a friend can be trusted, but an enemy multiplies kisses. (Prov. 27:5-6)

He who rebukes a man will in the end gain more favor than he who has a flattering tongue. (Prov. 28:23)

A man who remains stiff-necked after many rebukes will suddenly be destroyed—without remedy. (Prov. 29:1)

It is better to heed a wise man's rebuke than to listen to the song of fools. (Eccles. 7:5)

According to the Bible, godly rebuke is a sign of the Lord's love, and it should be warmly welcomed:

My son, do not despise the LORD's discipline and do not resent His rebuke, because the LORD disciplines those He loves, as a father the son he delights in. (Prov. 3:11-12)[1]

Those whom I love I rebuke and discipline. So be earnest, and repent. Here I am! I stand at the door and knock. If anyone hears My voice and opens the door, I will come in and eat with him, and he with Me. (Rev. 3:19-20)

Let a righteous man strike me—it is a kindness; let him rebuke me—it is oil on my head. My head will not refuse it. (Ps. 141:5a; this is an accurate rendering of the Hebrew)[2]

Biblical correction brings life:

Blessed is the man whom God corrects; so do not despise the discipline of the Almighty. For He wounds, but He also binds up; He injures, but His hands also heal. From six calamities He will rescue you; in seven no harm will befall you. In famine He will ransom you from death, and in battle from the stroke of the sword. You will be protected from the lash of the tongue, and need not fear when destruction comes. You will laugh at destruction and famine, and need not fear the beasts of the earth. For you will have a covenant with the stones of the field, and the wild animals will be at peace with you. You will know that your tent is secure; you will take stock of your property and find nothing missing. You will know that your children will be many, and your descendants like the grass of the earth. You will come to the grave in full vigor, like sheaves gathered in season. (Job 5:17-26; you may want to read this passage again. This is the fruit that comes from receiving divine correction!)[3]

Yes, godly, constructive correction is essential. In fact, as Paul states plainly, one of the central purposes of the Word of God (and the minister of the Word) is to bring correction and rebuke:

> All Scripture is God-breathed and is useful for teaching, rebuking, correcting and training in righteousness, so that the man of God may be thoroughly equipped for every good work. In the presence of God and of Christ Jesus, who will judge the living and the dead, and in view of His appearing and His kingdom, I give you this charge: Preach the Word; be prepared in season and out of season; correct, rebuke and encourage—with great patience and careful instruction. For the time will come when men will not put up with sound doctrine. Instead, to suit their own desires, they will gather around them a great number of teachers to say what their itching ears want to hear. They will turn their ears away from the truth and turn aside to myths. (2 Tim. 3:16–4:4)

> These, then, are the things you should teach. Encourage and rebuke with all authority. Do not let anyone despise you. (Tit. 2:15)

Thank God for righteous correction and rebuke! Thank God for those who speak the truth in love, regardless of the consequences, regardless of who rejects them or accepts them. These people are a vital gift to the Church, and we would all do well to listen to them when they speak—whoever and wherever they are.

This is especially important to remember in times of revival. Why? Because every revival will have its critics, and it is all too easy for those who are being used in a real move of God to reject *all* criticism and disagreement as coming from the devil or the flesh, thereby disregarding counsel and insight that could have been life-giving or life-saving. Because destructive criticism is often so loud and aggressive, constructive correction frequently goes unheard. You can easily get into the habit of simply ignoring everyone who differs with you, reasoning to yourself, "Since every revival has its critics and I am involved in real revival, those who disagree with me are therefore negative, harmful critics."

This kind of attitude quickly breeds pride, the insidious sin that can easily enter the hearts of those who are being powerfully used by the Lord, causing them to shut their ears to any kind of input, advice, or rebuke.[4] (By the way, pride is often the fleshly cover-up for insecurity, the sinful way of avoiding healthy and honest self-examination.) For these reasons, those involved in revival should be careful to maintain a humble, teachable attitude, welcoming constructive input and correction. This kind of "criticism" brings life.

The same cannot be said for destructive criticism. It does far more harm than good. (To be totally candid, some destructive critics wreak havoc on the Body and are so injurious in their tactics and techniques, that, even when they are correct they actually hurt people more than they help them.) Of course, there are many opposers of revival who do not denounce, demean, and denigrate those with whom they differ. They are teachable and open and do not think they have an exclusive handle on the truth. People like this will respond positively to honest interaction, often revising their positions when confronted with truth and even embracing the very thing they once rejected. As one such brother stated when he recanted his previous views, "I will be praying for the revival now, instead of trying to tear it down...[and] may God bestow upon me the wisdom and the knowledge to be able to impart credible and scholarly reasoning to those who may have justifiable concerns."[5]

Sadly, this kind of attitude is rarely seen among the destructive critics. In fact, although these critics strenuously deny the accusation that they are "Pharisaical," this description is often accurate, for the same attitude that Jesus denounced in the hypocritical leaders of His day—a proud, self-righteous, negative, picky, faultfinding, unthankful, unhappy, often stiff, never-satisfied attitude— can be found among our critical brothers and sisters today. Let's consider some of the characteristics of a critical spirit.

In my previous book, *From Holy Laughter to Holy Fire: America on the Edge of Revival*, I listed ten characteristics of religious hypocrisy. A religious hypocrite: 1) claims to have an exclusive corner on the truth, even among God's people; 2) is self-righteous; 3) is a slave to human praise and criticism; 4) is jealous, envious, and competitive; 5) is highly critical; 6) wants his spirituality to be seen; 7) is cynical and skeptical; 8) produces bondage instead of freedom; 9) is more concerned with outward forms and traditions than with the power of God, mercy, and compassion; 10) is narrowly nationalistic and dangerously denominational.[6] Most of these characteristics (really, all but numbers 3, 4, and 6) also describe some of the destructive tendencies of the negative critic, and *destructive* is the best way to describe the effects that these critics have. But we need to be careful! To the extent that these tendencies are found in any of our lives, we too will hurt the sheep and blemish the name of the Lord. So, though we may be quick to point the finger at the critics, we must also point it at ourselves, since any of us can fall prey to these destructive attitudes and biases.

As we look carefully at more specific aspects of this negative, critical spirit, we should keep looking *inward* as well as looking *outward*. In other words, these points are important for self-examination as well as for seeking to distinguish between constructive correction and destructive criticism. We must be diligent to never let these poisonous weeds sprout up in our own life or ministry, and we must never be intimidated by those opposers who bear these negative, destructive characteristics.

1) A destructive critic is often self-appointed rather than God-appointed. When rebuking the religious hypocrites, Jesus reminded His disciples, "The greatest among you will be your servant. For whoever exalts himself will be humbled, and whoever humbles himself will be exalted" (Matt. 23:11-12). Often, the critic falls prey to this very sin of self-exaltation, because, after feeling a "burden" to safeguard the Body from deception and error, he rigidly and dogmatically sets up his own beliefs as the standard by which everything else must be judged. Frequently, his "calling" was never confirmed by leaders who knew him, and he was not raised up and sent out by a home church or denomination as he would have been if he had been going to the mission field, planting a new congregation, or beginning a new evangelistic ministry. Rather, he has taken it upon himself to keep the Church straight.

Even though the motivation for this can be sincere and noble, the "ministry" it produces is often quite dangerous, since destructive critics like this are frequently *unaccountable and unsubmissive to authority*. They may be mavericks who were not properly nurtured, never getting their rough edges smoothed out and never learning essential ministry principles. Frequently, they fail to respect other leaders because they are fully convinced that they alone are right. And, because they have not endured the fire of practical church life and day-to-day ministry, they do not recognize their own shortcomings and flaws. (There is nothing like real-life, shoulder-to-shoulder ministry with a very human team of leaders and a still imperfect flock to show you your own frailty and weakness!) In fact, the precious, priceless quality of brokenness is often scarce among the negative critics.

These critics warn the Church about the alleged "cult-like" tendencies of certain contemporary Christian movements, yet their own exclusive attitude is actually somewhat cult-like. In fact, if you look at those who started cults and false religions, you will see that many of them began in the faith but then cast off spiritual authority, surrounding themselves with a small group of devoted followers before separating themselves from accountability to the rest of the Body, ultimately rejecting basic scriptural truths. Look out for this kind of attitude among the destructive critics, and don't be afraid to ask the critic to whom he is accountable (after first asking yourself to whom *you* are accountable!).

This aspect of self-appointed unaccountability certainly does not apply to all critics, but it is fairly common and, potentially, very dangerous. And because this kind of attitude revolves around self, a destructive critic can sometimes be more concerned with his own reputation than with the reputation of the Church. When he attacks the "false unity movements" in the Church (as many critics do, failing to distinguish between a genuine work of the Spirit to unite the people of God and works that are fleshly, compromised efforts) he betrays the fact that he has little concern for the overall unity of the Body. After all, aside from the critic and the holy remnant that hangs on his every word, not too many others are even saved![7]

2) A destructive critic frequently speaks out of limited (or no) personal experience in the matters on which he makes pronouncements. Jesus said to the Pharisees, "Woe to you, teachers of the law and Pharisees, you hypocrites! You shut the kingdom of heaven in men's faces. You yourselves do not enter, nor will you let those enter who are trying to" (Matt. 23:13). On a certain level, this applies to the critics as they speak about false revival, assuring the multitudes who claim to have been transformed through this current move of God that their experience is suspect. Yet the critics themselves have never experienced powerful sweeping revival, and they most certainly have never *ignited* this kind of a revival. (One critic with whom I spoke at length questioned whether a prominent, contemporary revival was really worthy of being called a "revival"—in light of the historic use of the term—but then said moments later, "Look, I witness to people and disciple them in the Lord. If that's not revival, what is?" So, a radical, widespread visitation of the Spirit that is impacting millions of lives is "not revival"—because this particular critic doesn't like a few of the manifestations he has seen—whereas normal Christian soul-winning *is* revival!)

It is a fact that the Holy Spirit has been moving powerfully around the world for years in nations like China and Africa, yet the critics, for the most part, have not participated in what the Lord is doing in places like these. Rather, they point to revivals of the past (which at this point exist only on paper) or to the "coming great revival" (which at this point exists only in theory) while vilifying the present-day visitation. They don't enter into God's current work themselves, and they try to stop those who do want to go in from making it past the front door. Instead of leading the way, they block the way without showing a better way. What a harmful position to take!

Often, negative critics revel in God's mighty moves of the past, while reviling His mighty move in the present. Jesus exposed this same raw nerve when He said:

Woe to you, teachers of the law and Pharisees, you hypocrites! You build tombs for the prophets and decorate the graves of the righteous. And you say, "If we had lived in the days of our forefathers, we would not have taken part with them in shedding the blood of the prophets." (Matt. 23:29-30)

Doesn't this sound familiar? "How wonderful the Great Awakening was! How awesome the Hebrides Revival was! How glorious the Welsh Revival was! We fully embrace these tremendous outpourings of the Spirit. But we reject that which you claim is a current, glorious outpouring. Yes, it's true that we're criticizing this so-called contemporary revival. But we're not like the critics of past revivals. If we had lived then, we would have welcomed them with open arms!" This sounds just like the religious leaders of Jesus' day who claimed to love the prophets of old ("We're not like our forefathers who resisted the true God-sent prophets") and yet killed the true, God-sent Prophet of their generation.

Dear critic, how do you know you would have embraced the great revivals of the past when you cannot point to a single, bona fide, widespread revival that meets with your approval anywhere in the world *today*? Something is wrong with this picture! Or, to bring this one step closer to home: Are *you* experiencing revival? Can you lead me (or my church) into the fullness of that "genuine revival" of which you speak?

Of course, this challenge applies only to those critics who actually believe that real revival will one day come. Some critics reject all claims of revival today because they are convinced that there will be no more revival— ever!—for the Church in this age. At least they are consistent: They are pessimistic and hopeless, and they lead others into their pessimism and hopelessness. To the rest I say: If you can't lead the way, then get out of the way. Maybe you really don't know where you are going after all! (And to those of us who are grieved by the negative fruit of the critics, I ask, are *we* leading the way?) And this is closely related to the next point:

3) A destructive critic is often an expert in tearing down but a novice in building up. Of course, it's easier to tear down than to build up. (It has been said that, "You have to be little to belittle," and someone else once commented, "Fault finding is like window washing. All the dirt seems to be on the other side."[8]) Unfortunately, many critics are loose cannons who freely and flippantly air their damning opinions and derogatory judgments for all to hear.[9] They speak first and consider the consequences later, hardly ever considering the amount of damage that their verbal and written attacks do. (This is in addition to the fact that their followers tend to emulate the destructive example they set. And so, while the critics mock the idea of a "highly transferable" anointing—a concept that has been both powerfully used and pitifully abused in the current revival—they certainly prove that a proud, judgmental attitude is "highly transferable" *and* quite contagious! Such attitudes spread like cancer, and kill like cancer too.)

Destructive critics fail to realize that they are often guilty of gossip and slander, all under the guise of strengthening the Church. Isn't this a characteristic of a blind guide? Yes, these critics are quick to point to individuals whom they claim have been hurt through the current revival while they are oblivious to the fact that they themselves are dampening and damaging the faith of many through their often slanderous, inaccurate, and exaggerated words. How great is the carnage of the critics!

James warned us plainly about the dangers and responsibilities of those who take it on themselves to be teachers of the Word. "Not many of you should presume to be teachers, my brothers," he wrote, "because you know that we who teach will be judged more strictly" (Jas. 3:1). In contrast with this, many critics begin their comments with statements like (all these are actual quotes or representative paraphrases), "While not being an expert on revival," or, "I am not a theologian or Bible scholar," or, "I am just a little sheep, with no ministry experience," or, when pressed to substantiate an accusation, "You really need to contact so and so. They have firsthand information. Mine is only secondhand." Yet they still attack and malign with a vengeance!

Ira Sankey, Moody's minister of music, once remarked, "It only takes half a man to criticize," and Paul himself spoke of his apostolic authority as "the authority the Lord gave me for building you up, not for tearing you down" (2 Cor. 13:10b). Even Jeremiah, the weeping prophet from Anathoth, the lonely messenger called to pronounce judgment on his sinning generation, was given a positive commission as well: "See, today I appoint you over nations and kingdoms to uproot and tear down, to destroy and overthrow, to build and to plant" (Jer. 1:10; see also Jer. 24:6; 31:28; 42:10).[10] My critical friends, you have certainly sought to tear down and destroy the current revival. Where is the revival that you have built up and planted?

4) A destructive critic can be a hairsplitter and nitpicker, straining out a gnat but swallowing a camel. Many of the Pharisees were scrupulous in the details of religious practice while neglecting the fundamentals of the faith, as Jesus said:

> Woe to you, teachers of the law and Pharisees, you hypocrites! You give a tenth of your spices—mint, dill and cummin. But *you have neglected the more important matters of the law*—justice, mercy and faithfulness. You should have practiced the latter, without neglecting the former. You blind guides! *You strain out a gnat but swallow a camel.* (Matt. 23:23-24)

This is one of the more ironic characteristics of the destructive critics. They will launch a holy war in the name of doctrinal purity and love for the Lord, subjecting revival preachers and teachers to the most rigorous scrutiny, examining their ministries with a fine-tooth comb and calling them to account for every little comment or anecdote that has ever proceeded from their mouths, yet they will do this in the most unChristlike manner imaginable. They will subject a revival service to their skeptical scrutiny, as contenders for the real faith, of course, and then mock it in the most ugly terms.

To give you one recent example, in a purportedly serious and thoughtful article expressing deep concerns with a major outpouring, two critics maligned a sacred night of intercession and repentance in the revival with the almost unthinkable description of an "orgy of voyeurism." They objected to the fact that young people under a tremendous burden of prayer were carried onto the church platform where they travailed on their faces before God, complaining that, "A biblical concept [i.e., intercession] is now being redefined in a totally sensual way and is identified with convulsions."[11] And these authors, who can put into print such an unseemly description (friend, when is the last time you used words like *orgy* or *voyeurism*?), somehow deem themselves capable of questioning the spiritual soundness of those who directed the wonderful meeting that night.[12]

One pastor who presents himself as having a deep burden for the Body of Christ attacked one revival leader in such sick, slanderous terms that it is inappropriate even to print the description here. Yet he published this trash in his national newspaper, and— God have mercy on this critic— explicitly identified the leader whom he defamed. Not only are his ugly and completely untrue judgments despicable in the eyes of the Lord, but they even call into question the purity of this critic's heart, since his very allegations were almost perverse. Yet this pastor, who dares to speak such biased, godless judgments, has appointed himself to keep the Church free from the dangers of false revival.[13]

Critics who claim to be sticklers for the Word will attack other Christian leaders with charges of "false prophet" or "heretic," claiming that many of these leaders are guilty of blaspheming the Spirit; yet in making horrific charges against their brothers, these destructive critics misinterpret the very Scriptures that they claim to follow so closely. We need to be careful! (The fact is, we should *never* call a fellow Christian a false prophet, since the New Testament makes it clear that false prophets are wolves in sheep's clothing and are *not* part of the Church [see Matt. 7:15-23; 24:10-11,24; 2 Pet. 2:1-3; 1 John 4:1-6]. It is one thing to prophesy falsely; it is another thing to be a false prophet. It is one thing to teach something that is false; it is another thing to be a false teacher. Study the Word on this!)[14]

When the critic claims that people involved in revival today are preaching another Jesus or another gospel, does he realize that he is pronouncing them hell-bound (see Gal. 1:6-9)? And if he dares to say that they are guilty of blaspheming the Spirit, does he recognize that, in his opinion, he is declaring them to be eternally condemned and without forgiveness (see Chapter Two, "Scorning the Sacred: When Critics Enter the Danger Zone")? Yet many critics freely fling these terms around—though few realize how serious such charges are— out of alleged loyalty to the Word. Instead, they misuse that very Word by condemning to hell those who are righteous in God's sight through the blood of His Son.

Similar to this unsound practice is the tendency of destructive critics to major on the minors. They will highlight an off-the-cuff, somewhat flippant, insignificant comment made by a minister years ago, while overlooking hundreds of hours of solid biblical teaching by that same man. And they will ignore the fact that the fundamental message and emphasis of the ministry (or minister, or movement) they attack is completely scriptural, as well as completely disregarding the truly Christian fruit that is produced. How is this honest or helpful? Is this practice really motivated by a spirit of love for the Lord, love for the Church, and love for the truth? Or is it just another aspect of that very spirit that Jesus described, pursuing the "purity" of the Church in an impure way? And why is it that an unusual—but not unscriptural—manifestation in a revival service is to be rejected like the plague, while the critics' unscriptural method of publicly mocking and denigrating fellow ministers (by name!) is to be accepted? What a destructive double standard![15]

This again points to the blindness of the critics. They will watch a video of a powerful meeting attended by thousands of people and go ballistic because one person at the altar suddenly falls to the floor, totally ignoring the fact that Jesus is being preached in clarity, that carnality and compromise are being rebuked, and that hundreds of backsliders and sinners are being transformed. What blindness!

This is reminiscent of the approach of Jesus' opponents: "Some of them were looking for a reason to accuse Jesus, so they watched Him closely to see if He would heal him on the Sabbath" (Mark 3:2). Note the text carefully: They were looking for a reason to accuse the Lord, not a reason to acclaim Him, and because they watched Him closely, with an adversarial, contrary eye, they failed to see the glory of God manifest in the miraculous healing that took place moments later (see Mark 3:3-5). All they could see was that He broke their tradition. That critical spirit stole their sight.

A negative critic will view the testimony of a trembling young woman who was sexually abused as a child, leading to a life of guilt, shame, and attempted suicide, but who is now totally free after meeting the Lord in a revival service; yet the critic doesn't hear these wonderful words, nor does his spirit rejoice when the Scriptures are proclaimed from this new convert's lips. Why? Because she is shaking as she speaks! Her head is bobbing a little! So these critics are unable to hear the God-exalting testimony that is being shared so wonderfully, and they cannot see the transforming power of the Spirit at work right before their eyes. All this is because they are focusing on outward nonessentials while ignoring essential inward changes resulting from the preaching of the truth. And yet we are somehow asked to believe that these critics are reliable guides who will steer us into a *true* visitation of the Spirit.

5) A destructive critic feeds on negativity and fosters unbelief, suspicion, and fear. Over and over again, the Scriptures urge us to fear God, telling us that this reverential fear is the beginning of wisdom and knowledge (see Prov. 1:7; Job 28:28) and the foundation of holiness and obedience (see Ex. 20:20; Eccles. 12:13; 1 Pet. 1:14-19). Proverbs tells us that the fear of the Lord is a refuge and strength, a source of life and protection (see Prov. 14:26-27), and Jesus taught us to fear no one and nothing except God Himself (Matt. 10:28). This is important to remember! He who fears God need not fear Satan or his works.

In the fear of the Lord (which includes a recognition of who He is, a careful lifestyle in light of His purity and power, and the security that comes from being under His covering) there is protection. This includes protection from deception. In the fear of the Lord, there is also liberty. Fearing Him sets us free from all other fears. Fearing Him gives us confidence. He will keep His own.[16]

Somehow the critics often miss this, and their hyper-suspicious, conspiracy-everywhere mentality breeds bondage to fear and begets spiritual paralysis and inertia. This approach to gospel living poisons faith rather than produces faith, for the critic is often vigilant when it comes to knowing what the devil is doing (actually, giving him more credit than he deserves) and negligent when it comes to knowing what God is doing. He is constantly gathering negative, discouraging information ("So many people are being deceived!"), looking eagerly for the latest destructive trend in the Church while being wary of everything that is alive and thriving. He spends precious little time gathering information about those who are being gloriously touched in the very movements he rejects. How does this strengthen faith in the Lord?

After digesting some of the critics' teaching, you feel afraid even to visit a church or listen to a minister who doesn't bear their highly selective seal of approval. "Watch out! You may get demonized if that person who just attended the revival meetings so much as brushes up against you, and you may get influenced by an alien spirit if that preacher even shakes your hand. Careful! There are dark spirits lurking everywhere, ready to pounce on you the moment you put down your cult-watch manual." Friends, this is not New Testament Christianity!

One dear woman who attended less than one hour of a powerful revival service was so frightened by a few people shaking a little and by some talk that night about "the river of God" (actually becoming concerned that the leaders there were into river-worship and not Jesus-worship!) that she fled the meeting in haste, her kids in tow, leaving in the parking lot the books and tapes she had just purchased. She didn't want anything unclean or deceptive to get on her children![17]

From whence does this kind of attitude come? Certainly not from above! Yet this fearful, paranoid mindset is becoming more and more common, to the point that brothers and sisters in Christ look at each other with deep distrust, as if one of them had spiritual rabies or an unholy plague. Why such suspicion and fear?

It is not surprising that different Christians may have different beliefs and convictions when it comes to the nonessentials, or that some zealous Christians may judge their more formal brothers to be somewhat cold, while their solid and steady fellow believers will judge *them* to be somewhat emotional. Such perceptions and differences, right or wrong, merited or unmerited, are completely under-standable. But to look at other saints whom you have known for years as if they have suddenly become unclean or contagious—just because they attended a renewal meeting somewhere and received prayer—this is inexcusable and immature.

Yet people today will turn on a dime against formerly trusted, cherished colleagues and co-workers simply because they went to a certain place or were blessed through a certain outpouring. "You went there?! That's the place where they work people into spasms and fits while others roll on the ground and bark. Stay away from me! You've got the 'cooties!' " (I recently returned home one night to find an *anonymous* message on my answering machine from a "concerned" friend. This sister, who said she greatly respected me in the past, was now grieved that I had fallen prey to "New Age" and "witchcraft" manifestations! And what was the great sin I had committed? It was becoming part of the leadership team in the Brownsville Revival, a revival about which I am sure she knew ab-solutely nothing.)

How can people believe that friends and leaders with whom they have labored for years have gone so quickly off the deep end? (This seems to be the spiritual equivalent of the invasion of the body-snatchers, if you know what I mean.) And why is it that some of these dear saints are afraid even to talk with you about their dif-ferences? (It seems these folks have completely forgotten John 7:51: "Does our law condemn anyone without first hearing him to find out what he is doing?")[18] This behavior is due to the fear-mongering tactics of the negative critics. They cause you to harbor suspicion about almost everyone (except themselves, of course). This is certainly *not* a Spirit-birthed frame of mind.

Look at 1 John 4:18: "There is no fear in love. But perfect love drives out fear, because fear has to do with punishment. The one who fears is not made perfect in love."[19] Believers who are envel-oped in the love of God are not fearful people. They do not cower before their Father in servile fear. (See Romans 8:15a: "For you did not receive a spirit that makes you a slave again to fear, but you re-ceived the Spirit of sonship.") Neither do those who know the love of their Father fear for their present or future well-being (see Is. 41:10; John 14:27). They certainly don't fear the devices of the devil. Rather, they follow Paul's admonition to the Ephesians to "put on the full armor of God so that you can take your stand against the devil's schemes" (Eph. 6:11). Paul also reminded the Corinthians that there was no reason for Satan to outwit them, since they were "not unaware of his schemes" (2 Cor. 2:11). We have a real, deadly, diabolical enemy, but he does not sit enthroned in the highest heavens, nor does he have the ability to suddenly take over the souls of devoted, Word-loving, Jesus-honoring children of God. Yet the destructive approach of the negative critics gives the impression that he can. For the good of the Church, this really needs to stop.

Listen to Paul's counsel to Timothy:

> As I urged you when I went into Macedonia, stay there in Ephesus so that you may command certain men not to teach false doctrines any longer nor to devote themselves to myths and endless genealogies. These promote controversies rather than God's work—which is by faith. The goal of this command is love, which comes from a pure heart and a good conscience and a sincere faith. Some have wandered away from these and turned to meaningless talk. (1 Tim. 1:3-6)[20]

Isn't it high time that we gave up the meaningless talk? Let's recognize destructive, critical attitudes and tendencies in our own lives and nail them to the cross, renewing our minds with the Word of God. And let's not be moved by the negative words of those who oppose real revival today. The Lord is certainly not slowing down because some people don't like what He's doing or how He's doing it. He is marching right on! And He is calling each of us to cooperate with His work (which is by faith, as Paul wrote) and to build and cultivate love—love for Him, love for His people, and love for this dying world.

And so, I urge you, dear critic, to put down your sword and to pick up your sickle. There's a harvest out there waiting to be reaped.

I have been saved 40 years, went through secular high school, universities, and my Doctorate is from Florida State University. I've been in the district for 20 years, I have been at this school for 9 years. I have never seen a move of God in schools like what we have since the [Brownsville] Revival began. Kids tell me, "I got saved, my attention deficit is gone, I can study. I've been released from getting up every morning hating my uncle for some abuse that occurred when I was younger. I've been released from drugs." One girl said she used to not want to live, she was controlled by drugs, depressed, and it's all gone.

> Dr. Charles Woolwine, Vice-Principal, Niceville High School
> where hundreds of students have been powerfully impacted by the revival

I have prayed for revival for 51 years, 5 months, and 15 days. I have led and raised up revival prayer movements through most of these years. At last I have seen it—at Brownsville. I felt like Simeon who saw God's salvation after many years, and then asked if he could depart in peace!! You can see how encouraged I was while with you.

> A letter from a British evangelical leader
> after visiting the Brownsville Revival

I must tell you that since attending the [Brownsville leadership] conference in November [1996], my own life has been profoundly affected. I feel like I have been born again all over again (I realize that's what is meant to happen in revival) and am experiencing the presence of God in a way I have never done before. The first Sunday I was back, I stood in front of the congregation here in Alton to greet the people and just broke down uncontrollably. Many in the congregation began to do the same....I did manage to deliver the Word the Lord had given me the night before. I knew I had to, as I was experiencing such a burden in my heart in a way I have never experienced before. I spoke from Isaiah 6..."I have seen the Lord...Woe to me, I am ruined! For I am a man of unclean lips and live among a people of unclean lips and my eyes have seen the King, the Lord Almighty." I gave opportunity to the people to respond and every single person came forward to repent and be cleansed....There are many things I could share, but just to say that there is a new spirit over the people. People want to worship and pray in a way they've never done before and have a whole new desire to see their families, friends and neighbours saved. Something has begun, I just know it.

> E-mail from a British pastor after his visit to the Brownsville Revival

It was like we had somehow fallen into a real life horror movie!!! I still can hardly believe what I saw with my own eyes!!! It was evil!!! Those people are not being saved; they can say the sinner's prayer all day long, but unless the true Holy Spirit is there to do the work of regeneration they cannot be saved. The Spirit of the Lord must draw people to Christ, and He was not there!!!!!!!!!!! This is the great deception!!!!!!!!

> Publicly circulated e-mail from a
> one-time visitor to the Brownsville Revival

Chapter Five

Let No One Deceive You

According to the New Testament, the possibility of deception is very real. In fact the Scriptures indicate that most of the human race—today as well as in the past—is deceived. Perishing sinners don't know they are hell-bound. They don't know the religion they are following is not the true religion and the "god" they are worshiping is not the one true God. They don't know they are guilty transgressors who will one day be held accountable for their deeds. They are sick and dying but think they are healthy and thriving. They are slaves to the devil but imagine they are free. That is the nature of deception, and most of the human race is deceived.

But that doesn't mean that everyone has to be deceived! We can be kept safe in Jesus (and following Him is not like walking through a mine field).[1] The Lord can bring us into a wide place where we can be firmly rooted and secure, and it is for that very reason that the Bible often says to us: "Be not deceived." God tells us not to be deceived because we don't need to be deceived! On the one hand, if we fail to heed God's warnings, we open the door wide to deception. But on the other hand, it's because we *can* be protected that we are forewarned. We don't need to be misled! Yes, God can set our feet on a rock and give us a firm place on which to stand (Ps. 40:2). He can *establish* us in the faith (Rom. 16:25; Eph. 3:17; Col. 1:23; 2 Pet. 1:12).

Following Jesus is not like walking a tight rope (one wrong move, even by a millimeter, and you're gone!). No. The Shepherd of our souls (1 Pet. 2:25) knows how to keep His sheep, and He will carefully guard His purchased possessions. In fact, the New Testament not only calls Jesus our Shepherd, but it also calls Him the

Good Shepherd (John 10:14) and the Great Shepherd (Heb. 13:20).[2] I think His sheep can trust His keeping power!

Of course, that doesn't mean we are untouchable and "untemptable." Nor does it mean we cannot possibly be misled or deceived. Perish the thought. As Paul wrote to the Corinthians, "So, if you think you are standing firm, be careful that you don't fall!" (1 Cor. 10:12) Or, as he expressed it to the Galatians: "If anyone thinks he is something when he is nothing, he deceives himself" (Gal. 6:3).

Yes, there are plenty of warnings about deception in the New Testament that are directed toward believers. God is telling His children to be careful and watch out. The Word warns us not to follow false messiahs or give credence to false miracles (which are designed to validate the claims of the false messiahs). It instructs us not to listen to false messages, not to play games with sin, and not to fool ourselves with empty religion. *But with all these scriptural warnings against deception, nowhere does the Bible warn us to be careful about things like "falling under the power," shaking, or being overcome by the Spirit.*

These things are simply not issues, unless, to say it again, they cause us to take our eyes off the Jesus of the Bible or to dilute our resolve against sin. Otherwise, they are simply peripheral matters, things not worthy of special attention; they are only outward manifestations which in and of themselves could just as easily be heavenly, human, or hellish. The real issue—and this is indisputable from a careful study of the Scriptures—has to do with the person and work of Jesus. That's where the rubber meets the road. If the gospel message is being proclaimed in purity, resulting in holy living and love for the Word of God, if the truth is being preached and lived out, *then deception is not at work in any significant way*. Period. Whether people shake or fall is not important.[3]

Let's take two hypothetical examples. In the first example, we'll say that an unbeliever comes into our assembly, is overcome by God's power (which, just like demonic power, is invisible to the human eye), falls to the ground, shakes and cries out, then two hours later arises radically transformed, thoroughly repentant, completely committed to Jesus, and lives out the rest of his life in faithful service to the Lord. The power that touched him was from above! On the other hand, let's say that a committed believer begins attending special meetings where people are supposedly "falling under the power" and where "prophetic" messages are being given which declare, "I am the Lord and I say to you My people, 'Do not worry about your sins. They are all forgiven! Just do what comes naturally. There is no more sin in Me. Nothing is unholy. Everything is now pure!' " Friend, the "spirit" at work there is not from God. Deception is rampant.

But there is something you must see in these illustrations. Outward manifestations of falling or shaking were not the deciding factor. It was the Spirit (or spirit) *behind* the manifestations that was critically important. That's where the Lord (or Satan) is doing His (or his) work. That's where people are being drawn toward (or away from) Jesus, toward (or away from) the Word, toward (or away from) holiness. The root is known by the fruit! What kind of fruit is being produced?

"But," you object, "what if someone took LSD, had a vision of Jesus, and became a believer? You'd say that taking LSD was from the Lord." Hardly! I'd say that God somehow brought good out of a sinful, demonic situation.

"Well, then," you reply, "I could say the same thing about your hypothetical example of the man who shook violently, fell to the ground in a heap, and arose converted two hours later. God somehow brought good out of a sinful, demonic situation"

Sorry, friend, but you're comparing apples with oranges. In fact, you've just demonstrated that you're still missing the whole point. *There is nothing necessarily wrong with shaking or falling to the floor.* This could be the result of the power of God or the power of Satan, the result of mass hysteria or a physical disorder. It could be good, bad, or neutral, in complete contrast with LSD, which is always bad and demonic. Also, the "fruit test" should be applied as widely as possible, looking for the clear, overwhelming evidence. If this would be done, it would be seen that LSD produces disastrous results in the lives of almost everyone who uses it, whereas the current revival is producing glorious results in the lives of almost everyone being touched by it.

"Now stop right there!" you might say. "You just don't get it. Deception is very subtle. It creeps in little by little, through the back door, not the front. The devil appears to be an angel of light, but he is really the prince of darkness. So, once you open yourself up to this whole thing being called revival—the loud, repetitive worship, the emotional altar calls, the prayer lines, and the people falling at the end—you're in trouble. The Bible tells us that deception is coming and that we shouldn't follow these kinds of false miracles and wonders. Be careful!"

Now *you* stop one second. *You* are the one who just doesn't get it. *Where is the deception?* Where is a false Christ being followed or another gospel being preached? If deception is at work, what is it doing? How are people being misled?

If we really want to understand just how misguided many of the critics of revival really are, we need to take a careful look at the New Testament warnings against deception. After all, one of the boasts of the critics is that *they* never go beyond the Word of God (as opposed to poor souls like us who apparently base our doctrine on angelic visitations, prophetic words delivered by unstable children, or revelations and dreams influenced by the Book of Mormon). And yet in spite of their claim to be the scriptural standard bearers of the day, much of the critics' theology of deception is not based on the Bible. It misses the real message of the Word, goes beyond the teaching of Scripture, and warns about things that God Himself does not see fit to warn about.[4]

The critics diligently look for demons lurking in every nook and cranny of any spiritual move in the Church, holding high the banner of "Don't be deceived!" almost the way an exorcist would make the sign of the cross before a vampire in an old movie. But is that really what the New Testament is warning us about—to be careful that the person shaking beside us in the church service is not actually flinging demons around the room? If this stuff is so dangerous, why didn't the Spirit see fit to warn us about it?

Let's study the key verses in the New Testament dealing with deception. First, we'll look at the words of Jesus in what is called the Olivet Discourse (found in Matthew 24, Mark 13, and Luke 21).

Three times Jesus warned His disciples to be on guard against deception. Jesus had just told them that the glorious temple buildings would be totally destroyed. They in turn asked Him, "Tell us...when will this happen, and what will be the sign of Your coming and of the end of the age?" (Matt. 24:3b) To this Jesus replied (and we focus here on His warnings relevant to deception):

> ...Watch out that no one deceives you. For many will come in My name, claiming, "I am the Christ," and will deceive many. ... Then you will be handed over to be persecuted and put to death, and you will be hated by all nations because of Me. At that time many will turn away from the faith and will betray and hate each other, and many false prophets will appear and deceive many people. ... At that time if anyone says to you, "Look, here is the Christ!" or, "There He is!" do not believe it. For false Christs and false prophets will appear and perform great signs and miracles to deceive even the elect—if that were possible. See, I have told you ahead of time. So if anyone tells you, "There He is, out in the desert," do not go out; or, "Here He is, in the inner rooms," do not believe it. For as lightning that comes from the east is visible even in the west, so will be the coming of the Son of Man. (Matt. 24:4-5,9-11,23-27)

Now, before we go any further, and without even addressing the specifics of this prophetic word (in other words, discussing to whom it is addressed and to what extent it applies to us today),[5] one simple question *must* be asked: What in the world do these warnings have to do with someone shaking or falling or getting excited in a revival meeting? What is the connection? How do these warnings about false messiahs and false prophets working false miracles relate in any way to contemporary issues of revival? And why is it that some critics think that by merely citing these verses ("Be careful! Jesus warned us about deception!") they have somehow demonstrated that the Bible is telling us to be very cautious about every form of renewal and outpouring?

Let's be sober and scriptural about this. Jesus is warning His disciples (we'll include ourselves here) about false messianic movements, in particular, about people claiming that *Jesus will not be coming in the clouds of heaven because He is already here.* Interestingly, in the last few years, Messianic fervor has risen greatly, and there have been some significant false messiahs in this very decade.

Most prominent was the highly influential Jewish leader Rabbi Menachem Schneerson, who was hailed by many of his followers as the Messiah before his death in 1992. (To this day, his loyal adherents still believe he is the Messiah and will soon "return.")[6] There are also various New Age "messiahs" who will supposedly be revealed soon (or, who are alleged to be already here) and who will bring the world into some kind of "Christ-consciousness," not to mention the notorious false messiah David Koresh of the Branch Davidian cult. All this could well point to the special relevance of Jesus' warnings for this day in which we live.[7]

But again, I must ask the critics honestly: What do His warnings have to do with the current revival? The outpouring of the Spirit of which I have been writing actually *centers* on the Jesus of the Scriptures, the Son of God who died for the sins of the world, the Savior and Lord who alone can forgive, the spotless Messiah who rose from the dead on the third day and who will one day return in the clouds of glory. Where is the deception?

It is one thing to point to the rise in counterfeit Christs (e.g., the Mormon "Christ" who is actually no Christ at all) and to say, "Let's remember the words of Jesus!" It is another thing entirely—in fact, it is a real misuse of the Word of God—to seek to call into question every renewal movement in the Church today just because it may come in a slightly different form than some of us are used to.

Paul warned the Corinthians about the dangers of deception, and his theme was similar to Jesus' words cited above:

> I am jealous for you with a godly jealousy. I promised you to one husband, to Christ, so that I might present you as a pure virgin to Him. But I am afraid that just as Eve was deceived by the serpent's cunning, your minds may somehow be led astray from your sincere and pure devotion to Christ. For if someone comes to you and preaches a Jesus other than the Jesus we preached, or if you receive a different spirit from the one you received, or a different gospel from the one you accepted, you put up with it easily enough. (2 Cor. 11:2-4)[8]

You see, the issue was one of receiving another Jesus, another spirit, or another gospel different than the genuine Jesus/Spirit/gospel they had accepted at the first. I have yet to hear a critic clearly explain where and by whom another Jesus or gospel is being preached in the current cross-centered, evangelistically driven revival that is impacting the nation. Where is it? I'm not interested in hearing about what someone felt in his heart or "discerned" in his spirit about the preaching he heard or the meeting he attended. (For everyone who "discerned" something wrong, I'm sure there is someone else who "discerned" something right.[9] Plus, the "discernment" argument can just be a battle of words. For example, one critic who visited a tremendous revival service later wrote, "I discerned no anointing on the worship." My reply was, "I discerned no anointing on your discernment!" Can you see how issues of *substance*—not just what I felt or you felt—need to be discussed?) I'm asking those who level the "other Jesus," "counterfeit Christ" charge to put the evidence on the table. *Show me according to the Word where the preaching emphasis has departed from the simple proclamation of the fundamental truths of the gospel.*[10] And if you can't, dear critic, quit throwing around such ugly and untrue charges.

Some "discernment ministries" are quick to quote verses like 1 Timothy 4:1 with reference to end-time deception: "The Spirit clearly says that in later times some will abandon the faith and follow deceiving spirits and things taught by demons." But they fail to quote the very next verse in which Paul states categorically that "such teachings come through hypocritical liars, whose consciences have been seared as with a hot iron" (for further discussion of these verses, see Chapter Nine, "Are We Living in the Last Days?"). What critic would dare say that the leaders in the current outpouring are "hypocritical liars" with "seared consciences"? Who is willing to make such horrific accusations?[11]

The fact is—and this is the bottom line on the issue—neither Paul nor Jesus warned us to beware of different types of spiritual manifestations. Rather, they warned us to beware of false messiahs and false messages along with false miracles that seemed to validate the false messiah and/or message. The Book of Revelation speaks about this too:

Then I saw another beast, coming out of the earth. He had two horns like a lamb, but he spoke like a dragon. He exercised all the authority of the first beast on his behalf, and made the earth and its inhabitants worship the first beast, whose fatal wound had been healed. And he performed great and miraculous signs, even causing fire to come down from heaven to earth in full view of men. *Because of the signs he was given power to do on behalf of the first beast, he deceived the inhabitants of the earth.* He ordered them to set up an image in honor of the beast who was wounded by the sword and yet lived. (Rev. 13:11-14)

I ask every critic again: What in the world does this have to do with revival today? If you say, "Well, I believe that it is all part of one great conspiracy that will eventually bring in the reign of the antichrist," I have only response for you: Don't you have anything better to do with your time? And how do you know that *you* are not part of that alleged conspiracy? How do you know that *you* haven't been duped?

Your response, I imagine, will be something like, "But I'm not following another Jesus or believing another gospel! I'm following the Word." Well, shake my hand, friend. It's looks like we're on the same side!

Of course, there is something else that exposes the total folly of the "conspiracy" theory. According to Revelation 13, the false miracles worked by the second beast are of colossal proportions, "even causing fire to come down from heaven to earth in full view of men." They are so amazing that the whole world is deceived by them. And yet there are critics today who actually equate a few people shaking in a meeting with these incredibly impressive counterfeit signs and wonders. Give me a break! Do you really think that the *whole world* will be deceived into following the antichrist because of someone trembling in church? Really, it would be hard to misuse the Word more seriously than this. (See further Chapter Eight, "Does the Devil Have a Monopoly on Miracles?")

Naturally, there will always be someone out there who will say, "Look, Paul also warned the Corinthians about receiving another spirit, and I'm sure that's exactly what's happening in these meetings today where people get worked up into a frenzy and shake and fall to the ground."

Well, putting aside the fact that it is just someone's opinion that
people are getting worked up into a frenzy, and not even dealing
here with the very obvious fact that the emphasis of the revival today is holiness and the harvest as opposed to shaking and falling,
the critics are still missing an essential point: When people receive
another spirit, it will ultimately lead to either wrong doctrine or
wrong practice. One way or another, a false spirit will lead people
astray. Therefore, I come back to my original question: Where is the
deception? Show me where the people who are being touched in the
revival are being led *away* from Jesus, *away* from the Word, *away*
from holiness, *away* from obedience. Show me!

To repeat again: Miracles themselves are not the issue. Signs
and wonders are not the problem. Departing from the truth is the issue. Embracing another Jesus is the problem. This is what the Bible
stresses. God forbid that we add to it or take away from it.

"But what about Matthew 7:21-23?" someone asks. "Didn't Jesus point to the dangers of miracles and signs there?" Not quite.
Let's see exactly what He said:

> Not everyone who says to Me, "Lord, Lord," will enter the kingdom
> of heaven, but only he who does the will of My Father who is in
> heaven. Many will say to Me on that day, "Lord, Lord, did we not
> prophesy in Your name, and in Your name drive out demons and per-
> form many miracles?" Then I will tell them plainly, "I never knew
> you. Away from Me, you evildoers!" (Matt. 7:21-23)

You see, in the early Church, healings, prophetic words, miracles, and spiritual gifts were quite common (they were actually the
norm).[12] Jesus had also taught that, in some sense, driving out demons in His name brought about a kind of spiritual validation, helping to identify a disciple as one of His own:

> "Teacher," said John, "we saw a man driving out demons in Your
> name and we told him to stop, because he was not one of us." "Do
> not stop him," Jesus said. "No one who does a miracle in My name
> can in the next moment say anything bad about Me, for whoever is
> not against us is for us." (Mark 9:38-40)

Therefore, it could have been very easy for someone to get caught
up in a kind of spiritual fervor, getting all excited about Jesus (see

Acts 19:13-17 for an example of this) and apparently demonstrating some level of unusual empowerment or gifting, while all the time this person had never surrendered to Him as Lord. So, the warning was not so much about the danger of spiritual gifts (remember, such things were the norm) but rather of failing to submit to Jesus as Lord. That was where the danger lay!

To put this in terms that many believers could relate to today, Jesus could have said something like, "Many will say to Me on that day, 'But Lord, we were baptized in Your name, and in Your name became faithful members of the local church, and in Your name prayed and saw many special things take place.' " And yet these people never truly knew Him or served Him. That's where the deception is found.

Of course, there are some who read the passage in Matthew 7 as a special warning about a great increase in counterfeit miracles *at the end of the age*, thereby getting around the argument I just raised concerning the common nature of miracles and spiritual gifts in the early Church. Still, even if you accept that point of view, it would not in any way call into question what is happening in revival today. Why? Because miracles are *not* the central issue; submitting to Jesus and doing the Father's will are the central issue. These are the very foundations of the present visitation.

The revival message that is being sounded today throughout the land says, "Repent! Get right with God! Turn from your sins and submit to His will. Jesus wants to save you and deliver you so that you can be free and clean. But if you want Him as Savior, you must serve Him as Lord." That's the message being preached. The focus is not on miracles or manifestations but on the Lord Jesus. Where is the deception in this? Where is the inherent danger? Where are we being led astray? Open your Bibles and tell me please. I'm asking you to look into the Word.

In point of fact, the majority of warnings about deception in the New Testament have to do with issues of holy living and are closely related to Jesus' words that, "Not everyone who says to Me, 'Lord, Lord,' will enter the kingdom of heaven, but only he who does the will of My Father who is in heaven" (Matt. 7:21). This underscores the fact that Jesus was warning us to beware of a "lordless," loose gospel message—not to beware of miracles in and of themselves. (Of course, anytime we put our trust in miracles without the Word, or to the exclusion of the Word, we are opening up the door to trouble, but when miracles occur in accordance with the Word or to reinforce the message of the Word we are on solid ground.)

James warned us plainly about the dangers of *self-deception*, and the issue clearly was not miracles or manifestations. The issue was obedience:

> Do not merely listen to the word, and so deceive yourselves. Do what it says. ... If anyone considers himself religious and yet does not keep a tight rein on his tongue, he deceives himself and his religion is worthless. Religion that God our Father accepts as pure and faultless is this: to look after orphans and widows in their distress and to keep oneself from being polluted by the world. (Jas. 1:22,26-27)

In a similar vein, Paul frequently exhorted his readers with the words: "Do not be deceived!"

> Do you not know that the wicked will not inherit the kingdom of God? *Do not be deceived:* Neither the sexually immoral nor idolaters nor adulterers nor male prostitutes nor homosexual offenders nor thieves nor the greedy nor drunkards nor slanderers nor swindlers will inherit the kingdom of God. And that is what some of you were. But you were washed, you were sanctified, you were justified in the name of the Lord Jesus Christ and by the Spirit of our God. (1 Cor. 6:9-11)

> The acts of the sinful nature are obvious: sexual immorality, impurity and debauchery; idolatry and witchcraft; hatred, discord, jealousy, fits of rage, selfish ambition, dissensions, factions and envy; drunkenness, orgies, and the like. I warn you, as I did before, that those who live like this will not inherit the kingdom of God. ... *Do not be deceived:* God cannot be mocked. A man reaps what he sows. The one who sows to please his sinful nature, from that nature will reap destruction; the one who sows to please the Spirit, from the Spirit will reap eternal life. (Gal. 5:19-21; 6:7-8)

> For of this you can be sure: No immoral, impure or greedy person— such a man is an idolater—has any inheritance in the kingdom of Christ and of God. *Let no one deceive you with empty words,* for

because of such things God's wrath comes on those who are disobedient. Therefore do not be partners with them. (Eph. 5:5-7)[13]

I find it painfully ironic that many of those who constantly warn us about deception today (quoting Jesus' words in Matthew 24) actually believe that, no matter how you live, once you ask Jesus to forgive your sins and save your soul, you are safe and secure. Yet Paul is almost shouting from the pages of the Word, "Don't be deceived! Those who live wicked and sinful lives will not make it into God's Kingdom." Jesus also raises His voice to these misguided critics saying, "I'm the one who told you that unless a professing believer does My Father's will, he will be cast out of My presence."

And yet these particular spiritual watchdogs have somehow fallen asleep at the gate, allowing a deceptive doctrine to infiltrate their ranks while they anxiously warn people being touched in revival—people who have repented of the very sins of which Paul spoke, people who embrace the lordship of Jesus—these critics warn them saying, "Look out! Jesus told us to be careful of deception." How blinded these dear critics are! They have failed to see the nature of Jesus' warnings and they have failed to understand how deception works.

Look at one more key passage where Paul writes in detail about the nature of the end-time deception of the antichrist:

> The coming of the lawless one will be in accordance with the work of Satan displayed in all kinds of counterfeit miracles, signs and wonders, and in every sort of evil that deceives those who are perishing. They perish because they refused to love the truth and so be saved. For this reason God sends them a powerful delusion so that they will believe the lie and so that all will be condemned who have not believed the truth but have delighted in wickedness. But we ought always to thank God for you, brothers loved by the Lord, because from the beginning God chose you to be saved through the sanctifying work of the Spirit and through belief in the truth. (2 Thess. 2:9-13)

Once again, there is an emphasis on counterfeit signs and wonders, but this time Paul tells us precisely who it is that will be misled. It is those who "perish because they refused to love the truth and so be saved"; therefore, God sends them a powerful delusion because they "have not believed the truth but have delighted in wickedness." This is in stark contrast with the Thessalonian believers who were "saved through the sanctifying work of the Spirit and through belief in the truth."[14]

Do you see the significance of this? Deception is for those who refuse the message of the gospel, who do not love the truth, who delight in wickedness. *They* are the ones who will be duped by the devil. Their whole foundation was built on falsehood; therefore, they will be easy prey for false miracles pointing to a false messiah. They rejected the Truth Himself, choosing instead to embrace a lie; therefore, they will align themselves with the father of lies. They hated God's law; therefore, they will hail the lawless one. Not so the Thessalonians! They were holy-living, God-fearing, Word-loving believers. If they continued walking down the path of righteousness, they would not be misled. Deception ought *not* deceive the elect! It is those who are perishing who are sitting ducks for deception. Isn't this what the Word says?

The real truth is that one of Satan's greatest tactics today is "deception-mania," a paralyzing, fear-laden attitude that causes God's people to withdraw from the front lines rather than attack. Instead of breeding faith for revival, it fosters pessimism, fear, and suspicion. Rather than encouraging believers to avail themselves of the fullness of the Spirit's power, it raises questions about the whole supernatural realm. It dampens, not deepens, gospel work, and instead of helping those immature and weak—yet quite genuine!—believers whose "renewal" emphasis may be a little off, it is quick to call them deceived, questioning their very salvation experience. And worst of all, it puts more confidence in the devil's power to steal and destroy than in God's power to keep and deliver.

Tragically, it is the critics who have failed to heed one of the most important New Testament warnings about Satan's wily ways. Speaking of those who had duped many of the Corinthian believers, Paul wrote:

> For such men are false apostles, deceitful workmen, masquerading as apostles of Christ. And no wonder, for Satan himself masquerades as an angel of light. It is not surprising, then, if his servants

masquerade as servants of righteousness. Their end will be what their actions deserve. (2 Cor. 11:13-15)[15]

The principle here is obvious: Satan will not come in an overtly deceptive way. Rather, he and his servants will masquerade as angels of light. While people are expecting him to sneak in through some back door or side window, he may instead knock loudly at the front door, claiming to be someone he is not.

Now, I am not hinting, implying, or stating that the critics of revival are false apostles or deceitful workmen or children of the devil or servants of Satan. God forbid that any of us think of our brothers and sisters in the Lord in such terms! But I am saying that deception, once again, may be at work in an unexpected way. It may be coming through those who most strenuously warn the Church *against* deception! Again we must ask, Who is deceiving whom?

Dear critic, is it possible that a careless use of the Word has caused you to be misled in your attack against revival? Is it possible that pride entered your heart when you dogmatically and inflexibly decided that your discernment—or that of someone whose word you accepted without question or evidence—was accurate while the discernment of thousands of godly leaders and hundreds of thousands of hungry believers was untrustworthy and undependable? Could it be that a negative mentality ("The only thing left for the Church is darkness and defection!") predisposed you to reject, rather than accept, a wonderful move of God?[16] Could it be that a small-minded, "my group alone is right" attitude hindered you from seeing the work of the Spirit in a way that was unusual to you? And is there a chance, even a slight chance, that stubbornness, not sincerity, is the main driving force that keeps you from recognizing the error of your ways? Are you the one who is deceived?

I urge you in the words of Paul to "let no one deceive you with empty words." A national awakening of monumental proportions is at hand. Whatever you do, don't be left out.

If a prophet, or one who foretells by dreams, appears among you and announces to you a miraculous sign or wonder, and if the sign or wonder of which he has spoken takes place, and he says, "Let us follow other gods" (gods you have not known) "and let us worship them," you must not listen to the words of that prophet or dreamer. The LORD your God is testing you to find out whether you love Him with all your heart and with all your soul. It is the LORD your God you must follow, and Him you must revere. Keep His commands and obey Him; serve Him and hold fast to Him. That prophet or dreamer must be put to death, because he preached rebellion against the LORD your God, who brought you out of Egypt and redeemed you from the land of slavery; he has tried to turn you from the way the LORD your God commanded you to follow. You must purge the evil from among you.

Deuteronomy 13:1-5

The next day, the one after Preparation Day, the chief priests and the Pharisees went to Pilate. "Sir," they said, "we remember that while He was still alive that deceiver said, 'After three days I will rise again.' So give the order for the tomb to be made secure until the third day. Otherwise, His disciples may come and steal the body and tell the people that He has been raised from the dead. This last deception will be worse than the first."

Matthew 27:62-64

Chapter Six

Was Jesus a False Prophet?

For all of you who are really worried about being deceived, I have good news. This is not the first time God's people have had to deal with the issue of deception on a life-and-death scale. We experienced a trial run 2,000 years ago. In fact, the scenario was quite similar. The Jewish people had the Word of God (the Hebrew Scriptures, which were later called the Old Testament by the Church), and it was the measure and rule by which everything had to be tested. Every claim to prophetic inspiration or miraculous power had to be evaluated by the written Word. That alone was the final arbiter.

Throughout Israel's history, many false prophets had been exposed. They were either guilty of speaking prophetic words in the Lord's name that did not come to pass (see Deut. 18:14-22), prophesying in the name of other gods (see Jer. 23:13), or encouraging the wicked and discouraging the righteous through their message, thereby violating the moral code of Scripture (see Jer. 23:14; Ezek. 13:22). For a God-fearing, Scripture-revering Israelite, it wasn't too hard to recognize a false prophet over the course of time. Naturally, there was often a deceptive mixture, and some false prophets delivered some messages that were in harmony with the Word and seemed to exalt Yahweh. But soon enough, their oracles were found to be either empty, idolatrous, or immoral.[1]

It was because of the possibility of this deceptive mixture that the warning in Deuteronomy 13 was especially urgent: A prophet or miracle worker may come with a validating sign or prophetic word (the people of Israel knew the value of validating miracles and words—remember Moses and the exodus?), and the word he spoke may come to pass and he may, in fact, work a miracle. The bottom line is that if he says in the end, "Let's follow other gods," they were to stone him to death. He's a false prophet. God has sent him to test His people, to see if they will really cleave to Him alone.[2]

Now, let's put today's revival critics back in the first century when Jesus came into the world. After all, if their methods are truly scriptural, those same methods would have worked just as well then as now. If the critics can separate the counterfeit from the true today, surely they could have done it then. In fact, it should have been much easier to recognize the real Messiah Himself—the living Word walking and talking among us, the Son of God in the flesh—than to sort out the counterfeit from the genuine in a contemporary revival movement.

Let's see how Jesus would have passed their test. Remember, the Israelites were already warned about false prophets, counterfeit miracles, and deception (see also Zech. 13:1-6, and note passages such as 1 Kings 22:1-38), just as we have been warned about false prophets, counterfeit miracles, and deception. If the true Messiah could pass the critics' test, true revival should also be able to pass their test. But if the criteria by which the critics evaluate contemporary claims of revival would also have disqualified Jesus, then something is wrong at a very basic level.

Shall we give it a try? Brother and Sister Critic, meet Jesus!

It begins in Galilee, where the hillside villages of Nazareth are astir. There is a man in their midst making unusual claims about Himself, saying that the prophetic Scriptures are fulfilled in Him. Could He be the one we have been waiting for? Soon enough, you are following in His footsteps, watching, praying, studying. The reports of healings and deliverance seem genuine enough, but was it right for Him to cause such a stir in the synagogue in Capernaum? The demon-possessed man screamed out right in the middle of the meeting! That never happened before Jesus came. It seems confusing! Anyway, it's too early to tell. Let's keep watching.

You follow Him to Cana where He attends a wedding. To your absolute shock, He turns water into wine. "My God! Where is that in our Scriptures? Where does it say that the Messiah will do such a thing? And our Bible is very clear: 'Wine is a mocker and beer a brawler; whoever is led astray by them is not wise' " (Prov. 20:1). Your suspicions are already beginning to rise; you had better watch Him extra carefully!

You follow Him into the region of the Gerasenes. "What's this? He seems to have gone off the deep end. He's making deals with de- mons! He's agreeing to give them a second chance! Instead of ban- ishing them to the pit (why *wouldn't* He do that unless He's secretly working with them?), He sends them into a herd of pigs...and they rush headlong into the river.... They're all destroyed...the owners have lost their income...and village life is in complete chaos. Then the people beg Him to leave their region. My God! This is more se- rious than I thought. Of course, the demonized man *was* delivered, but this has all the earmarks of a counterfeit miracle.

"In fact, I think I had better investigate further. Let's see what His family thinks about all this. What? They think He's out of His mind? They're trying to take Him away? And the religious leaders? What do they say? They say He's working with the devil himself? Little wonder. And this poor Jesus fellow keeps pointing to His mir- acles and His deliverances as if they somehow proved something. We were already forewarned about all this!

"I had better check into this guy's origins. They say He was born in Bethlehem. Well, that lines up with the Word. But He was born in a stable? Our Messiah and King born in a stable? Where is that written? I tell you, something's funny here!

"Of course, I've only heard excerpts of His teaching so far. Let me listen a little more closely. Oh no, I can't believe my ears. He's saying that if we want to follow Him, we have to *hate* our own par- ents. My Bible says that I am to honor them! But wait. This is the worst thing yet. He claims that if we want to have eternal life, we have to *eat His flesh and drink His blood.* Heretic! False prophet! Deceiver! No one in His right mind would ever utter such words. Even if He meant them metaphorically or symbolically, they are the absolute height of irreverence and a total mocking of the Word.

How can anyone possibly follow this guy? It's those miracles! They are so misleading.

"Well, He's made His way into Jerusalem. This should be His downfall. The religious leaders there are so deep in the Word. They are real contenders of the faith, sticklers for biblical accuracy. He won't stand a chance with them.

"What's this? Controversy already? He healed a lame man on the Sabbath? Well, I know there's always been a big argument about that, and He did make some valid points in His favor the last time He did it. But now it's different. Jesus instructed the man to *carry his mat*. We have laws against carrying on the Sabbath! Jeremiah specifically forbade it in the name of the Lord. But wait…He's done something else? He just spat on the dirt, made it into mud (with His own spittle!), and put it on a blind man's eyes? That's not just gross and bizarre, that's working on the Sabbath. And now, get this— they're saying that the blind man went to the pool of Siloam, washed the mud off, and can see perfectly. The uneducated masses are now hailing Jesus as the Messiah! Don't they have any discernment? Don't they know the Word?"

* * *

Well, by the time Jesus dies on the cross you're already back home, content that *you*, at least, exposed this counterfeit messiah. Of course, you know that when He was crucified last week He was claiming support from the Scriptures that the Messiah had to die and rise from the dead. But those are just isolated proof texts, hardly in harmony with the biblical picture of the Messiah as a reigning King. And you have heard, of course, that people are already stating that He rose on the third day, perpetuating His messianic claims. This deception was far more grave than you ever imagined![3] Still, the Word is perfectly clear:

> If a prophet, or one who foretells by dreams, appears among you and announces to you a miraculous sign or wonder, and if the sign or wonder of which he has spoken takes place, and he says, "Let us follow other gods" (gods you have not known) "and let us worship them," you must not listen to the words of that prophet or dreamer. The Lord your God is testing you to find out whether you love Him

with all your heart and with all your soul. It is the LORD your God you must follow, and Him you must revere. Keep His commands and obey Him; serve Him and hold fast to Him. That prophet or dreamer must be put to death, because he preached rebellion against the LORD your God, who brought you out of Egypt and redeemed you from the land of slavery; he has tried to turn you from the way the LORD your God commanded you to follow. You must purge the evil from among you. (Deut. 13:1-5)

But wait one second. There's something you seemed to have missed. Jesus never said, "Let us follow other gods and worship them." He never failed the test of a true prophet. Why then did you fail to recognize Him as the true Messiah? It is for the exact same reasons that the critics fail to recognize the Holy Spirit's work in true revival today: 1) misuse of the Scriptures (and related to this, abuse of the concept of "historical precedent"); and 2) a hostile, unsympathetic evaluation of the teaching in question. Let me explain.

One of the most common objections of the critics is: "Show me that in the Bible!" In other words, if you can't provide a specific chapter and verse that backs up a particular practice or manifestation, then it can't possibly be from God. Of course, in many cases, there *are* specific chapters and verses that back up the phenomenon under attack, but other times there are not. Does that disprove the divine origin of the movement or manifestation? Of course not. Remember, Jesus Himself did things that had no precedent in the Hebrew Scriptures—the Bible of His day—but that did not disqualify Him. Why? Because having a specific chapter and verse to back up every deed and manifestation has *never* been necessary.

It is one thing to back up every point of *doctrine* and *faith* with specific chapters and verses from the Word. This is essential. It is another thing to try to validate every *practice* or *manifestation* with specific Scripture citation. This is not only unnecessary, it is virtually impossible. (By the way, I find it ironic that one of the complaints of the critics is that some contemporary renewal leaders use the Scriptures [what do you know!] to support certain manifestations—the very thing they were challenged to do! It is also ironic that many critics who say, "Show me that in the Bible!" are actually cessationists—that is, Christians who believe that many of the spiritual gifts and manifestations recorded in the Scriptures are not for today—so, when you *do* "show them that in the Bible," they reject it anyway!)[4]

You see, if everything had to have a clear precedent in Scripture, then there would have been no way for God to have done anything different or new once the first few books of the Bible were written. In other words, if Isaiah (or Jeremiah or Ezekiel or Hosea) did something that was not recorded in the Torah (and they sure did!) someone could have said to them, "Where's that in the Word of God? I don't see anywhere where Abraham or Moses were ever commanded to marry a prostitute [Hosea was], or forbidden to marry [Jeremiah was], or directed to walk around stripped [Isaiah was], or cut their hair, throw it in the air, and chop it up before it hit the ground [Ezekiel was]."

If this line of reasoning were correct, it would have been impossible for the Lord to have commanded His prophets and servants to do anything beyond what was explicitly written in the first recognized "canonical" Word of God, the Five Books of Moses, the Torah. In the same way, Jesus did things that were without precedent or explicit example in the Old Testament, and the apostles did things that were without precedent or explicit example in the Gospels. But everything the prophets, the Messiah, and the apostles did was *in harmony* with the Word or *not in conflict* with the Word.

"But," you say, "there's a difference. Today, we have the whole Bible; the ancient Israelites (or, the first followers of Jesus) only had it in part." Sorry, friend, but your argument doesn't work. Why? Because neither the ancient Israelites nor the first followers of Jesus knew that they only had the Bible in part! The contemporaries of Joshua had no way of knowing that there would be books called Psalms and Proverbs added to the Torah. The contemporaries of Zephaniah had no way of knowing that there would be books called Haggai, Zechariah, and Malachi added to the prophetic writings. And the contemporaries of Jesus had no way of knowing that a whole series of scriptural books called the New Testament would become part of the Word of God.[5]

How then could these different generations of believers evaluate prophetic messages, unusual manifestations, and messianic claims if not by the Scriptures extant in their time? A false prophet could have simply claimed that he was bringing a completely new and previously unknown revelation, just like a false teacher today could say, "The reason you can't find support for my teaching in the New Testament is because I'm bringing a *newer testament,* the *final revelation.*" (By the way, that's just what the Koran claims to be.) Instead, *doctrinal or moral teaching* must always be directly *confirmed* or *contradicted* by the Word, but the *specific practices* associated with the teaching in question—maybe the prophet or teacher had no beard, and we were used to bearded prophets only; or perhaps he jumped up and down when he spoke, and we were used to a more subdued style; or possibly people fell to the ground as he delivered his message, and we had never seen that before—these things could not necessarily (and cannot necessarily) be evaluated by the Word. Other factors would have to be considered.

That's why the right question was not and is not, "Where is this practice, phenomenon, or manifestation explicitly spoken of in the Word of God?" Rather, the question has always had to be, "Is this practice, phenomenon, or manifestation *contrary* to the Word of God?" Or, as Derek Prince asks in his practical little book, *Protection Against Deception*:

> Is the manifestation in question in harmony with Scripture? In 2 Timothy 3:16, Paul says, *All Scripture is given by inspiration of God.* In other words, the Holy Spirit is the author of all Scripture, and He never says or does anything to contradict Himself. Every genuine manifestation of the Holy Spirit will, in some way, harmonize with Scripture.[6]

Nothing else would—or could—work without completely paralyzing God's activity at different times and places and in different cultures and settings.

Just think of the Book of Acts. There were *many* unusual things that took place without any precedent in either the Old Testament or the Gospel accounts (and remember, as we have already mentioned, there were many unusual things that took place in the Gospels that had no precedent in the Old Testament). For example, in Acts, there were the tongues of fire on the day of Pentecost; Ananias and Sapphira fell dead for lying to the Spirit about their giving; Peter's shadow healed the sick; Paul was converted through seeing a light and hearing a voice; something like scales fell from his eyes when he was healed of temporary blindness; an angel opened prison doors; a jailhouse was rocked with a divine earthquake; handkerchiefs and aprons were taken from Paul and used for healing and deliverance: These are just a sampling! And how does Luke describe the last miracle we just cited? "God did *extraordinary miracles* through Paul, so that even handkerchiefs and aprons that had touched him were taken to the sick, and their illnesses were cured and the evil spirits left them" (Acts 19:11-12). Yes, Luke called them "extraordinary," not unbiblical.[7]

There's another point to be made here as well. The Bible only tells us a portion of Jesus' mighty deeds, as John explained at the end of his Gospel: "Jesus did many other things as well. If every one of them were written down, I suppose that even the whole world would not have room for the books that would be written" (John 21:25). And, as if this were not enough, Jesus taught that we who believed in Him would not only do the *same* things He did (and only a fraction of them were written down for us) but *greater* works (John 14:12). This is saying something!

As I stated before, we must back up our *message* and our *doctrine*, the substance and core of our preaching and teaching, with explicit, clear Scripture. But, if the message is biblically based, there is nothing in the Word that says, for example, that a pastor can't use an overhead projector to illustrate his points, or that an evangelist can't walk up and down the aisles while he speaks. In the same way, the fact that a particular phenomenon or manifestation isn't recorded in the Word—as long as it is not contrary to the Word (in other words, as long as it is merely *extra*-biblical as opposed to *un*biblical)—does not necessarily bring it into question. This is the only rule that could possibly be deduced from a careful study of the Scriptures.

Did the fact that demons sometimes shrieked when Jesus cast them out—a striking manifestation without any Old Testament precedent—make Him a false prophet? Of course not. Why? Because His teaching was in accordance with the Bible, His miracles glorified the God of Israel, and there was nothing *contrary* to the Word in these occurrences. "Show me that in the Bible" would not have worked then!

Did the fact that Peter's shadow healed the sick—a miraculous act without any Gospel precedent—call into question his faithfulness to Jesus? Of course not. Why? Because his preaching was in accordance with the Bible, the healings glorified Jesus, and there was nothing contrary to the Word in what took place. Once more, "Show me that in the Bible" would not have worked.

Does the fact that today, in many revival meetings, prayer workers lay their hands on believers who sometimes fall to the ground prove that the revival in question is not real, since there is no example in the Scriptures of such a practice producing comparable results? Of course not. Why? Because the revival teaching and preaching is in harmony with the Bible, the fruit produced in the lives of those prayed for glorifies the Lord, and there is nothing *contrary to the Word* in this phenomenon. Simple! If you think it through, you will see that this is the only way things could have been judged in David's day, in Joel's day, in Jesus' day, in Paul's day, in Finney's day, in Spurgeon's day, or today. To repeat again the wise words of Jonathan Edwards, "We ought not to limit God where He has not limited Himself."[8] (This short saying is worth chewing on. It's profound *and* true.)

You see, the God we serve is a God of great variety, a God who, as to His essential nature, never changes at all (see Mal. 3:6; Jas. 1:17), but who is continually doing new things. Just look at these verses that express the wonderful diversity and vitality of our Lord:

> See, the former things have taken place, and new things I declare; before they spring into being I announce them to you. (Is. 42:9)

> Forget the former things; do not dwell on the past. See, I am doing a new thing! Now it springs up; do you not perceive it? I am making a way in the desert and streams in the wasteland. (Is. 43:18-19)

> You have heard these things; look at them all. Will you not admit them? From now on I will tell you of new things, of hidden things unknown to you. They are created now, and not long ago; you have

not heard of them before today. So you cannot say, "Yes, I knew of them." (Is. 48:6-7)

Behold, I will create new heavens and a new earth. The former things will not be remembered, nor will they come to mind. (Is. 65:17)

He who was seated on the throne said, "I am making everything new!" Then He said, "Write this down, for these words are trustworthy and true." (Rev. 21:5)

This brings us to another argument of the critics that, like the "Show me in the Bible" approach, is also misunderstood and overplayed. What I'm referring to here is the argument of historical precedent, the line of reasoning that says, "I accept the fact that certain phenomena relative to revival are not explicitly found in the Scripture. Just show me where the things you talk about today have occurred before in classic, historic revivals." In other words, even though the Scriptures do not record that anyone fell to the ground under conviction when Peter preached in Acts 2, contemporary critics state that they would have no problem—at least theoretically—with such responses to revival preaching today if similar things had occurred in past revivals. However, since there is no record of Jonathan Edwards, Charles Finney, or Evan Roberts laying hands on people who then fell to the ground, such practices today are called into question.

Of course, just as there is great value in carefully studying the Word when seeking to evaluate a particular manifestation or movement (see Chapter Ten, "All Shook Up Over a Little Shaking" for an example of this), there is also great value in studying the history of revival when seeking to evaluate specific contemporary claims. In fact, it is *ignorance* of the past that has robbed many believers today of so much of their spiritual heritage. As I have written and stressed for years, we American believers are notorious for calling every little puddle a mighty river and every meager trickle an awesome outpouring. If three people fall down after prayer in a service, we call it revival, and if five people are saved, we call it a visitation. This exposes our ignorance of the great revivals of the past, not to mention our ignorance of God's Word and God's power.[9] Also, it is comforting to know that some of the intense and unusual things that we often see in times of revival have happened before. In that sense, the unusual is really quite *usual*!

Still, there is a serious flaw in the whole "historical precedent" argument, and it is simply this: The first time something happens it has no historical precedent! There has to be a beginning somewhere, and the very examples that we cite today as "historic" were, at one time or another, brand-new, unprecedented occurrences. Consider what would have happened if the very first time someone in a meeting cried out under conviction and fell to the floor, some critic said, "When has that ever happened before? Show me that in the history of revival!"

Once again, if this approach were totally valid, God's work would have been paralyzed and it would have been impossible for Him to do anything new. Therefore, we must come to the very same conclusion regarding historical precedent that we came to regarding scriptural precedent. The ultimate question has to be: "Is this practice, phenomenon, or manifestation *contrary* to the Word of God or *in clear contradiction* to past revivals?"

Even when we ask this question, we must remember that there may be *many* things that God has done in many places over the course of many years of which we may be completely unaware. It could well be that the very thing we write off as bizarre and without historical precedent has happened hundreds of times in true revivals in India, Africa, or Europe, but that our limited knowledge has caused our so-called authoritative assessment to be narrow and misguided.[10] We must be just as careful not to throw out the baby with the bath water as to be sure that we don't put the baby into polluted waters. Both errors are to be avoided. Unfortunately, just as there are all too many believers who embrace every *apparent* move of the Spirit without even a trace of discernment or wisdom, there are all too many critics who reject every *true* move of the Spirit in the name of discernment and wisdom. As the respected New Testament scholar D.A. Carson wrote, "Empty-headed credulity is as great an enemy of true faith as chronic skepticism. Christian faith involves the sober responsibility of neither believing lies nor trusting impostors."[11]

Of course, someone could agree with me that it is impossible to reject a particular phenomenon based exclusively on the "historical precedent" argument, yet claim that it is right to look for a *pattern* of God's moving in history or for *repeated* occurrences of similar things over the years. In other words, although you can't reject something the first time it occurs simply because it never occurred before (obviously!), you could say, "When has such a thing become a pattern?" Once again, the point has some validity. How often does God do something only once?

And yet here too there is a trap. First, God *might* do something awesome and wonderful just one time, never making it into a pattern for the future. Second, the very thing some critics now reject—for example, people falling to the ground after having hands laid on them—has been a Pentecostal/charismatic pattern for some time now![12] What once had little or no precedent (although, once again, there is absolutely nothing in the phenomenon of people genuinely "going down under the power" that is *un*scriptural or *contrary* to the Word) now has ample precedent. So the "historical precedent" argument has some glaring weaknesses.

This leads to the next problem in the critics' methodology. It is their seriously flawed, "tear the teaching to pieces" approach, a practice that tends to find fault with the teaching at any cost, looking for the exceptional and presenting it as the normal, and never taking time to ask, "Could this guy (or, these people, or, this movement) really be that off the wall? Is it possible that there is an angle that I'm missing?" Perish the thought. This might blunt the critic's blow![13] And the critic must always refuse to consider the supernatural evidence, no matter how God-glorifying it may be. The supernatural is just too dangerous! Jesus had no right to point to His miracles for verification (of course, He thought otherwise; see, for example, Matthew 11:1-6,20-24; John 10:24-26,31-32,37-38; 14:11; 15:24; note also Acts 2:21, among many other verses),[14] and we have no right to point to God's mighty works in revival today. (It's a good thing this doesn't bother the Lord. *He* keeps on moving, regardless of what anyone says.)

Looking back at Jesus, everyone knew that He was a faithful, law-abiding Jew, and He was called "rabbi" by His contemporaries.[15] When He was brought before the High Priest, no two witnesses could agree on any clear accusation against Him (see Matt. 26:59-61). And He taught plainly that we were to keep the commandments, including honoring our father and mother (see Matt. 15:1-9). So, when He uttered His famous words, "If anyone comes to Me and does not hate his father and mother, his wife and children, his brothers and sisters—yes, even his own life—he cannot be My disciple" (Luke 14:26), it would have made perfect sense for the critics in our story to have inquired as to what He really meant, instead of immediately rejecting Him as a false teacher. And when He said, "...I tell you the truth, unless you eat the flesh of the Son of Man and drink His blood, you have no life in you" (John 6:53), it would have been logical for our critical, too-quick-to-draw-negative-conclusions friends to pursue Him on this and say, "Rabbi, are you advocating cannibalism with Yourself as the victim? Please clarify!" After all, there was not the slightest hint that Jesus was in favor of such a bestial practice, especially when it came to crowds of people eating His own flesh and blood. In fact, it would have been mind-boggling for any honest, sympathetic hearer to really think that *this* was what the Lord meant.[16]

In the same way, it is nothing less than mind-boggling when some critics actually think that ministers involved in the current revival—ministers who have faithfully preached the Word for decades—would now teach things like, "You don't need the blood of Jesus to cleanse you from sin. All you need to do is shake!" And it shows poor judgment on the part of the critic when he views tiny excerpts of videos or disjointed snippets of teachings (put together, of course, by staunch opponents of the current revivals) and then uses these biased, unexplained, and unrepresentative segments to form his entire view of the movement he questions. How would the critic like to be judged in this way?

I assure you, I could take excerpts of the tapes, books, or articles of major critics and make them look like complete jerks. (This is not an overstatement.) I could also run every syllable of their teachings through the toughest, most unforgiving gauntlet of biblical scholarship imaginable and make them look either ignorant or idiotic.[17] Yet if this type of treatment were applied to these critics, they would strongly object, calling it totally unfair—and they would be right! But it is just as unfair when the critic works like this, using a dishonest double standard that it is a hindrance, not help, to determining truth.[18]

The same holds true for the critics' attack on Jesus for allegedly breaking the Sabbath. If the relevant Scriptures (e.g., Jeremiah 17, dealing with "carrying" on the Sabbath) would have been studied in a careful, not cursory, manner, then no accusation would have been raised. Also, if it had been recognized that the issue was primarily one of human tradition, not biblical commandments, there would have been room for diversity.[19] Alas for the critics— of yesterday and today—they are sometimes "out to get you," so the Word is either interpreted: 1) in the most narrow possible way (so as to stand *against* whatever it is they are seeking to "expose"), in spite of the fact that other interpretations are equally plausible; 2) in a way that goes beyond what the text actually says, as if it directly applied (in a negative way, of course) to the situation under the critic's microscope; or, 3) in a highly individualistic way, as if the critic's view was the mainstream, "orthodox" view, and any deviation from this was almost heretical.[20] It is unfortunate but true that the critics are not always as sound and scholarly as they would like you to think they are (this is actually a kind statement).

And so, coming full circle, we return again to the crucial passage in Deuteronomy 13:1-5, a passage that mirrors the New Testament warnings against deception (see Chapter Five, "Let No One Deceive You"). The warning in Deuteronomy 13 pertains to following *other gods*, just as the New Testament warns against following another gospel, another Jesus, another message. There is nothing ambiguous here! *If a particular revival movement leads people to the Jesus of the Word and not away from Him, if it reinforces the claims of Scripture rather than negates them, if it is doing damage to the kingdom of darkness by producing holiness, righteousness, and reformation of life, then it is from Heaven, as surely as Jesus is the Messiah.* The Word of God makes it clear! And so we can say with unshakable confidence that the current revival that is causing millions to follow the Lord God more closely and forsake devotion to all other "gods" is absolutely Heaven-sent.[21]

Tragically, the same negative, narrow, and nit-picking spirit that would have rejected Jesus—failing to hear Him out sympathetically, looking to accuse and disprove, disregarding the overall tenor of the scriptural message in the name of loyalty to the Word—today rejects bona fide, Spirit-empowered revival sent by Jesus Himself.

I would gently challenge all critics reading this book to ask yourselves again in what way you are different in spirit than the fault-finding Pharisees of the Gospels (you may need to re-read Chapter Four of this book). Have you been guilty of the same rigid and inflexible criticism that marked many of the religious leaders of Jesus' day? Have you refused to give a sympathetic ear to teaching that at first strikes you as unfamiliar? Have you chosen not to consider the weight of tens of thousands of reports from around the world testifying to the God-ordained nature of the current revival? Have you exaggerated the biblical warnings against deception (or, at the very least, misapplied them)? Really there is much for you to weigh before the Lord.

The good news is that He is more than ready to meet you and send revival fire into your soul in harmony with His Word and to the glory of His Son. Open your heart to Him! He is pouring out His Spirit today just as surely as Jesus came 2,000 years ago in the power of His Spirit. You could be the next one He touches. Why not?

But it may at first appear surprising, to find men of renown, men supposed to be endowed with knowledge, and with abilities of every kind, flatly, openly, peremptorily denying, that there has been any unusual work of God at all! Yea, a late eminent writer goes farther yet; accounts it an instance of downright enthusiasm [i.e., religious fanaticism], to imagine that there is any extraordinary work now wrought upon the earth....

It avails not to say, "No; he does not deny this, but he denies it to be the work of God." This is palpably trifling; for the work under consideration is of such a nature, (namely, the conversion of men from all manner of sins, to holiness of heart and life,) that if it be at any time wrought at all, it must be the work of God; seeing it is God alone, and not any child of man, who is able to "destroy the works of the devil."

John Wesley, *A Farther Appeal to Men of Reason and Religion*

Why should the Devil suddenly start doing this kind of thing? Here is a church in a period of dryness and drought, why should the Devil suddenly do something which calls attention to religion and Jesus Christ? The very results of revival, I would have thought, completely exclude the possibility of this being the action of the Devil...There is nothing so ridiculous as this suggestion that this is the work of the Devil.

D. Martyn Lloyd-Jones, *Joy Unspeakable*

Sitting down, Jesus called the Twelve and said, "If anyone wants to be first, he must be the very last, and the servant of all." He took a little child and had him stand among them. Taking him in His arms, He said to them, "Whoever welcomes one of these little children in My name welcomes Me; and whoever welcomes Me does not welcome Me but the one who sent Me." "Teacher," said John, "we saw a man driving out demons in Your name and we told him to stop, because he was not one of us." "Do not stop him," Jesus said. "No one who does a miracle in My name can in the next moment say anything bad about Me, for whoever is not against us is for us."

Mark 9:35-40

Chapter Seven

Did Satan Get Saved?

If you listen to the cry of the critics long enough—"Beware of deception! Jesus told us that deception was coming! This is the great deception!"—you can easily get the feeling that almost everybody in the Church has been duped, that, even though it *seems* clear that God is moving and the Spirit is being poured out and lives are being transformed for His glory, in reality, it is the devil who is doing the work.[1]

Unfortunately, the critics have forgotten a cardinal principle of the Word: Satan cannot cast out Satan! The prince of darkness cannot work against himself. If the devil heals, it is only to bring a more serious affliction. If he leads someone out of drugs into a false religion, the final bondage is worse than the first. Satan never truly helps anyone. It's a fact. Whatever he does must ultimately aid and abet his diabolical purposes. Otherwise, he would be working with the Lord. Jesus used this very powerful argument against those who falsely accused Him:

> Then they brought Him a demon-possessed man who was blind and mute, and Jesus healed him, so that he could both talk and see. All the people were astonished and said, "Could this be the Son of David?" But when the Pharisees heard this, they said, "It is only by Beelzebub, the prince of demons, that this fellow drives out demons." Jesus knew their thoughts and said to them, "Every kingdom divided against itself will be ruined, and every city or household divided against itself will not stand. If Satan drives out Satan, he is divided against himself. How then can his kingdom stand? And if I drive out demons by Beelzebub, by whom do your people drive them out? So then, they will be your judges. But if I drive out

demons by the Spirit of God, then the kingdom of God has come upon you. (Matt. 12:22-28)[2]

There is substance to this argument! Yet, if you listen to some critics, you would think that they cut these verses out of their Bibles. How so? They have rendered them virtually meaningless. They simply do not accept the plain meaning of the text.

Let's think this through for a minute. What if the vast majority of the converts of the current revival go on with the Lord for years, bearing fruit as sound Bible believers? Was this the work of Satan, the flesh, or God? What if many of them become missionaries, pastors, and Christian educators? Was this the work of Satan, the flesh, or God? What if the revival ultimately results in millions of new citizens of Heaven? Was this the work of Satan, the flesh, or God? Has the devil now switched sides? Has the flesh become divine in its transforming power? Stop for a moment and think.

I know it's easy to throw around terms like "deception," "emotionalism," "flesh," "counterfeit," "socio-psychological manipulation," "shamanism," and "New Age manifestations"—to name just a few of the buzz words being used these days by the critics. But the fact is that *none* of these things, in and of themselves, advance the Kingdom of God or help the cause of Christ in the least, whereas the present revival is furthering the work of the gospel by leaps and bounds.

The Word states plainly that flesh gives birth to flesh and that the devil produces nothing of eternal value and good. The Bible is absolutely clear! Yet the critics would somehow have us believe that Satan's troops are scurrying around the world right now, encouraging the lost to attend revival meetings and hear the message of repentance and the preaching of the cross, urging these sinners to respond to the altar calls and cast off their evil ways, pushing them to embrace the Word of God and commit themselves to the lordship of Jesus, then inspiring them to tell their friends about their newfound Savior and best Friend. How preposterous! With demons like these, the devil is in big trouble! Come to think of it, the critics are in big trouble too. These "demons" are producing more good fruit than they are!

Other critics would somehow try to persuade us that it is *the flesh* (if not Satan himself) that is causing hundreds of thousands of backslidden, compromised, worldly, carnal, uncommitted, lukewarm, slumbering Christians to suddenly become on-fire, disciplined, cross-bearing, forward-marching, Bible-reading, Jesus-glorifying believers. Nonsense! The flesh doesn't do that! Jesus made this absolutely plain:

> ...I tell you the truth, no one can enter the kingdom of God unless he is born of water and the Spirit. Flesh gives birth to flesh, but the Spirit gives birth to spirit. (John 3:5-6)

> The Spirit gives life; the flesh counts for nothing. (John 6:63a)[3]

That's pretty clear, wouldn't you say? And yet the critics must argue that *lots* of flesh (after all, they claim that masses of Christians are being deceived these days by spurious revival) is somehow resulting in lots of devotion to Jesus. This cannot be!

Paul made himself totally clear regarding the spiritually useless nature of the flesh:

> I know that nothing good lives in me, that is, in my sinful nature [Greek *sarx*, flesh]. (Rom. 7:18a)

> Those who live according to the sinful nature [flesh] have their minds set on what that nature desires; but those who live in accordance with the Spirit have their minds set on what the Spirit desires. The mind of sinful man is death, but the mind controlled by the Spirit is life and peace; the sinful mind is hostile to God. It does not submit to God's law, nor can it do so. Those controlled by the sinful nature [flesh] cannot please God. (Rom. 8:5-8)

> Do not be deceived: God cannot be mocked. A man reaps what he sows. The one who sows to please his sinful nature [flesh] , from that nature will reap destruction; the one who sows to please the Spirit, from the Spirit will reap eternal life. (Gal. 6:7-8)

Yes, fleshly, sinful nature is *hostile* to God and the things of the Spirit, producing a harvest of destruction.[4] Yet the critics have made the flesh (and/or the devil) into the greatest ally (or allies) of the Holy Spirit in this generation.

Of course, such a scenario is totally unscriptural and utterly impossible (in reality, these kinds of arguments actually expose the folly of the critics' denial of the reality of revival today). Satan can not cast out Satan! The devil does *not* produce love for the truth and reverence for the Word. The truth of the Word is his downfall! He does *not* produce desire for prayer and intercession. Those are the very weapons that he dreads! Neither does the flesh cause homosexuals to abandon their perversions and live in purity, nor God haters to become God lovers, nor lost cult members to become saved church members.

No, my friend, it is not that hard to determine which spirit/ Spirit is behind the work when you carefully examine the lasting fruit. Andrew Murray noted last century that:

> The enemy uses all his power to lead the Christian—and above all the ministers—to neglect prayer. He knows that however admirable the sermon may be, however attractive the service, however faithful the pastoral visitation, none of these things can damage him or his kingdom if prayer is neglected.[5]

Yet according to the critics, the enemy of our souls is actually *spurring* us to prayer.

The Puritan author Richard Sibbes observed that, "When we go to God by prayer, the devil knows we go to fetch strength against him. Therefore he opposeth us all he can."[6] Yet if the critics are right, the devil today is *motivating* believers to fetch that very strength against him! No, no, and a thousand times no. Satan is not divided! In fact, he is far more logical and consistent in his methods than many of the critics are in their arguments.

Jesus taught plainly that the devil "was a murderer from the beginning, not holding to the truth, for there is no truth in him. When he lies, he speaks his native language, for he is a liar and the father of lies" (John 8:44b). The fact is that all true conversions are the work of the Holy Spirit, not demonic spirits and not the flesh, and where true conversions abound, the Spirit's work is evident.[7]

Naturally, the critic has an answer here too. "The revival conversions," he claims, "are *not* true but rather spurious, and the reformation of character merely temporary. There is no depth to the experience and no foundation in the Word that will last." Of course, the plain facts are against the critics, since the fruit of much of the current revival is now several years old and getting *more* solid, mature, biblically grounded, and Christlike by the day (which naturally leads to the question, *at what point does a critic admit that he or she was sadly mistaken?*). And the Word itself stands against the critic, since the Bible tells us clearly how we can recognize genuine converts.

Look, for example, at John's teachings:

> Whoever loves his brother lives in the light, and there is nothing in him to make him stumble. ... No one who denies the Son has the Father; whoever acknowledges the Son has the Father also. ... If you know that He is righteous, you know that everyone who does what is right has been born of Him. (1 John 2:10,23,29)

> No one who is born of God will continue to sin, because God's seed remains in him; he cannot go on sinning, because he has been born of God. This is how we know who the children of God are and who the children of the devil are: Anyone who does not do what is right is not a child of God; nor is anyone who does not love his brother. (1 John 3:9-10)

> This is how you can recognize the Spirit of God: Every spirit that acknowledges that Jesus Christ has come in the flesh is from God, ... No one has ever seen God; but if we love one another, God lives in us and His love is made complete in us. ... If anyone acknowledges that Jesus is the Son of God, God lives in him and he in God. (1 John 4:2,12,15)

> Everyone who believes that Jesus is the Christ is born of God, and everyone who loves the father loves his child as well. (1 John 5:1)[8]

What can the critic say after he interviews countless revival converts who are now more than two years old in the Lord (or, by the time you read this, five or ten years old in the Lord), who demonstrate real love for their brothers and sisters in Jesus, openly and freely confess Jesus as the Son of God and only Savior and Lord, do what is right in their public and private lives, hold firmly to the fundamentals of the faith, and walk in purity and freedom from habitual sin, thereby meeting the criteria of true conversion according to the Word? How can these be dismissed as the results of satanic spirits or the flesh? What will happen as time goes by and we are looking at converts of 20 or 30 years duration? What will the critics say then?[9]

Jesus explained in the parable of the sower that "...the seed that fell on good soil is the man who hears the word and understands it. He produces a crop, yielding a hundred, sixty or thirty times what was sown" (Matt. 13:23). This is in contrast with those whose hearts were not fully given to the Word, resulting in immediate apostasy in times of testing or defective fruit bearing over a period of time.

> The one who received the seed that fell on rocky places is the man who hears the word and at once receives it with joy. But since he has no root, he lasts only a short time. When trouble or persecution comes because of the word, he quickly falls away. The one who received the seed that fell among the thorns is the man who hears the word, but the worries of this life and the deceitfulness of wealth choke it, making it unfruitful. (Matt. 13:20-22)

The overwhelming majority of converts in this present awakening are clearly "good soil" hearers! Many of them have already been seriously tested, having their loved ones turn on them, being ridiculed and excluded at school, losing substantial income formerly earned through sinful means, resisting temptation even in difficult times. And they grow stronger still! They are hardly "rocky soil" hearers. Nor are they "thorny-hearted" hearers, seduced by the love of this world and the cares of this life. To the contrary, there are now millionaires who serve as church ushers, wealthy businessmen who are preparing for ministry, and former earthly minded worriers who are now heavenly minded worshipers.[10] The seed they received did not fall among thorns!

According to statistics compiled in recent decades, only about three to ten percent of those who "make decisions for Christ" in mass rallies or special evangelistic services are actually added to the churches, despite the best follow-up plans and discipleship programs. In stark contrast to this, in some congregations experiencing revival today, as many as 90 percent of the converts who get into discipleship programs are going on with God and being added to the local churches.[11]

I'm sorry, dear critic (actually, I'm not sorry, I'm glad!), but sooner or later you will have to admit that what you have been rejecting as alien, counterfeit, and mixed has been God-birthed and Heaven-sent. Granted, no one would claim that the work is perfect or that some people have not, on occasion, taken things to extremes. But there can be no doubt to the honest, Spirit-led student of the Word that the Lord is now sending revival to His Church.

John Wesley dealt with similar objections from the critics of his day. He also pointed to the undeniable evidence of the fruit (after all, Jesus was the one who emphasized the importance of judging the tree by checking the fruit; see Matthew 7:15-20; 12:33; Luke 6:43-44; and John 15:1-8). Listen to Wesley's wise words to one of his more vocal critics:

> That, whenever God revives his work upon earth, many tares will spring up with the wheat, both the word of God gives us ground to expect, and the experience of all ages. But where, Sir, have you been, that you have heard of the tares only; and that you rank among the consequences of my preaching, "a neglect and contempt of God's ordinances, and almost of all duties?" Does not the very reverse appear at London, at Bristol, at Kingswood, at Newcastle? In every one of which places, multitudes of those (I am able to name the persons) who before lived in a thorough neglect and contempt of God's ordinances and all duties, do now zealously discharge their duties to God and man, and walk in all his ordinances blameless.[12]

Therefore the work is of God!

You see, it is possible for a good tree to have some rotten fruit here and there. But if the tree is good, most of the fruit it bears will be good. And when a move of the Spirit results in scripturally sound converts who are serving the Lord and awakened saints who have turned away from the world and back to God, when its fruit is passion for Jesus and His Word and hatred for Satan and sin, then that is proof that the "tree" (in this case, the current revival) is good.

Listen again to Jesus: "No good tree bears bad fruit, nor does a bad tree bear good fruit. Each tree is recognized by its own fruit. People do not pick figs from thornbushes, or grapes from briers"

(Luke 6:43-44). These words are just too simple and straightfor-ward to deny. Countless figs and grapes are not being picked from thornbushes and briers!

Biblical truth is biblical truth. The devil *does not* depopulate the kingdom of darkness in order to populate the Kingdom of light. He *does not* cultivate devotion to his archenemy Jesus, nor does he inspire reverence for the God who will one day condemn him, nor interest in the Word that exposes his lies. Satan's hellish, unholy tree *cannot* bear such heavenly, holy of fruit!

Of course, good fruit is something that the critics often choose to ignore as they examine with a microscope one piece of fruit that seems to be slightly defective, while ignoring hundreds of pieces of excellent fruit that fall right on their head. The obvious conclusion—that the tree is a divine, not devilish, tree—is hardly obvious to them.

But this is nothing new. When the blind man was healed by Je-sus in John 9, not everyone recognized this as the work of God. There were some who went into denial, since they couldn't possibly believe that a blind man could be healed. "It's not really the same man," they reasoned. "No, he only looks like him" (see John 9:9a)! Unfortunately for the deniers, the healed man had no doubts: "…he himself insisted, 'I am the man' " (John 9:9b).

For the Pharisees, who were still not sure the man had really been healed (how could he have been healed by Jesus when He did not belong to their camp?), the issue was a little different. This so-called Messiah violated their traditions!

> Some of the Pharisees said, "This man is not from God, for He does not keep the Sabbath" [meaning, according to their customs and laws]. But others asked, "How can a sinner do such miraculous signs?" So they were divided. … [After Jesus taught…] the Jews were again divided. Many of them said, "He is demon-possessed and raving mad. Why listen to Him?" But others said, "These are not the sayings of a man possessed by a demon. Can a demon open the eyes of the blind?" (John 9:16; 10:19-21)

In these few verses, we have the three most common, critical responses to the miraculous works of Jesus, past and present: 1) nothing really happened (in other words, in John 9 the blind man wasn't really healed, and in today's revival, the conversions aren't real and won't last); 2) something probably did happen, but it can't be from God because the methods used deviate from our way of doing things; 3) something very powerful happened, but it was performed by demon power![13]

The words of the once-blind man rebuke all critics and unbelievers, past and present:

> We know that God does not listen to sinners. He listens to the godly man who does His will. Nobody has ever heard of opening the eyes of a man born blind. If this man were not from God, He could do nothing. (John 9:31-33)

Amazingly enough (and it is nothing less than amazing), there are still those who claim—against all factual, verifiable evidence—that the conversions of the current outpouring are really quite questionable, the result of practices like hypnotism. Of course, as James Edwin Orr and others have said, the only proof of the new birth is the new life, and, consequently, the genuine nature of the new birth is proved out by the genuine nature of the convert's walk. This fact alone, as we have emphasized, demonstrates clearly the reality of the Spirit's converting work in the present outpouring.

But is there actually widespread hypnotism taking place in revival meetings? Is this the real source of the revival's power?[14] And, for that matter, are there courses on "holy hypnotism" taught in our revival-birthed schools of ministry, and do we raise up and send out "hypnovangelists" (to coin a term)?

Forgive me for being sarcastic, but it's hard not to be. Such questions and charges are absolutely ludicrous, hardly worthy of a response. If the critics are right, hypnotism is more powerful than the Word and the Spirit combined! They claim that what God's true evangelists cannot do *intentionally* with the sword of the Spirit, deluded, misled evangelists can do *unintentionally* through hypnosis. Not only so, but the changes resulting from the "hypnovangelist's" ministry include deep repentance from sin, sound scriptural faith in the Lord Jesus, complete submission to God, sober and holy living, and a burden to reach the lost. And the changes last!

Still, as absurd as the claims of "hypnotism" are, and despite the fact that medical doctors, through their scientific observations, have discounted the notion of mass hypnosis in the current revival (as well as mass hysteria),[15] you might find it interesting to learn that charges of hypnosis have been leveled against revival leaders in the past. Yes, there's nothing new under the sun!

For example, Charles Parham, the Pentecostal pioneer who rejected Azusa Street with a vengeance (possibly fueled by some racist attitudes as well), claimed that he found there "hypnotic influences, familiar-spirit influences, mesmeric influences, and all kinds of spells, spasms, falling in trances, etc."[16] Yes, William "Daddy" Seymour apparently was a great hypnotist too![17]

D.L. Moody's son notes that his father was likewise accused:

> In another city Mr. Moody said to me: "There seems to be something here out of the ordinary, obstructing the work and hindering a great blessing." I found out the next day that the town had a considerable number of freethinkers, or theoretical infidels, and they were out at the meetings to see Mr. Moody, as they said, hypnotize the converts.[18]

That's right! Moody was successful because he too learned the secret of "hypnotizing" his converts. Come to think of it, he must have cast a pretty strong spell, since a good number of those converts gave their lives to foreign missions, becoming some of the great leaders of their generation.[19] Who knew that hypnotism was so powerful?

Even John Wesley was subjected to the charge of "exercising a hypnotic influence on his audiences" by one of his later, critical biographers:

> Brushing his hair back with his hand, the face he presented to his hearers would fill them with awe, and he used his eyes in such a way that each felt that they pierced him alone, that his words were meant especially for him. He seems to have exercised a sort of hypnotic influence on his audiences. Perhaps he was conscious of this power, and liked to use it, for God had given it him to convert with, and convert he would. For though he might speak the words of humility as much as he liked, the spirit of pride was there, pride that he had been chosen to do this

work. And perhaps also the hysterical displays satisfied his hungry emotionalism, cheated by his failure to love and to be loved humanly, a longing he professed to have eradicated. And above all he could rule, rule in hell while serving in heaven. His doubts vanished, his fits of unhappiness disappeared.[20]

Doesn't this negative, judgmental, highly biased account seem pathetic when you read it today? Yet it is just as pathetic when the modern critics of revival mistakenly attribute the work of the Spirit and the Word to hypnosis, socio-psychological manipulation, emotionalism, or demonic power. The truth is that Satan doesn't save and hypnotists don't make people holy—unless the devil and his gang got converted somewhere along the line.

One theologian recently made some penetrating observations when challenging those who claimed that a worldwide spiritual move was from below:

Here we have hundreds of thousands of Christians, all over the world, testifying to an experience which causes them to fall in love with Jesus all over again, have a renewed desire to read the scriptures, to pray, to witness. We have literally hundreds of testimonies of remarkable healings, some physical, many emotional. We have churches where the people do not want to go home and stay there for hours in worship. We have worship going into depths of love and joy we have never seen before. We have an outpouring of new worship songs coming out of the midst of this move, songs which focus on total surrender, holiness, love for God, longing for revival. We have a wonderful increase of unity between churches and Christian leaders affected by it. Sadly, as with the beginning of the Pentecostal movement and the charismatic renewal, those who aggressively oppose it cause division. To attribute such things, in such intensity, in such volume, to the devil, is really to divinise the devil....Further, if the devil was behind this, we would not have to think of a mild attack, but of total possession, because the phenomena are not mild. They indicate people being totally overcome. Were anyone to be totally overcome by the devil, repeatedly, for months, they would by now be showing signs of insanity, carnality, heresy, etc. We see no such thing. The idea [is] simply ridiculous. If the devil is doing this, then the devil has just been converted.[21]

We must remember that, "Every good and perfect gift is from above, coming down from the Father of the heavenly lights, who does not change like shifting shadows" (Jas. 1:17). We can recognize the Giver by His gifts! And Jesus Himself encouraged us to approach our heavenly Father with boldness and confidence, knowing that He will not give His own children something destructive and unseemly:

> Ask and it will be given to you; seek and you will find; knock and the door will be opened to you. For everyone who asks receives; he who seeks finds; and to him who knocks, the door will be opened. Which of you, if his son asks for bread, will give him a stone? Or if he asks for a fish, will give him a snake? If you, then, though you are evil, know how to give good gifts to your children, how much more will your Father in heaven give good gifts to those who ask Him! (Matt. 7:7-11)

And do you know how one critic responded to this argument (the argument that if we ask our Father for bread, He will not give us a stone)? (See also Luke 11:9-13, where Jesus ends these same words by saying, "If you then, though you are evil, know how to give good gifts to your children, how much more will your Father in heaven give *the Holy Spirit* to those who ask Him!") Well, in the opinion of that critic, since people who asked God to touch them and fill them afresh with the Spirit were receiving answers to their prayers that were not listed among the fruit or gifts of the Spirit, then the "gifts" received could not possibly have come from God! Therefore, the "father" who answered their prayers (called by this critic "unbiblical" prayers) was another father, Satan, the father of lies.[22] (I know it sounds like I'm making this up to make the critics look bad, but the fact is, when it comes to some critics of revival, truth is stranger than fiction!)

It is bad enough that this Christian brother uses an absurd, unbiblical test to judge someone's experience. (If someone asked God for help during a time of despair and received new hope—something not specifically listed among the fruit or gifts of the Spirit—would that mean that the devil sent the hope?) But this author, praised as a fine teacher of the Word by one of his colleagues, actually turns the Word of God, and specifically the promise of Jesus, on its head. All confidence in God has been stolen!

According to this twisted, new version of these verses, if you pray to your gracious, compassionate, kind, faithful heavenly Father, putting your confidence in Him and Him alone, asking Him for blessing according to His promise, and you then receive a wonderful, life-transforming touch—if this critic doesn't approve of your experience, then it was the devil who heard and answered your prayer! And bear in mind that the specific people this critic came against were not asking God to "bless" them with cocaine and whiskey; they were asking Him for a fresh filling of His Spirit! And the answer they received was not drugs and alcohol but rather joy and refreshing. How was this a satanic answer to an unbiblical prayer?

And there you have the terrible tragedy of the critical, negative mentality: It magnifies the powers of darkness and minimizes the power of Light. It glorifies Satan's ability and denigrates the Lord's ability. It sees demons at work everywhere and the Spirit at work almost nowhere. It pictures the devil sitting on his throne, sending counterfeit, destructive "gifts" in answer to the heartfelt, dependent prayers of the people of God while our heavenly Father sits idly by, shaking His head because His children are so deceived.

Dear critic, that "God" is not the God whom I serve, nor is that "devil" the devil whom Jesus defeated. The God of the Bible, the God we worship, is worthy of our total adoration and absolute trust, and in Him, we overcome the wicked one (see 1 John 2:14; 5:4,19; Luke 10:19). That is why I, for my part, am lifting my eyes to Heaven with confidence. Why should you keep looking down?

We are given no miraculous signs; no prophets are left, and none of us knows how long this will be. How long will the enemy mock You, O God? Will the foe revile Your name forever? Why do You hold back Your hand, Your right hand? Take it from the folds of Your garment and destroy them!

Psalm 74:9-11

The angel of the Lord came and sat down under the oak in Ophrah that belonged to Joash the Abiezrite, where his son Gideon was threshing wheat in a winepress to keep it from the Midianites. When the angel of the LORD appeared to Gideon, he said, "The LORD is with you, mighty warrior." "But sir," Gideon replied, "if the LORD is with us, why has all this happened to us? Where are all His wonders that our fathers told us about when they said, 'Did not the LORD bring us up out of Egypt?' But now the LORD has abandoned us and put us into the hand of Midian." The LORD turned to him and said, "Go in the strength you have and save Israel out of Midian's hand. Am I not sending you?"

Judges 6:11-14

Men of Israel, listen to this: Jesus of Nazareth was a man accredited by God to you by miracles, wonders and signs, which God did among you through Him, as you yourselves know. ...God anointed Jesus of Nazareth with the Holy Spirit and power, and...He went around doing good and healing all who were under the power of the devil, because God was with Him. ... I tell you the truth, anyone who has faith in Me will do what I have been doing. He will do even greater things than these, because I am going to the Father.

Acts 2:22; 10:38; John 14:12

You see, one of Satan's tactics is to discredit that which is good by its misuse.

Derek Prince, *Protection from Deception*

Chapter Eight

Does the Devil Have a Monopoly on Miracles?

You can read the Bible from Genesis to Revelation and never find a single passage that says that the *absence* of God's signs and wonders is a good thing, a thing to be believed for, a thing to expect. Rather, the absence of divine signs and wonders is an indication that something is wrong, that something is missing, that the Lord is not demonstrating His power. From a biblical perspective, it is good when the Lord acts in a pronounced, public way and bad when He doesn't.[1] Therefore, the prayer of the believers in Acts was a good prayer then, and it remains a good prayer to this day:

> Now, LORD, consider their threats [i.e., of those who oppose the gospel] and enable Your servants to speak Your word with great boldness. Stretch out Your hand to heal and perform miraculous signs and wonders through the name of Your holy servant Jesus. (Acts 4:29-30)

The fact that there were counterfeit signs and wonders in the Bible never negated the importance and reality of *true* signs and wonders, anymore than the presence of false prophets and teachers invalidated the importance and reality of *true* prophets and teachers. Moses and Aaron were able to demonstrate to all of Egypt that Yahweh alone was God because Egyptian magicians and miracle workers were unable to duplicate the signs and wonders performed by the Lord's servants:

> The LORD said to Moses and Aaron, "When Pharaoh says to you, 'Perform a miracle,' then say to Aaron, 'Take your staff and throw it

down before Pharaoh,' and it will become a snake." So Moses and Aaron went to Pharaoh and did just as the LORD commanded. Aaron threw his staff down in front of Pharaoh and his officials, and it became a snake. Pharaoh then summoned wise men and sorcerers, and the Egyptian magicians also did the same things by their secret arts: Each one threw down his staff and it became a snake. But Aaron's staff swallowed up their staffs. (Ex. 7:8-12)

The Lord then turned all the water in Egypt into blood through the hand of Moses and Aaron (Ex. 7:17-22). But the magicians were able to duplicate—not counteract—the miracle (thanks a lot, guys!). Then the Lord sent the plague of frogs, and the Egyptian magicians also made frogs come up on their land (not exactly the right move, fellows!), but they were unable to *stop* the frogs. Pharaoh had to appeal to Moses and Aaron for deliverance (Ex. 8:1-14). Next came the horrible plague of gnats, as "all the dust throughout the land of Egypt became gnats" (Ex. 8:17b). This time the magicians were completely stymied: "But when the magicians tried to produce gnats by their secret arts, they could not. And the gnats were on men and animals. The magicians said to Pharaoh, 'This is the finger of God.' " (Ex. 8:18-19a). From there on, it was all downhill for the workers of secret arts. They didn't stand a chance! The Lord alone was God—God of nature, God of life and death, God of all.[2]

It is no wonder that Moses and the children of Israel sang these words of adoration to the Lord after crossing the Sea: "Who among the gods is like you, O LORD? Who is like You—majestic in holiness, awesome in glory, working wonders?" (Ex. 15:11) There is none like the Lord! He is a God of holy power and signs and wonders. Counterfeit signs and wonders only highlight His greatness.

The Israelites never ceased to praise the Lord for His mighty deeds and wondrous works. Here is a representative sampling of verses:

I will praise You, O LORD, with all my heart; I will tell of all Your wonders. I will be glad and rejoice in You; I will sing praise to Your name, O Most High. (Ps. 9:1-2)

I will remember the deeds of the LORD; yes, I will remember Your miracles of long ago. I will meditate on all Your works and consider all Your mighty deeds. Your ways, O God, are holy. What god is so great as our God? You are the God who performs miracles; You display Your power among the peoples. (Ps. 77:11-14)

I will open my mouth in parables, I will utter hidden things, things from of old—what we have heard and known, what our fathers have told us. We will not hide them from their children; we will tell the next generation the praiseworthy deeds of the LORD, His power, and the wonders He has done. (Ps. 78:2-4)

Let me understand the teaching of Your precepts; then I will meditate on Your wonders. (Ps. 119:27)

Give thanks to the LORD, for He is good. His love endures forever. Give thanks to the God of gods. His love endures forever. Give thanks to the Lord of lords: His love endures forever. To Him who alone does great wonders, His love endures forever. (Ps. 136:1-4)

And this Sovereign Lord—the God of Moses, the God of Elijah, the God of Daniel, the God of the apostles, the God of the Church in every age—has not changed. He still performs signs and wonders. He still stretches out His hand and acts. He still confirms His Word in power.

"But," you say, "the New Testament specifically warned us that there would be counterfeit signs and wonders occurring on an unprecedented scale before the return of Jesus, so we should be especially suspicious of the miraculous at this critical time in which we live."

Of course, I could ask you to prove conclusively from the Word that we are living in the very last of the last days, the end of the end-times immediately preceding the Lord's coming, the final generation (see Chapter Nine, "Are We Living in the Last Days?"). But let's just say that I agree with you that we are in that specific, prophesied time of unusual deception. Your argument still doesn't hold water. The fact is, Jesus warned us that before His return, false christs would come in His name saying, "I am he!" Does this mean that there will be no *true Christ*? God forbid! Rather, it is *because* the true Messiah is about to return that many false messiahs will arise. In the same way, it is because there will be true signs and wonders in the end of the age that the counterfeit will come in abundance. The exact same principle holds true in 2 Peter 2:1a, where the apostle warns his readers, "…there were also false prophets among the people, just as there will be false teachers among you." Does the fact that *false* teachers will infiltrate the Church mean that there will be no *true* teachers in the Church? Hardly! (If so, where would this leave the critics, even in their own view?)

The bottom line is that you can't have it both ways. Either the warnings to beware of false miracles, false teachers, and false messiahs invalidate all claims of true miracles, true teachers, and a true Messiah, or the warnings to beware of false miracles, false teachers, and false messiahs cause us to embrace only the *true* miracles, teachers, and Messiah.

Of course, you may accept the logic behind my line of reasoning but still ask, "Where does the Bible say that there will be a profusion of divine signs and wonders in the end of the age?" Well, I could just as well as ask you, "Where does the Bible say that there will *not* be a profusion of divine signs and wonders in the end of the age?"[3] But I won't raise that question yet, because there *is* biblical evidence that God's Spirit will move in supernatural power before Jesus returns.

I remind you of Peter's Pentecost sermon, discussed in Chapter Nine, as he quoted from Joel's prophecy:

> …this is what was spoken by the prophet Joel: "In the last days, God says, I will pour out My Spirit on all people. Your sons and daughters will prophesy, your young men will see visions, your old men will dream dreams. Even on My servants, both men and women, I will pour out My Spirit in those days, and they will prophesy. I will show wonders in the heaven above and signs on the earth below, blood and fire and billows of smoke. The sun will be turned to darkness and the moon to blood before the coming of the great and glorious day of the Lord. And everyone who calls on the name of the Lord will be saved." (Acts 2:16-21)

As we will examine more closely in Chapter Nine, this prophecy applies to "the last days" (i.e., the entire period from the cross to the return of Jesus), promising an outpouring of the Spirit on "all people" (i.e., young and old, men and women, even servants—in other words, not just the "prophetic elite"). We should also note that the prediction that God would show "wonders in the heaven above and signs on the earth below, blood and fire and billows of smoke" cannot be limited to what He did on the day of Pentecost (contrary to the opinion of some).[4] Instead, it speaks of still-to-come miraculous signs of cosmic proportions that are to take place "before the coming of the great and glorious day of the Lord," in all probability meaning "immediately before." And, lest you think that the last sign spoken of is purely a judgment sign ("the sun will be turned to darkness and the moon to blood"), as if there will be only gloom and doom at the end of the age, Peter explicitly states, "And everyone who calls on the name of the Lord will be saved."[5] The door to salvation will be opened wide! This age—right up to the very end—is to be a time of great harvest and miraculous wonders.

Peter promised the gift of the Holy Spirit to all who would hear the Word of the Lord in his generation and in every generation to come, saying:

> ...Repent and be baptized, every one of you, in the name of Jesus Christ for the forgiveness of your sins. And you will receive the gift of the Holy Spirit. The promise is for you and your children and for all who are far off—for all whom the Lord our God will call. (Acts 2:38-39)

Now here is something very important: There is not the slightest hint in Peter's words that the Holy Spirit received by believers in each subsequent generation would be any less of a supernatural, miracle-working Spirit than the Holy Spirit the 120 received in the upper room. And remember that the context of this "promise" of the Spirit in Acts 2:39 is found in the previous verses in this chapter, namely, the powerful, miraculous outpouring described in Acts 2:1-21, 32-33. (You should go back and re-read these verses to get the full impact of just what Peter's hearers—and by extension all subsequent hearers—understood when he made reference to receiving "the gift of the Holy Spirit.")

But there's more. Once you recognize that believers in every age receive the same Spirit as the first century believers, then you must accept that, on some level, the same power is available to the Church in every generation. Let me explain.

The Greek word used by Luke (in his Gospel and in Acts) to describe the miracle-working, healing power of the Spirit is *dunamis*, and he frequently utilized this word in this very specific sense.[6] According to Luke 5:17, "One day as He was teaching, Pharisees and teachers of the law, who had come from every village of Galilee and from Judea and Jerusalem, were sitting there. And the power [*dunamis*] of the Lord was present for Him to heal the sick." Luke 6:17-19 tells us that as crowds of sick and demonized people came from everywhere to hear Jesus and be healed, "the people all tried to touch Him, because power [*dunamis*] was coming from Him and healing them all." This is the same power that healed the woman with the issue of blood, as the Lord said, "Someone touched Me; I know that power [*dunamis*] has gone out from Me" (Luke 8:46), and it is the same power that Jesus gave to His disciples to heal and drive out demons: "When Jesus had called the Twelve together, He gave them power [*dunamis*] and authority to drive out all demons and to cure diseases, and He sent them out to preach the kingdom of God and to heal the sick" (Luke 9:1-2).

After His resurrection, Jesus promised His disciples a lasting enduement of the Spirit's power, telling them, "I am going to send you what My Father has promised; but stay in the city until you have been clothed with power [*dunamis*] from on high" (Luke 24:49).[7] Note carefully those words: "what My Father has promised" (literally, "the promise of My Father"). Peter referred to this explicitly in Acts 2:33 ("the promised Holy Spirit") in explanation of the miraculous phenomena taking place that day. He spoke of it again in Acts 2:39 as belonging to *everyone* who would be saved ("The promise is for you and your children and for all who are far off—for all whom the Lord our God will call"). All of which means this: The Spirit in power was not just a promise to the early Church![8]

Before His ascension to Heaven, Jesus said to His disciples, "...you will receive power [*dunamis*] when the Holy Spirit comes on you; and you will be My witnesses in Jerusalem, and in all Judea and Samaria, and to the ends of the earth" (Acts 1:8). Now I ask you: Is there any way to separate the promise of the power of the Spirit in Acts 1:8a (the same miracle-working, healing power spoken of throughout Luke's Gospel) from the declaration in Acts 1:8b that Jesus' disciples would be His witnesses *to the ends of the earth*? Of course not. Then there can be only one conclusion: As long as the Great Commission is still in effect, this promise of empowerment must also be in effect. In other words, since the gospel message is still being declared "to the ends of the earth" (there are almost two billion people yet to hear the message), then, according to Acts 1:8, the promised supernatural power of the Spirit that is to enable us to testify of the death and resurrection of Jesus must be available to this day.[9]

The very thing that happened in Acts 4:33 ("With great power [*dunamis*] the apostles continued to testify to the resurrection of the Lord Jesus...") is happening today around the world. And I remind you once more: This was the same power with which Jesus was endued, seen clearly in Peter's recounting of "How God anointed Jesus of Nazareth with the Holy Ghost and with power [*dunamis*]: who went about doing good, and healing all that were oppressed of the devil; for God was with Him" (Acts 10:38, KJV).

So we see that Jesus healed the sick and drove out demons through the *dunamis* of the Spirit, and He told His disciples that they too would receive this *dunamis* when the Holy Spirit came on them, supernaturally empowering them to be His witnesses throughout the world. He referred to this gift of the Spirit as a "promise" of His Father, and at Pentecost, the disciples received the promised Holy Spirit (which is when Jesus said they would receive *dunamis*), and Peter explicitly declared that this promise—the reception of the very same Spirit that had filled the first disciples—was for *all* who would repent and believe in every generation. Yes, the *power* (*dunamis*) of the Spirit would enable the disciples to take the gospel "to the ends of the earth" (Acts 1:8); therefore, it must be a continuing empowerment. And the *promise* of the Spirit was "for all who are far off—for all whom the Lord our God will call" (Acts 2:39); therefore, it must be a *continuing* promise.

So, the Spirit in power will be given to those who *bring* the gospel "to the ends of the earth" and the Spirit in power will be given to those who *receive* the gospel in the ends of the earth. Yes, these are the ones who "are far off," those to whom the promise of the Spirit is also given. Do you see it clearly?[10]

And all this simply expands on the promise given by Jesus when He said to His disciples:

> Don't you believe that I am in the Father, and that the Father is in Me? The words I say to you are not just My own. Rather, it is the Father, living in Me, who is doing His work. Believe Me when I say that I am in the Father and the Father is in Me; or at least believe on the evidence of the miracles themselves. I tell you the truth, anyone who has faith in Me [or, more exactly, whoever believes in Me] will do what I have been doing. He will do even greater things than these, because I am going to the Father. (John 14:10-12)

Jesus is teaching clearly that *everyone* who believes in Him will do the same miraculous works He did (the context is indisputably clear) and even greater things, because He goes to the Father.[11] (By the way, I don't fight over the issue of exactly what Jesus meant when He spoke of doing "greater things" than He did. I'm content for now to concentrate on simply doing the *same* things He did!) And note carefully that the *universal nature* of this promise is undeniable, since the Greek phrase, "Whoever believes in Me" (*ho pisteuon eis eme*) cannot be limited to the first disciples only. Just look at these verses from John:

> Then Jesus declared, "I am the bread of life. He who comes to Me will never go hungry, and he who believes in Me [*ho pisteuon eis eme*] will never be thirsty. (John 6:35)

> Whoever believes in Me [*ho pisteuon eis eme*], as the Scripture has said, streams of living water will flow from within him. (John 7:38)

> ...I am the resurrection and the life. He who believes in Me [*ho pisteuon eis eme*] will live, even though he dies; and whoever lives and believes in Me will never die. Do you believe this? (John 11:25-26)

> ...When a man believes in Me [*ho pisteuon eis eme*], he does not believe in Me only, but in the one who sent Me. When he looks at Me, he sees the one who sent Me. I have come into the world as a light, so that no one who believes in Me [*ho pisteuon eis eme*] should stay in darkness. (John 12:44-46)

Is there any possible way to limit these promises to the first believers only? Absolutely not! Then there is no way to limit John 14:12 to the first believers only. To the contrary, Jesus gives us His word that *whoever* believes in Him can do the same miraculous things He did—and it's time we start believing!

So, the promise of ongoing, supernatural power for service remains unbroken to every generation of believers, and it is no more possible to exclude this promise from believers living in the end of the age than it is to exclude the other promises in John from believers living in the end of the age. "Whoever" means *whoever.*

Of course, we could take much more time to develop these biblical arguments that demonstrate the Church's promised ongoing inheritance of the power of the Spirit.[12] But enough has been said for the moment to enable us to turn the tables and put a serious question to our critical friends. We have presented some explicit scriptural promises and foundational theological evidence. Where is yours? Can you show me *one explicit verse* in the New Testament that states that the gifts and power of the Holy Spirit were given to the first generation of believers only? Where is the clear, conclusive evidence?[13]

Someone might ask, "So? Even if you're right, what's all this got to do with counterfeit miracles at the end of the age?" Simply this: Most critics who warn us to beware of end-time counterfeit signs and wonders have become suspicious of *all* "end-time" signs and wonders, believing somehow that as we get closer to the return of Jesus, it will be the devil who will have a monopoly on miracles. God forbid! Our heavenly Father has acted in glorious power in the past, He is acting in glorious power in the present, and He will act in glorious power in the future...right up to the very moment His Son returns to this earth to establish His Kingdom. In fact, you can argue that it is *because* God's mighty acts will be on the increase at the end of this age that the satanic counterfeits will also abound. Study the Scriptures on this. You will see that this has been the pattern throughout biblical history.

When true prophets were on the rise, false prophets were on the rise; when true miracles increased, counterfeit miracles increased.

And when true signs and wonders were on the decline (for example, in times of extreme rationalism in Church history), Satan's signs and wonders also declined. Why would Satan want to call attention to the supernatural? Why would he want Christians to realize that there must be more? Why would he want to expose the absence of divine power by displaying his devilish power? Instead, when God's Spirit is moving, Satan tries to mimic the move. When all is quiet, he does his dirty work in other ways.[14]

Anyway, if we throw out a particular spiritual phenomenon because it has pagan parallels or demonic counterfeits, then we would have to throw out the born-again experience because numerous cults and sects claim to have a born-again experience. We would have to reject the witness of the Spirit because Mormons claim to have the inner witness. We would have to throw out tongues because various demonically inspired groups speak in tongues. Laying on of hands would cease because African shamans practice the laying on of hands. We could no longer practice fasting and separating one's self for spiritual empowerment because the witches and warlocks of Latin America fast and separate themselves for spiritual empowerment. There would be no miraculous healings of any kind because Hasidic Jews claim that their leaders miraculously heal. We would have to reject receiving words and insights from the Spirit of God because psychics receive words and insights from a spirit. Even prayer would have to be completely thrown out because every religion in the world practices prayer.

We would also have to reject the biblical creation and flood accounts because they have parallels with Mesopotamian creation and flood accounts. The biblical story of the birth of Moses would be invalid because it resembles the story of the birth of king Sargon of Akkad. The New Testament teaching of the Son of God who died and rose from the dead could no longer be accepted because the Egyptians believed that Osiris was a dying and resurrecting god and the Canaanites believed the same about Baal. In fact, we would have to reject our entire belief in Jesus the Messiah because there are many cults that believe in a semi-divine, savior-messiah figure; and even within Judaism, there have been numerous counterfeit messiahs. We would be required to de-emphasize the importance of the blood of Jesus because satanists emphasize the importance of blood. Also, we would have to reject many specific practices such as door-to-door witnessing (because Jehovah's Witnesses do this) and even—God forbid!—taking up offerings (because charlatans do this).[15]

No, common sense, along with sound scholarship, would tell you that just because a particular phenomenon, manifestation, doctrine, or practice has pagan, demonic, or worldly parallels or precedents doesn't mean that it should be automatically rejected. The fact is, critical Old Testament scholars often claim that Solomon's Temple was simply an amalgamation of Canaanite religious symbols, while an influential New Testament scholar wrote a famous study entitled *Jesus the Magician*, based on alleged similarities between the ministry of Jesus and magical practices.[16]

Trust me, friends. When you deal with these issues on a serious academic level and you see how just about every biblical miracle or practice is written off by some scholars as a pagan rite or tradition borrowed by the Israelites, you will not be troubled in the least by revival critics who warn us to beware of claims of end-time miracles because of Satan's counterfeits.

"But," you ask, "isn't it true that true miraculous gifts and powers ceased when the last apostle died?" Absolutely not. This is completely inaccurate from a historical standpoint, and, even more importantly, there is no biblical support for this view.[17] The *facts* are completely opposed to it. Even logic is against it, as can be readily (and humorously) seen through the following, caricatured scenes.

Imagine a prayer meeting taking place in Corinth 1,900 years ago in Corinth. People are prophesying and speaking in tongues. Suddenly the words freeze on their lips. Their mouths are moving, but nothing is coming out. What happened? "Brothers, it looks like the last of the apostles just died!"

Or consider this scene from Ephesus around the turn of the first century: A bold disciple has been preaching the Word to a lame man when, perceiving the cripple's faith, he takes him by the hand and, instantly, the lame man begins to walk, taking the first steps of his life. Suddenly, he collapses to the ground in a heap, all healing virtue having left him. What happened? "Sorry, but the last of the apostles just died!" How preposterous.

Of course, I doubt anyone would argue that such a sequence of events ever occurred, but it really does underscore just how strained the argument is that "the gifts of the Spirit died out with the apostles." What would have happened to believers who were mightily empowered with the Holy Spirit as young children when the last of the apostles (presumably John on the Isle of Patmos) was an old man? Did they continue to exercise these spiritual gifts through their lifetime? And what of those for whom they prayed for the Spirit's touch? Was the chain somehow broken with them?

"But," you respond, "isn't it a fact that the miraculous gifts of the Spirit gradually died out over the first few centuries of Church history?" Now you're getting a *little* closer to the truth.[18] There are still accounts—too numerous to mention here—of miraculous healings, deliverances from demonic power, and even resurrections from the dead well into the *fifth century* of the Church. Accounts of healings and miracles have continued virtually without interruption throughout Church history (documented by men like George Fox and John Wesley, to name a few). However, it is true that as the Church grew more formalistic and worldly these powerful gifts became far less common. But remember: During much of this time, foundational biblical truths like justification by faith were also hardly heard! During much of this same time, the Bible itself was taken from the common people. In fact, things got so bad that the "Church" persecuted and even killed those who tried to translate the Scriptures into the language of the people. *Why in the world then should we point to Church history as the ideal model, the pattern which we are to emulate?*

Thank God that, for the last 500 years, the Church has been in a process of restoration (although it has sometimes taken two steps forward and one step back and called some things "restoration" that have not truly been restoration). Through these centuries, fundamental truths have once more become fundamental, the missionary mandate has come again to the forefront, and the power of the Spirit is being poured out afresh.

Let me put this in perspective for you. When John Hus took a stand in the fifteenth century for what we would now call basic principles of the faith, he was burned at the stake. William Tyndale was *martyred* for translating the Bible into English in the sixteenth century. Yes, not only biblical truth, *but the Bible itself* was virtually stolen from much of the Church for centuries. In the eighteenth century, when the English cobbler William Carey suggested to his church board that he take the gospel message to India, tradition has it that he was rebuffed with the comment, "Sit down, young man! When God is ready to convert the heathen, He will do so without any help from you or me." And so, even world missions, the very heartbeat of the Church, had once become a forgotten truth. Why then should it surprise us that, with some of the most fundamental principles of the faith neglected, the power of the Spirit—a sign of divine vitality and action—should also have waned through these very same centuries?

But again, thanks be to God, over the past 120 years, the Spirit's miracle-working power has been and is being restored to the people of God. And so while history records a dramatic *decrease* in healings and miracles over the course of medieval Church history, it records a dramatic *increase* in these healings and miracles in modern Church history.[19]

Of course, it is true that there have been numerous excesses, extremes, and errors in the name of the gifts of the Spirit, right up to this very moment. But this was the case in the early Church too (remember the Corinthians?). And even when it comes to the restoration of the *message* of the gospel to the Church, there have been plenty of excesses, extremes, and errors in the name of doctrinal purity (the Reformation was far from perfect). Do we therefore throw out Reformation truths because of Reformation extremes? Of course not. In the same way, we do not throw out the reality of the present-day ministry of the Spirit because of "charismatic" extremes.[20]

Now, let me bring this historical perspective home even more clearly. Around the world, the fastest growing religious faith is not

Islam, nor is it some cultic, New Age ideology or atheistic philoso-
phy. Not at all. Rather, on every continent on the globe, the fastest
growing religious faith—far and away—is Spirit-empowered, signs
and wonders Christianity. In fact, just to give you a feel for what
this means, for every Baptist on the earth today, there are *four*
Pentecostal/charismatics.[21] (Of course, I'm fully aware that there are
plenty of "Spirit-filled" Baptists and more than enough "Spirit-
frilled" Pentecostals, but I'm dealing with recognized religious labels
here.) Or, to put this another way, the largest identifiable Protestant
group in the world today consists of those who would call themselves Spirit-baptized, tongue-speaking believers. God is moving!
(For more on this, see Chapter Thirteen, "Is Good News Bad News
for the Gloomers and Doomers? Exposing the Laodicean Lie.")

Unless you are willing to write off *the majority of fundamental-
ist, Bible-believing Christians around the world today*, calling them
part of an end-time counterfeit conspiracy, you will have to admit
that the Spirit is still confirming the Word in power. As Paul wrote
more than 1,900 years ago, "For the kingdom of God is not a matter
of talk but of power" (1 Cor. 4:20). (For clarification regarding the
kind of power Paul was talking about, read 1 Corinthians 2:1-5.)[22]
Thank God for His mighty, present-day power! The devil does *not*
have a monopoly on miracles.

To repeat what we have been saying: Nowhere does the Word
of God tell us that the miraculous powers of the Holy Spirit would
be withdrawn after the days of the apostles, and therefore, there is
absolutely no basis for the argument that all miracles, signs, and
wonders since the first century should be suspected of being counterfeit. And, as we have emphasized elsewhere, nowhere does the
Word of God tell us to beware of every miracle, utterance, and sign.
Rather we are to *test* and *try* them. To put it another way, the New
Testament does not say, "Beware of every spirit," but rather, it
teaches, "Believe not every spirit" (1 John 4:1-6, KJV).[23]

Paul's guidelines sum it up: "Do not put out the Spirit's fire; do
not treat prophecies with contempt. Test everything. Hold on to the
good" (1 Thess. 5:19-21). But with the negative scenario painted by
some critics, with a devil who has a thriving miracle industry and a

God who seems to have retired from the miracle business, I wonder what "the good" is (to use Paul's words) that the critics are "holding on to"? What *is* the Spirit doing? Anything?

"All right," you say. "You've made your point. Still, I'm concerned with the fact that there are so many other verses warning us about counterfeit miracles at the end of the age. Shouldn't we look at some of those passages?" That's a good idea (although I warn you in advance: There aren't as many verses dealing with counterfeit miracles as you may think). We'll start with the Book of Revelation, an end-time "favorite." Does the devil have a monopoly on miracles there? Not in the least! Consider this detailed description of the miraculous powers of the two Heaven-sent witnesses:

> If anyone tries to harm them, fire comes from their mouths and devours their enemies. This is how anyone who wants to harm them must die. These men have power to shut up the sky so that it will not rain during the time they are prophesying; and they have power to turn the waters into blood and to strike the earth with every kind of plague as often as they want. (Rev. 11:5-6)

These verses argue *against* those who feel that there will be no true, heavenly signs and wonders before the return of the Lord, but only counterfeits. If you say, "But this passage in Revelation 11 pertains to the period of the tribulation after the Church has been raptured" (a reading based on a futurist, pre-tribulation understanding of the book), then I say in reply, "Then so do all the verses in Revelation and elsewhere pertaining to the counterfeit miracles of the false prophet and antichrist! So why all the fuss about these things now if the believers will already be gone?"

The same logic must also apply to any other interpretation of Revelation 11:5-6. If the passage speaks symbolically of past events in the Church (the preterist viewpoint), then the references to the false prophet and antichrist also refer symbolically to past events. If the passage speaks of miraculous events occurring during the tribulation and believers are *not* raptured before that time (the futurist, post-tribulation viewpoint), then that means we will be here to see both true miracles *and* false miracles on a gigantic scale.[24]

This, in fact, applies to other important passages dealing with counterfeit signs and wonders. They apply clearly to the "antichrist" and "false prophet," figures who come to the fore in the "tribulation" period. So, for those who hold to a pre-tribulation rapture, the warnings are hardly relevant; for those who hold to a post-tribulation rapture, there will be both true and counterfeit miracles in abundance.

There is also something else of real importance in the description of false signs and wonders in Revelation. Look at the relevant verses:

> Then I saw another beast, coming out of the earth. He had two horns like a lamb, but he spoke like a dragon. He exercised all the authority of the first beast on his behalf, *and made the earth and its inhabitants worship the first beast,* whose fatal wound had been healed. And he performed great and miraculous signs, even causing fire to come down from heaven to earth in full view of men. *Because of the signs he was given power to do on behalf of the first beast, he deceived the inhabitants of the earth. He ordered them to set up an image in honor of the beast* who was wounded by the sword and yet lived. He was given power to give breath to the image of the first beast, so that it could speak and cause all who refused to worship the image to be killed. (Rev. 13:11-15)

> The sixth angel poured out his bowl on the great river Euphrates, and its water was dried up to prepare the way for the kings from the East. Then I saw three evil spirits that looked like frogs; they came out of the mouth of the dragon, out of the mouth of the beast and out of the mouth of the false prophet. They are spirits of demons performing miraculous signs, and they go out to the kings of the whole world, *to gather them for the battle on the great day of God Almighty.* (Rev. 16:12-14)

Did you read these verses carefully? Aside from the fact that, for the pre-tribulation Christian, these passages have nothing to do with the Church (in other words, the pre-tribulationist believes the Church will be raptured before these events take place), the demonic activities spoken of in Revelation 13 are designed to deceive the whole earth into worshiping the "beast" (normally equated with the antichrist), while the miraculous signs and wonders spoken of in Revelation 16 are aimed at gathering the kings of the whole world into battle against God Almighty! They are counterfeit miracles *performed overtly* in the name of "the beast" and in open rebellion against the Lord. That's why they seem to be so powerful and persuasive. Their demonic design is huge, since they are part of Satan's plot to convince people to follow him and fight against Jesus. That's pretty bold!

This leads us to something that must be embarrassingly obvious to the critic: These verses have *nothing whatsoever* to do with someone being dramatically touched in a contemporary renewal or revival movement. Even if that person did not have a true experience in the Lord and instead had become worked up into a mere emotional frenzy, that unfortunate situation would still not change the fact that these verses in Revelation are *completely unrelated* to that particular experience.[25] My critical colleague, let's not be silly here. If you desire to base yourself on the Bible, be consistent. The counterfeit signs and wonders spoken of here—accomplished, I remind you, in the name of the antichrist—are designed to align the world in a final battle against the Almighty. How then can you use these very passages to warn believers to beware of all supernatural manifestations in the Church today? Get a grip, friend!

It's one thing to say, "Look. The devil is a deceiver, and in the end of the age, he will try to lure the whole world into allegiance with him, using all kinds of counterfeit miracles. This should caution us to *always* be faithful to the Word and walk closely with our Lord Jesus." That I can accept (although the logic is hardly flawless). It's another thing to say, "The Bible tells us that in the end of the age there will be all kinds of false signs and wonders. Therefore we should be suspicious of all signs and wonders in our day."

Let's get back to truth. According to Revelation 19:20, it was the "false prophet" (whose signs are probably alluded to in Matthew 24, a passage to which we'll turn in a moment) who through his signs "had deluded those who had received the mark of the beast and worshiped his image" (Rev. 19:20). Is there anyone who can tell me what in the world this has to do with someone shaking in a revival meeting? Plus, as we just saw, the miracles of the antichrist and false prophet are on a gigantic, cosmic scale, hardly related to a few people shaking or falling. Critical friends, you haven't seen anything yet!

"But," you ask, "what about all those other passages about counterfeit miracles in the last days?" Well, here's the punch line. There are only two other passages! The first is Matthew 24, with parallels in Mark 13; the second is 2 Thessalonians 2. Let's go to this second passage right now:

> For the secret power of lawlessness is already at work; but the one who now holds it back will continue to do so till he is taken out of the way. And then the lawless one will be revealed, whom the Lord Jesus will overthrow with the breath of His mouth and destroy by the splendor of His coming. The coming of the lawless one will be in accordance with the work of Satan displayed in all kinds of counterfeit miracles, signs and wonders, and in every sort of evil that deceives those who are perishing. They perish because they refused to love the truth and so be saved. For this reason God sends them a powerful delusion so that they will believe the lie and so that all will be condemned who have not believed the truth but have delighted in wickedness. (2 Thess. 2:7-12)

I emphasize again: For those who hold to a pre-tribulation rapture (and many of the critics do), these verses all pertain to events that will take place *after* the Church is taken out of the way. Therefore, on this interpretation, we will not be around to see these counterfeit miracles. More importantly, regardless of the particular end-time scheme to which you hold, the false wonders spoken of here, just like those in Revelation, are miracles performed to establish the cause of the antichrist.

To ask the obvious once more (I apologize for being redundant, but I have to make the point), what do these verses have to do with supernatural manifestations taking place in revival meetings in which Jesus is being glorified and adored, Satan is being resisted and rejected, and the Word of truth is being exalted? Please!

And look again at those who are deceived (for more on this, see Chapter Five, "Let No One Deceive You"): They are "those who are perishing...because they refused to love the truth and so be saved." They "have not believed the truth but have delighted in wickedness." Therefore they will be "condemned"! How can this possibly be applied to Word-loving, God-fearing, Jesus-adoring, holy-living believers who are being supernaturally touched in revival meetings? Friends, is it any wonder that some of us who study the Word carefully have a problem taking the critics seriously when they so pitifully misapply the Scriptures, especially when they claim to be following the example of the Bereans of Acts 17?

There is one more point of interest in this passage in 2 Thessalonians 2, specifically, verses 9-10. There we learn that "the coming of the lawless one will be in accordance with the work of Satan displayed in all kinds of counterfeit miracles, signs and wonders, and in every sort of evil that deceives those who are perishing."[26] In other words, the devil will do what he has been doing all along! He'll perform false miracles (as he has for thousands of years) and lead perishing people into every sort of evil (as he has for thousands of years). His final act will be just a bigger and "badder" version of the same old show. But where is there a hint that in the end of the age, for the very first time, Satan will now have a monopoly on miracles? Where is this written or even suggested?

And what about Matthew 24? Are the key verses in that passage any more relevant? Hardly! As we saw in our earlier discussion of Matthew 24:4-5, 9-11, and 23-27 (see 64-67), in this passage Jesus was warning His disciples (which, by extension, includes us today) about *false messianic movements*, in particular, about people claiming that *Jesus will not be coming in the clouds of heaven because He is already here.* Behind these false messianic movements will be false prophets working false wonders. That's what the warnings are about!

Once more, then, we must ask, Where is the connection between Jesus' warnings here and the current cross-centered revival, a revival that has for one of its central themes the *return of Jesus in the clouds of heaven*? It is true that the Lord warned us about coming great deception accompanied by false signs and wonders, but it is equally true that the warnings have absolutely *nothing* to do with today's repentance-based, get-the-sin-out-and-live-for-God, follow-the-Word Holy Spirit visitation. There is no correlation! (I would encourage you to review our discussion of these verses in Chapter Five, "Let No One Deceive You.")

Of course, I could also point out that, according to many pre-tribulational interpreters, the warnings in Matthew 24 apply specifically to Jewish believers who will be alive in the tribulation period, not to believers living today. Yet revival critics who are pretribulationalists still point to these very passages to warn us about alleged deception in the Church in this day and hour. So, not only do they misapply the *meaning* of these verses, but according to their own theology, they misapply the *timing* of these verses. To be candid, it really is a pretty poor job of biblical interpretation.[27]

The fact is, as we have seen through a review of the relevant Scriptures, there is no basis for the claim that, in the end of this age, the devil will have a monopoly on miracles. His carefully crafted counterfeits will only serve to underscore the purity and power of the Lord's sovereign signs, and the backdrop of gross darkness will cause the true light to be seen all the more clearly. Almighty God has not yet retired from the miracle-working business, and He has no plans on retiring any time soon.

Of course, if you want to, you can keep your eyes locked on the deceiving works of the enemy as he seeks to draw humanity away from the Son of God. I prefer to keep my eyes fixed on Jesus, listening daily to His Word, walking in reverent fear before Him, spreading the good news of His death and resurrection, and living holy until He comes in the sky for His own. Is this the path to deception?

And Trypho said, "I believe, however, that many of those who say that they confess Jesus, and are called Christians, eat meats offered to idols, and declare that they are by no means injured in consequence." And I replied, "The fact that there are such men confessing themselves to be Christians, and admitting the crucified Jesus to be both Lord and Christ, yet not teaching His doctrines, but those of the spirits of error, causes us who are disciples of the true and pure doctrine of Jesus Christ, to be more faithful and steadfast in the hope announced by Him. For what things He predicted would take place in His name, these we do see being actually accomplished in our sight. For He said, 'Many shall come in My name, clothed outwardly in sheep's clothing, but inwardly they are ravening wolves.' And, 'There shall be schisms and heresies.' And, 'Beware of false prophets, who shall come to you clothed outwardly in sheep's clothing, but inwardly they are ravening wolves.' And, 'Many false Christs and false apostles shall arise, and shall deceive many of the faithful.' There are, therefore, and there were many, my friends, who, coming forward in the name of Jesus, taught both to speak and act impious and blasphemous things; and these are called by us after the name of the men from whom each doctrine and opinion had its origin.

Justin Martyr's *Dialogue with Trypho*, mid-second century

After me there is no prophecy, but only the end of the world.

The "prophetess" Maximilla, who died in A.D. 179

Of a truth it was proclaimed of old through the Apostle John, Little children, it is the last hour (1 John 2:18), according as the Truth foretold. And now pestilence and sword rage through the world, nations rise against nations, the globe of the earth is shaken, the gaping earth with its inhabitants is dissolved. For all that was foretold is come to pass.

Letter from Gregory the Great
to John of Constantinople, fourth century

Another of the "Signs of the Times" is the revival of what is called the "GIFT OF TONGUES," in which the recipient claims that he is taken possession of by the "Spirit of God" and empowered to speak in an "unknown" or "foreign tongue." But the conduct of those thus possessed, in which they fall to the ground and writhe in contortions, causing disarrangement of the clothing and disgraceful scenes, is more a characteristic of "demon possession," than a work of the Holy Spirit, for the Holy Spirit does not lend Himself to such vile impersonations.

From what has been said we see that we are living in "Perilous Times," and that all about us are "Seducing Spirits," and that they will become more active as the Dispensation draws to its close, and that we must exert the greatest care lest we be led astray.

Clarence Larkin, *Dispensational Truth*, published in 1918

Chapter Nine

Are We Living in the Last Days?

Every "Spirit-filled" believer is familiar with Peter's Pentecost sermon. His quotation of Joel's prophecy is a favorite:

> Then Peter stood up with the Eleven, raised his voice and addressed the crowd: "Fellow Jews and all of you who live in Jerusalem, let me explain this to you; listen carefully to what I say. These men are not drunk, as you suppose. It's only nine in the morning! No, this is what was spoken by the prophet Joel: 'In the last days, God says, I will pour out My Spirit on all people. Your sons and daughters will prophesy, your young men will see visions, your old men will dream dreams. Even on My servants, both men and women, I will pour out My Spirit in those days, and they will prophesy. I will show wonders in the heaven above and signs on the earth below, blood and fire and billows of smoke. The sun will be turned to darkness and the moon to blood before the coming of the great and glorious day of the Lord. And everyone who calls on the name of the Lord will be saved.' " (Acts 2:14-21)

Yes, Peter's words were powerful and inspirational. But they were also precise and interpretive. He actually changed the original wording of Joel's prophecy! While preaching under the leading of the Spirit, he explained that when the Lord said through Joel, *"And afterward*, I will pour out My Spirit on all people," He really meant, *"In the last days...*I will pour out My Spirit on all people" (Joel 2:28a; Acts 2:17a).[1] Do you see it? Peter is telling us that the "and afterward" of Joel refers to "the last days," and according to Peter, *the last days began almost 2,000 years ago*. That is more important than you may realize. The last days have been here for a long time![2]

Listen to the testimony of the authors of the New Testament. Hebrews 1:1-2 states, "In the past God spoke to our forefathers through the prophets at many times and in various ways, but *in these last days* He has spoken to us by His Son, whom He appointed heir of all things, and through whom He made the universe." Notice those key words: "in these last days." The last days were inaugurated by Jesus Himself! This is underscored again in Hebrews 9:26 where it is written that He "has appeared once for all *at the end of the ages* to do away with sin by the sacrifice of Himself."

Paul writes in 1 Corinthians 10:11: "These things happened to them [the Israelites] as examples and were written down as warnings for us, on whom the *fulfillment of the ages* has come." The "fulfillment of the ages" had already come on the Corinthians, and they lived more than 1,900 years ago!

Peter could already inform his readers that Jesus, who was "chosen before the creation of the world…was revealed in *these last times* for your sake" (1 Pet. 1:20), warning them that "*the end of all things is near*. Therefore be clear minded and self-controlled so that you can pray" (1 Pet. 4:7). And James strongly rebuked the worldly rich, saying, "Your gold and silver are corroded. Their corrosion will testify against you and eat your flesh like fire. You have hoarded wealth *in the last days*" (Jas. 5:3, which is a literal translation from the Greek). Yes, these greedy people who died 19 centuries ago were guilty of hoarding wealth *in the last days*.

And what about the testimony of John? "Dear children, this is *the last hour*; and as you have heard that the antichrist is coming, even now many antichrists have come. *This is how we know it is the last hour*" (1 John 2:18). Could anything be more clear? Was John mistaken in what he wrote?[3]

There can be no possible question that the New Testament authors understood that they were living in the last days. Their words are perfectly clear. The last days are here right now and the last days have been here for many years! As John Calvin expressed it, "…the whole period of the new dispensation, from the time when Christ appeared to us with the preaching of his Gospel, until the day of judgment, is designated by the last hour, the last times, the last days...."⁴ That's why some preachers like to say that we are living in the last of the last days, the closing minutes of the final hour.

On a practical level, it means that both the New Testament warnings about the evil nature of the last days and the promises of the glorious outpouring of the last days applied then and continue to apply today. Therefore it would be wrong to think that believers today are dealing with something totally different than what the early Church dealt with. The basic problems remain the same, the basic warnings remain the same, and the same principles that worked then will work now.

When Paul wrote to Timothy, "But mark this: There will be terrible times *in the last days*" (2 Tim. 3:1), he wasn't just talking about things that would happen 1,500 or 2,000 years later. He was talking about things that Timothy himself would have to deal with. Otherwise it would be ludicrous to say, "But mark this, Timothy. Note this and remember it well. This is very important for your life and ministry. Be careful and be on guard: 2,000 years from now terrible times will come!" How absurd. Rather, the prophetic words he spoke to Timothy proved true then and prove true today.

You say, "Are you sure about your interpretation of the passage? Isn't there another way to look at it?" Well, let's not worry about my interpretation or your interpretation. Let's read the whole section and let the Word speak for itself:

> But mark this: There will be terrible times in the last days. People will be lovers of themselves, lovers of money, boastful, proud, abusive, disobedient to their parents, ungrateful, unholy, without love, unforgiving, slanderous, without self-control, brutal, not lovers of the good, treacherous, rash, conceited, lovers of pleasure rather than lovers of God—having a form of godliness but denying its power. *Have nothing to do with them.* (2 Tim. 3:1-5)

"Timothy, have nothing to do with these kind of people! These are evil days in which we live, days in which sin will abound and sinners will become more brazen. Avoid these godless transgressors."

Because Timothy was living in the last days (in the verses we just quoted, "the last days" clearly means "these last days"), and because it is possible that he may have been expecting everything to get better and brighter, Paul wanted to make sure his spiritual son understood the perilous nature of the hour.[5]

In a similar way, he gave practical instructions to Timothy in his first letter to him, emphasizing how important it was that his young disciple hold fast to his wise words. Why? "The Spirit clearly says that in later times some will abandon the faith and follow deceiving spirits and things taught by demons" (1 Tim. 4:1). Was this more end-times trivia for Timothy? Not at all. Rather, after outlining what some of those demonic doctrines would be, he wrote, "If you point these things out to the brothers, you will be a good minister of Christ Jesus, brought up in the truths of the faith and of the good teaching that you have followed" (1 Tim. 4:6). This is down-to-earth counsel from a father in the faith.

"Timothy, stick to the Word. Beware of strange new doctrines. In the days to come—days which you will experience—there will be lots of demonic activity and false revelation. That's why you must always remember: These last days will be treacherous!"[6]

Not surprisingly, by the time Paul wrote his second letter to Timothy, some already *had* departed from the faith:

Do your best to present yourself to God as one approved, a workman who does not need to be ashamed and who correctly handles the word of truth. Avoid godless chatter, because those who indulge in it will become more and more ungodly. Their teaching will spread like gangrene. Among them are Hymenaeus and Philetus, who have wandered away from the truth. They say that the resurrection has already taken place, and they destroy the faith of some. (2 Tim. 2:15-18)

Defection is nothing new. Apostasy is nothing novel. There have been "the deceivers" and "the deceived" as long as there has been truth:[7]

In fact, everyone who wants to live a godly life in Christ Jesus will be persecuted, *while evil men and impostors will go from bad to worse, deceiving and being deceived.* But as for you, continue in what you have learned and have become convinced of, because you know those from whom you learned it, and how from infancy you have known the holy Scriptures, which are able to make you wise for salvation through faith in Christ Jesus. (2 Tim. 3:12-15)

"Yes, Timothy, there will be plenty of self-deceived, evil people out there. You just be sure to cleave to the Word. That's your strength and foundation."

At this point, you may still be trying to figure out where I'm going with all this, wondering what the punch line is. It is simply this: There is a last-days frenzy in the air today, a hyper-deception craze that has no biblical basis. It is a spirit and attitude found throughout much of the Body—the critics thrive on it—that says, "Because we are living in the last days, and because these days will be particularly dangerous and treacherous, we must be specially wary of any type of intense spiritual movement, of any unusual activity attributed to the Holy Spirit. We must be suspicious of *all* supernatural phenomena." But this view is not scriptural! It is an exaggerated and often paralyzing position that is actually one of *Satan's tools*.[8]

The facts are as follows: Since the beginning of the New Testament era, we have been living in the last days, and we are warned to beware of the peril of deception in our day just as the early believers were warned to beware of the peril of deception in their day. There were counterfeits then and there are counterfeits now, and the same antidotes to deception that worked then will work today. Even if the days in which we live reflect an *acceleration* of both outpouring and deception (and I certainly believe this), the careful application of the same biblical principles will still provide the same safeguards.[9]

"Exactly!" the critic says. "That's why we must go to the Word and the Word alone. All the other things—the so-called manifestations of the Spirit, the falling and shaking, the crying out in prayer, the dancing and shouting—these are just diversions that Satan sends to get our eyes off the Bible."

Poor critic! How can you read the Bible and say such things? God's Word is full of examples of unusual, Heaven-sent spiritual manifestations that are designed to get our eyes on *Him*. The fact is, our dear critics would have had quite a hard time living in the days of Jesus and the apostles (not to mention the days of Moses or Elijah) using the very same principles by which they reject genuine revival today. (See also Chapter Six, "Was Jesus a False Prophet?")

To illustrate this more clearly, let's apply this critical mentality to the believers in the Book of Acts (after all, Peter told us emphatically that they were living in the last days). We'll put the critic back in the Upper Room (maybe with his spouse and children too):

> Brothers, fellow disciples, be careful! Do you hear that sound of a blowing, violent wind? Do you see those tongues of fire? Look at how quickly these bizarre manifestations have come! It's a good thing Jesus warned us to beware of false miracles. We could have easily been duped! The wind can't be from God because it's too loud and violent. Plus, where does the Word tell us to put our trust in wind? And those tongues are obviously counterfeits. Jesus never told us to look for tongues of fire hovering our heads! Something is wrong here, men....
>
> Oh no, what's this? Guys, what are you doing? Why are you acting like that? Everybody is going to think you're drunk. It will make a mockery of our message! And what's that gibberish you are all speaking? I can't understand a single word....And you can't understand what you're saying either? This is from the devil! Honey! Kids! Let's get out of here! The last-days deception is here! The false miracles are here already! Everybody else has gone crazy! They've already gotten their eyes off the Bible and put their trust in some experience. Help! We're the only ones left.

Does this sound far-fetched? Hardly! A Christian author (and former critic) who originally grouped the current revival with "paranormal" phenomena such as UFO's, New Age wonders, and modern apparitions of Mary, once wrote to me with reference to the Pensacola Outpouring:

> Dr. Brown, I am not a theologian, but I do know the scriptures which cite Jesus Christ warning Christians of deceptions that will befall Christendom during the end time. And so, Jesus warns in Matthew 24:24, "For false christs and false prophets will rise and show great signs and wonders to deceive, if possible, even the elect."

Dr. Brown, if we truly believe that the end time is upon us, we also must heed the warnings of Jesus Christ of the deceptions which will befall Christendom during the end time.

To illustrate the gravity of these deceptions presently active, I implore you to visit the following page: http://www.eclipse.it:80/medjugorje/0_Civit/Civitavecchia.html. This web page is just one of many, of testimonies of peoples profound experiences while on pilgrimage in Medjugorje. These testimonies far exceed the testimonies of the Pensacola outpouring, both in volume and in effectiveness. And yes, if one deems good fruit to be only healings and the release of one's guilt of sin, then like Brownsville, Medjugorje is also producing good fruits.

In closing, I am in no way condemning the people (victims) whom are entrapped in these powerful deceptions, it is my love and God's love for them, the reason I do this. Thank you, and may God bless you, brother.[10]

Notice that key sentence: "Dr. Brown, if we truly believe that the end time is upon us, we also must heed the warnings of Jesus Christ of the deceptions which will befall Christendom during the end time." And so anything supernatural (dubbed "paranormal" by that author) taking place in the name of Jesus is suspected of being part of the "end-time deception." (Thank God that, in this case, after honest dialogue and careful investigation, this truly sincere Christian gentleman publicly renounced his erroneous position, recognizing the divine origin of the current visitation.)

One can only wonder out loud: Is the Holy Spirit doing *nothing* supernatural at the end of this age? Does not the Bible itself tell us to expect great and mighty things from our God in every generation?[11] Really, it's hard to figure out whether to laugh or to cry after reading some of the latest anti-revival literature. But it's out there in abundance. Anything supernatural is suspect, and because people living in Medjugorje have had alleged visions of Mary, today's revival is not of God. (For further discussion, see Chapter Eight, "Does the Devil Have a Monopoly on Miracles?")

But this is not an isolated instance of outlandish criticism in the name of faithfulness to the Word of God. There's plenty of trash on the Internet, on the air, and in print that will make your insides churn. For example, another critic on the Internet says that the types of manifestations that he has heard take place in one particular revival:

> ...are seemingly identical to many counterfeit movements which have infiltrated and destroyed genuine Revivals down through history. Such manifestations are also identical to those found in the modern 'Kundalini' cults of Ramakrishna, Rajneesh, etc, as well as the occultic Chinese 'Qigong' movement, Franz Mesmer's occultic healing practice and other New Age type groups around the world. And yet, such manifestations are found nowhere in the Bible! As I said [in a previous article], if these are the days of "great deception" amongst Christians spoken of in the Scriptures, then shouldn't we be a little more careful about what we allow into God's church?[12]

And just what are some of the manifestations that he labels as occultic, New Age, and demonic? They are: falling on the floor, laughter, shaking, and deep bowing. Yes, these are the days of deception, and if you see anyone doing any of these things in a Christian meeting, beware. Satan's gonna getcha!

Of course, anyone who has attended one of today's typical, repentance-based revival services would know that the three major emphases of every single meeting are: 1) extended times of praise, worship, and adoration; 2) powerful, Christ-centered preaching of the Word, stressing holiness and repentance; 3) huge altar calls with sinners and backsliders getting right with God. That's what it's all about! That's the reason revival leaders are laboring night after night with great joy and thanksgiving. And, in most of these revival meetings, it is only *after* the altar ministry is completed—by that time, often more than *four hours* into a typical meeting—that there is prayer for all the hungry believers who want a refreshing touch from the Lord. Whatever manifestations there may be (during the main part of the service or at the end) are hardly central (except to the critic!). What *is* central is that people are being changed for the glory of God and the honor of Jesus.[13]

But there are other serious problems in this Internet critic's negative perspective. Where does he get the right to label the manifestations to which he refers as demonic counterfeits? It's simple, he would say. Such manifestations are found nowhere in the Bible! Shades of our friend who managed to run out of the Upper Room just before the deception got hold of him too! "The wind...the tongues of fire...the different languages.... They're not found in the Bible!"

And yet the very manifestations this critic attacks *are* found in the Bible. (Of course, even if they weren't, that, in and of itself, would not prove that they were not from God. For more on this, see again Chapter Six, "Was Jesus a False Prophet?") People fell to the ground because of God's presence in the Bible; people laughed to express great joy in the Bible; shaking was hardly uncommon in the Bible; and deep bowing before the Lord is actually admirable (we're *exhorted* to "bow down before Him" in the Word)![14] So, our "discerning" critic has not only missed the whole point and thrust of the current revival; he has not only chosen to ignore the fruit of the revival; he has not only turned a deaf ear to the central message of the revival; but he has claimed that manifestations that are hardly alarming and certainly not unbiblical are thoroughly devilish. Poor critic!

But the story doesn't end here. *Who told these critics that we were living in special days of great deception? Who told them that this period of time was a unique period of deception?*

"Now hold on!" you say. "I've got to object. Of course, I'll admit that you had me going there for a while. You had me pretty well convinced that the last days began in the New Testament era. But now you seem to be throwing out the baby with the bath water. Didn't Jesus Himself warn us that at the end of the age there would be special and unusual deception on an unprecedented scale? Doesn't this describe the day and age in which we live?"

Yes and no. You see, Jesus was warning His disciples about great deception that they would be facing in their day too. Before the temple was destroyed in A.D. 70, there were many false messiahs, many claiming, "I am he," but they were not.[15] And what happened then will happen again on an even greater scale before Jesus returns. What you really need to see is this: Throughout Church history, leaders have quoted the words of Jesus about end-time deception, believing that *they* were living close to the days of the Lord's return.

Take a good look at this lengthy quote from the third century:

> But after a long time we visited the brethren, and confirmed them with the word of piety, and charged them to avoid those who, under the name of Christ and Moses, war against Christ and Moses, and in the clothing of sheep hide the wolf. For these are false Christs, and false prophets, and false apostles, deceivers and corrupters, portions of foxes, the destroyers of the herbs of the vineyards: "for whose sake the love of many will wax cold. But he that endureth steadfast to the end, the same shall be saved. Concerning whom, that He might secure us, the Lord declared, saying: "There will come to you men in sheep's clothing, but inwardly they are ravening wolves. Ye shall know them by their fruits; take care of them. For false Christs and false prophets shall arise and shall deceive many."

This evil, most faithful brethren, had long ago begun, but now the mischievous destruction of the same evil has increased, and the envenomed plague of heretical perversity and schisms has begun to spring forth and shoot anew; because even thus it must be in the decline of the world, since the Holy Spirit foretells and forewarns us by the apostle, saying, "In the last days," says he, "perilous times shall come, and men shall be lovers of their own selves, proud, boasters, covetous, blasphemers, disobedient to parents, unthankful, unholy, without natural affection, truce-breakers, false accusers, incontinent, fierce, hating the good, traitors, heady, high-minded, lovers of pleasures more than lovers of God, having a sort of form of religion, but denying the power thereof. Of this sort are they who creep into houses, and lead captive silly women laden with sins, which are led away with divers lusts; ever learning, and never coming to the knowledge of the truth. And as Jannes and Jambres withstood Moses, so do these also resist the truth; but they shall proceed no further, for their folly shall be manifest unto all men, even as theirs also was." Whatever things were predicted are fulfilled; and as the end of the world is approaching, they have come for the probation as well of the men as of the times. Error deceives as the adversary rages more and more; senselessness lifts up, envy inflames, covetousness makes blind, impiety depraves, pride puffs up, discord exasperates, anger hurries headlong.[16]

Do you see what they were saying? "We're approaching the end of the age! These are the last days! It's getting darker! These are days of deception!"

"But they were wrong!" you say. Yes and no. As I pointed out before, the same principles and warnings that applied then apply now. *They* needed to be on their guard and *we* need to be on our guard. We, like they, are not to follow another Jesus; we, like they, are not to believe in another gospel; we, like they, are to wait patiently for the Savior's return in the clouds of heaven. Any claim that "He has already returned" is false. This is nothing new! We are using the same weapons to fight deception that the first believers (along with believers in every generation) used.

You see, there is no other way to approach this whole matter of end-time deception *because there is no way to know for sure that a given generation is the final generation until the end actually comes*. Do you follow?

Christian leaders 100 years ago were concerned about end-time deception just as Christian leaders 1,700 years ago were concerned about end-time deception (re-read the quotes at the beginning of this chapter!). On the one hand, you can see how some leaders took totally ridiculous stands in the name of guarding against deception. This should say something to today's "trustees of the truth." On the other hand, leaders throughout the centuries have done well to watch out for Satan's wily ways. The devil has been working overtime ever since his defeat at the cross and the empty tomb.

Unfortunately, many believers have been ignorant of one of his greatest deceptions. In every generation the father of lies says: "There will be no revival in this generation." He's used this lie for more than 50 generations now—because this is the last generation, a time of unprecedented deception and darkness. Satan himself proclaims to every new crop of believers: "Be careful! Don't get too spiritual now. Be on guard! Watch out for anything powerful that comes in the name of Jesus. It's probably counterfeit. After all, darkness is everywhere and deception abounds. These days are certainly not days of revival."

Liar! You've been throwing around this trash for 2,000 years now, and it's no more true today than it was the day you hatched it in your hellish mind. I reject it in Jesus' name. *Revival is in the land. The true Light is shining in the midst of the darkness. A sweeping visitation is near.* No wonder Satan is trembling in his boots. No wonder he's doing everything he possibly can to tell anyone who will listen, "These are not the days of revival! These are the days of deception!" Pity the poor souls who listen to his lies.

As for me, I'd much rather concentrate on what God says in His Word than on what the devil tries to say in our minds: Jesus will build His Church—a glorious Church—and the gates of hell shall not prevail against it (Matt. 16:18, KJV).[17] The gospel of the Kingdom will be preached in all the world before the end comes (Matt. 24:15),[18] and the last days will be marked, not only by increased satanic activity, but by increased Holy Spirit activity. That's where this whole chapter started, Peter's sermon at Pentecost, quoting from the book of Joel:

> In the last days, God says, I will pour out My Spirit on all people. Your sons and daughters will prophesy, your young men will see visions, your old men will dream dreams. Even on My servants, both men and women, I will pour out My Spirit in those days, and they will prophesy. I will show wonders in the heaven above and signs on the earth below, blood and fire and billows of smoke. The sun will be turned to darkness and the moon to blood before the coming of the great and glorious day of the Lord. And everyone who calls on the name of the Lord will be saved. (Acts 2:17-21)

You see, the critic can't have it both ways. If these indeed are the very last days, then what Peter said about them will also be true. They will be days of great and universal spiritual outpouring, of highly unusual and momentous *divine* signs and wonders, and of widespread salvation along with widespread delusion, wickedness, and counterfeit miracles. Would the critic dare argue that what Peter said about the last days applied *only* to that generation? Then he would also have to argue that what Paul and Jesus said about the last days applied only to their generation! It won't work. There was outpouring along with deception then and there will be outpouring along with deception today.

And so, I'm keeping my guard up, depending on Jesus, and following the proven, biblical guidelines for avoiding deception. But I'm keeping my hope much higher than my guard! I'm trusting in Jesus' power infinitely more than the devil's power. I'm putting far more faith in my Father's ability to keep His promise than in Satan's ability to thwart it. I'm trusting that truth will triumph over lies and that light will triumph over darkness, that the Spirit's end-time work will be much more effective than the enemy's final assault. And if, indeed, we are living in the very last of the last days, then all the more do I expect great things from above. God will save the best for last. (Did you ever read Ecclesiastes 7:8a, "The end of a matter is better than its beginning"?) Hear the Word of God!

> Dear friends, I am not writing you a new command but an old one, which you have had since the beginning. This old command is the message you have heard. Yet I am writing you a new command; its truth is seen in Him and you, *because the darkness is passing and the true light is already shining.* (1 John 2:7-8)

> And do this, understanding the present time. The hour has come for you to wake up from your slumber, because our salvation is nearer now than when we first believed. *The night is nearly over; the day is almost here.* So let us put aside the deeds of darkness and put on the armor of light. (Rom. 13:11-12)

Yes, more than 1,900 years ago, the darkness was passing and the true light already shining. More than 1,900 years ago, "the day" had almost dawned.[19] And now, in these treacherous and yet glorious times, the Morning Star is ready to appear. Keep looking up! The best is yet to come.

Men and women, whites and blacks knelt together or fell across one another; frequently a white woman, perhaps of wealth and culture, could be seen thrown back into the arms of a "buck nigger" and held tightly thus as she shivered and shook in freak imitation of Pentecost. Horrible, awful shame!

Impressions on the Azusa Street Outpouring
by Pentecostal pioneer Charles Parham

After I had finished preaching and was earnestly inviting all sinners to enter into the holiest by this new and living way, many of those who had heard began to call upon God with strong cries and tears. Some sank down, having no strength remaining in them. Others trembled and quaked exceedingly. Some were torn with a kind of convulsive motion in every part of their bodies, often so violently that sometimes four or five persons could not hold one of them. I have seen many hysterical and many epileptic fits, but in most respects none of them were like these. I immediately prayed that God would not allow those who were weak to be offended.

However, one woman was greatly offended, being sure those so affected could stop the shaking if they wished. No one could persuade her to the contrary. She had gone only three or four yards when she also dropped down in as violent an agony as the rest. Twenty-six had been so affected. Most of them were filled with peace and joy during the prayers which were made for them....

John Wesley, *Journal*, June 15, 1739

A work is not to be judged of by any effects on the bodies of men; such as tears, trembling, groans, loud outcries, agonies of body, or the failing of bodily strength.

Jonathan Edwards
The Distinguishing Marks of a Work of the Spirit of God

...any strained exertion of body, mind, or voice is not the work of the Holy Spirit.

Charles Parham

Tremble before Him, all the earth! The world is firmly established; it cannot be moved.

1 Chronicles 16:30

The LORD reigns, *let the nations tremble*; He sits enthroned between the cherubim, *let the earth shake*.

Psalm 99:1

Chapter Ten

All Shook Up
Over a Little Shaking

Revival is not about shaking. It is not about falling. It is not about physical manifestations. It is about God visiting His Church in power. It is about the exaltation of Jesus, the outpouring of the Spirit, the renewal of the saints, and the salvation of sinners. It is about restoration and change. But, when God *does* visit His Church in power, when His Spirit *is* poured out in abundance, when human lives *are* dramatically impacted, unusual things may happen. Trembling is not uncommon. Falling is hardly exceptional. Physical manifestations are often the order of the day. Why? God is shaking us up! He is awakening saints who are asleep in the light and arousing sinners who slumber in darkness. He is touching His people in power.

There is a reason why the early Quakers received their name. (In case you never realized it, just as the Methodists were so named because of their rigid and methodical lifestyles and the Lutherans were so named because of their devotion to the teachings of Luther, the Quakers received their name because they quaked with religious fervor.)[1] Yes, radical renewal can be heavy. After all, in revival, God is arresting our attention. He is convicting the complacent, converting the comatose, and bringing back the backslider. And even for those of us who have been walking closely with Him for years, His powerful touch may still overwhelm and overpower our weak human flesh. What's so odd about this? Revival is jarring and jolting. God's presence can be intense!

D. Martyn Lloyd-Jones, who was a medical doctor before becoming an internationally noted biblical expositor, clearly expressed just what can happen in times of divine visitation:

> It comes near to the rule that in revival phenomena begin to manifest themselves...Sometimes people feel the power of the Spirit to the extent that they faint and fall to the ground. Sometimes there are even convulsions, physical convulsions. And sometimes people fall into a state of unconsciousness, into a kind of trance, and many remain in that kind of state for hours...There phenomena are not essential to revival...yet it is true to say that, on the whole, they do tend to be present where there is revival.

> We must never forget that the Spirit affects the whole person. You see, man is body, soul and spirit and you cannot divide these. Man reacts as a whole. Something is happening which is so powerful that the very physical frame is involved.[2]

Look at this dramatic account from Exodus, immediately before and after the Ten Commandments were given:

> On the morning of the third day there was thunder and lightning, with a thick cloud over the mountain, and a very loud trumpet blast. *Everyone in the camp trembled.* Then Moses led the people out of the camp to meet with God, and they stood at the foot of the mountain. Mount Sinai was covered with smoke, because the Lord descended on it in fire. The smoke billowed up from it like smoke from a furnace, *the whole mountain trembled violently*, and the sound of the trumpet grew louder and louder.... (Ex. 19:16-19)

> *When the people saw the thunder and lightning and heard the trumpet and saw the mountain in smoke, they trembled with fear.* They stayed at a distance and said to Moses, "Speak to us yourself and we will listen. But do not have God speak to us or we will die." (Ex. 20:18-19)

This was quite a scene! And, on one level or another, it was repeated several times in the Scriptures. The world shakes when Almighty God moves in power:

> In my distress I called to the LORD; I called out to my God. From His temple He heard my voice; my cry came to His ears. *The earth trembled and quaked, the foundations of the heavens shook; they*

trembled because He was angry. Smoke rose from His nostrils; consuming fire came from His mouth, burning coals blazed out of it. (2 Sam. 22:7-9)

Your thunder was heard in the whirlwind, Your lightning lit up the world; the earth trembled and quaked. Your path led through the sea, Your way through the mighty waters, though Your footprints were not seen. You led Your people like a flock by the hand of Moses and Aaron. (Ps. 77:18-20)

May the glory of the LORD endure forever; may the LORD rejoice in His works—*He who looks at the earth, and it trembles, who touches the mountains, and they smoke.* I will sing to the LORD all my life; I will sing praise to my God as long as I live. (Ps. 104:31-33)

Tremble, O earth, at the presence of the Lord, at the presence of the God of Jacob, who turned the rock into a pool, the hard rock into springs of water. (Ps. 114:7-8)

He shakes the earth from its place and makes its pillars tremble (Job 9:6).

"Now, Lord, consider their threats and enable Your servants to speak Your word with great boldness. Stretch out Your hand to heal and perform miraculous signs and wonders through the name of Your holy servant Jesus." After they prayed, *the place where they were meeting was shaken.* And they were all filled with the Holy Spirit and spoke the word of God boldly. (Acts 4:29-31)

About midnight Paul and Silas were praying and singing hymns to God, and the other prisoners were listening to them. *Suddenly there was such a violent earthquake that the foundations of the prison were shaken.* At once all the prison doors flew open, and everybody's chains came loose. (Acts 16:25-26)

There is no doubt that, according to the Word, God's power and presence can cause the whole earth to quake and the foundations of the heavens to shake. Yet according to the critics, if a few people shake under God's power in a meeting, it's either the work of the devil or a sign of mental instability. Where is the scriptural logic in all this? According to the Word, God's power shook the believers' meeting place in Acts 4 and rocked the foundations of the jailhouse in Acts 16, yet according to the critics, it's totally unscriptural for Christians to ever shake in a meeting. By what authority do they make this judgment? What is the line of reasoning that validates this view?[3]

When God came down on Mount Sinai the whole mountain trembled violently and everyone in the camp trembled. My critical friends, I assure you: If you were there, you would have trembled as well! You would have been shaking too violently to even pull out your list of "Sure signs of deception," which, no doubt, would have included shaking. The Book of Hebrews actually tells us, "The sight was so terrifying that Moses said, 'I am trembling with fear' " (Heb. 12:21). At the mountain *everyone* was trembling because of the awesome presence of the Lord, but today, even a *few* cannot tremble because His glorious presence is near? Says who?

The question is not whether every person who shakes in a "revival meeting" is really being shaken by the Lord (it is certainly not unlikely that some people will "shake in the flesh"). The question is, Why is it impossible or unlikely that any stable believers will shake? Is there a critic who can provide a decisive, clear, biblical answer?

What do you think happened to the believers in Acts 4 when their meeting place was shaken after they prayed? Do you somehow imagine that the whole place shook but they didn't shake? (And notice: They were filled afresh with the Spirit and spoke the Word boldly.) Do you think that when the earthquake jolted the jailhouse in Acts 16, so that the prison doors "flew open" and "everybody's chains came loose," that Paul and Silas sat still and unmoved?[4] Really now! Why is it that *everything* can shake, sometimes violently, when God comes (including mountains, the pillars of the earth, and buildings), but frail little human beings cannot shake? What's the problem? Isn't the same Power at work?

"But," you say, "that kind of shaking is different!" How do you know? Were you there when it happened? What do you think it looked like on Mount Sinai when God Almighty came down among His people? What kind of shaking was it?

"But," you object, "if the whole building was shaking because of God's power, or the very ground was quaking, I would have no problem with people shaking too. But for people to just shake during a worship service or while responding at the altar, that's totally different."

Is it really totally different? What did the psalmist mean when he said, *"My flesh trembles in fear of You; I stand in awe of Your laws"* (Ps. 119:120)? What do these verses from Jeremiah mean?

> *"Should you not fear Me?" declares the Lord. "Should you not tremble in My presence?* I made the sand a boundary for the sea, an everlasting barrier it cannot cross. The waves may roll, but they cannot prevail; they may roar, but they cannot cross it. But these people have stubborn and rebellious hearts; they have turned aside and gone away." (Jer. 5:22-23)

"But that's Old Testament!" you say, as if people shook differently then than now. Really, friend, stop and think for a moment. What are you saying?

Of course, we just quoted Acts 4 and 16, where God shook things up a little in the New Testament too. And notice in particular Acts 16:29-30, the response of the jailer to the earthquake: "The jailer called for lights, rushed in and *fell trembling* before Paul and Silas. He then brought them out and asked, 'Sirs, what must I do to be saved?' "

The fact is, when God does something dramatic— Old Testament, New Testament, or today—it dramatically impacts us and, weak human beings that we are, we just may shake a little. Really, it's not that hard to understand.

We quiver when our bodies are cold, we tremble when a brisk wind blows right through us, we shake when we are afraid, and we jerk because of sudden, shooting pain. Those are just human responses to common natural stimuli. Is it crazy to think that something spiritual might also cause a bodily response? Does God's Spirit *never* affect us physically? Does He *never* touch our emotions so strongly that there is an accompanying outward reaction? What's so bizarre about this?[5]

"But," you interrupt, "even if I accept that some people may sometimes shake because of God's Word or presence or power, be it a natural or supernatural response, I have a real problem with people who *keep* shaking. In fact, I know someone in my church who went to a so-called revival meeting, and now she shakes every time she's in a service—and it's getting a lot of attention. That's strange!"

Of course, there is always the possibility that the *lady herself* is strange and that she's just getting herself worked up. On the other hand, why *can't* it be God's Spirit at work and a genuine sign of His presence? Why *can't* it be an ongoing attention-getter, just like Ezekiel's or Zechariah's dumbness (see Ezek. 3:24-27; 33:21-22; Luke 1:5-23,57-66)? And why can't God simply move on a person without explaining all the details to us?[6]

The bottom line is this: Not only is there nothing strange about someone shaking in a spiritually charged atmosphere, but *from a purely scriptural perspective*, shaking is simply not a big deal in the overall scheme of things (although from listening to many critics, you would think that the question of trembling or shaking is on an equal level to that of the person of Christ or His work of atonement).[7] If anything, we should not be in the least bit surprised if all kinds of shaking—spiritual, emotional, and physical—take place in times of revival.

In fact, as intense as the presence of God was at Mount Sinai, the New Testament promises something even more intense in the age in which we live:

> See to it that you do not refuse Him who speaks. If they did not escape when they refused Him who warned them on earth, how much less will we, if we turn away from Him who warns us from heaven? At that time His voice shook the earth, but now He has promised, "Once more I will shake not only the earth but also the heavens." The words "once more" indicate the removing of what can be shaken—that is, created things—so that what cannot be shaken may remain. Therefore, since we are receiving a kingdom that cannot be shaken, let us be thankful, and so worship God acceptably with reverence and awe, for our "God is a consuming fire." (Heb. 12:25-29)

If God's thundering voice on the earth caused His people to shake then, how much more will His thundering voice from Heaven cause *everything* to shake now?

Of course, the verses in Hebrews are not speaking about revival services, but the scriptural inference is clear: If God's overpowering Sinai presence could shake the earth and the people, how much more might His overpowering New Testament presence—a presence that shakes the earth and the heavens—shake some people too?

Simply stated, according to the Word, shaking under, or before, or because of God's glory or power is not the least bit unusual or uncommon. And when Hebrews 12:28-29 urges us to "worship God acceptably with reverence and awe, for our 'God is a consuming fire,' " it is reminding us that the God of the Old Testament is also the God of the New Testament, and He should be approached with care:

> Serve the LORD with fear and *rejoice with trembling*. (Ps. 2:11, an alternate translation is "shake with trembling")[8]

> Worship the LORD in the splendor of His holiness; *tremble before Him, all the earth*. (Ps. 96:9)

> This is what the LORD says: "Heaven is My throne, and the earth is My footstool. Where is the house you will build for Me? Where will My resting place be? Has not My hand made all these things, and so they came into being?" declares the LORD. *"This is the one I esteem: he who is humble and contrite in spirit, and trembles at My word."* (Is. 66:1-2)[9]

> Hear the word of the LORD, *you who tremble at His word*: "Your brothers who hate you, and exclude you because of My name, have said, 'Let the LORD be glorified, that we may see your joy!' Yet they will be put to shame." (Is. 66:5)

> Then everyone who *trembled at the words of the God of Israel* gathered around me because of this unfaithfulness of the exiles. And I sat there appalled until the evening sacrifice. (Ezra 9:4)

Look at what the Word says! It is the hard-hearted and stubborn, the irreverent and the godless who do *not* tremble before God and His Word, but it is the humble, contrite, reverent God-fearers who tremble in His presence.

"But that kind of trembling is different too!" shouts the critic. Get a life, friend! You claim to be so devoted to the Word, yet you refuse to accept the testimony of dozens of straightforward verses. When you want to cite Scripture in an attempt to disprove the reality of revival today, every syllable is to be taken literally. But when we, the proponents of today's revival, provide biblical evidence, the verses just become metaphorical figures of speech, not really meaning what they seem to mean. How inconsistent and biased!

Is there *no* shaking today that is scriptural? Enough with trying to find logical loopholes and exegetical escapes. The Scriptures are clear: God's presence is sometimes so overwhelming that people and things shake because they are overpowered; His presence is sometimes so awesome and terrifying that people and things quake with reverent fear before Him; and the fact that God is God and that His Word is holy is enough to cause us to tremble. As Jonathan Edwards wrote (with reference to the Queen of Sheba being overcome when she saw the glory of Solomon's kingdom), "I know of no reason why a being affected with a view of God's glory should not cause the body to faint, as well as being affected with a view of Solomon's glory."[10]

Just as "the elders of the town trembled" when Samuel came to Bethlehem (1 Sam 16:4), God's people often tremble when His Spirit comes in power. Just as the Roman guards at the garden tomb "were so afraid of [the angel of the Lord] that they shook and became like dead men" (Matt. 28:4), sinners often shake and fall like dead people because of the holy presence of the One who will judge the living and the dead. There are many good reasons why people shake!

I could give you hundreds of examples of this kind of shaking and trembling from the history of revival (in fact, I provide some in my book, *From Holy Laughter to Holy Fire*, Chapter Ten, "Jerkers, Jumpers, and 'Holy Disorder'," and others have written on this in much greater length);[11] however, I emphasize the *Word of God* here. Either accept it or reject it. (By the way, there is some semantic overlap in the Hebrew verbs translated "tremble" and "shake" and "quake" in most of the verses cited; in other words, for the most part, there is not a pronounced difference in meaning between them.)[12]

At times all nature quivers because of the wrath of God: *"The earth trembled and quaked, and the foundations of the mountains shook; they trembled because He was angry"* (Ps. 18:7). Is it surprising that sinners sometimes shake violently when they become aware of the crimes they have committed against a holy God, and for the very first time, get a glimpse of the wrath that is due them if they don't repent? This kind of shaking is quite common in times of true revival, past and present.

Once I was talking with a young Christian woman who was about to turn her back on God and go into the world. I asked her if she would pray with me, and she consented. While my eyes were closed in prayer, I received a strong word of rebuke and warning for her, and delivered it to her in the fear and love of the Lord. I said to myself, "When I open my eyes, if this girl is not moved, our talk is over." Instead, tears were streaming down her cheeks and her whole body was trembling. Needless to say, I continued to minister to her. Her shaking was a sign that the word hit home. She trembled because she heard and she feared. That kind of response is good!

And did you know that there is even a biblical shaking due to the goodness of God? His grace can also be overwhelming:

> Then this city will bring Me renown, joy, praise and honor before all nations on earth that hear of all the good things I do for it; *and they will be in awe and will tremble at the abundant prosperity and peace I provide for it.* (Jer. 33:9)[13]

What God will do will be so amazing that His people will be literally moved.

"But may I ask an honest question?" you say. "I can't argue with the fact that the Word talks a lot about shaking and trembling and the like. But I've seen some really weird things in some so-called revival services, and I've heard that even in meetings where the leaders try to keep things in control, there are some weird people acting in weird ways."

Let me say three things in response: First, not everything that is called revival is really revival, and even when God genuinely *is* moving, there are some superficial believers who just want to run with the latest fad. They might get really stupid with "renewal" or "revival" just like they have gotten stupid with other spiritual emphases in the past. I have written about this for years, and I share your concern. That's one of the reasons that it is so important during times of real outpouring to constantly major on the majors—repentance, holiness, salvation, and worshiping and loving the Lord.[14]

Second, I can personally verify that sometimes weird people can be spotted in revival meetings. They were weird before they came in. (The good news is that many of them are normal when they leave!) When you consider the fact that a church experiencing true revival may have hundreds or thousands of visitors every week or month, it's not surprising that some oddballs may also slip in. (I think I may have spotted one or two in your church too!) And it's just not possible to police everybody and everything all the time. You would also do well to remember the wise counsel of Jonathan Edwards: "We should distinguish the good from the bad and not judge of the whole by a part."[15] (Critics, may I encourage you to take this to heart? Following this sound advice would make quite a difference in your perspective!)

Third—and this is the other side of the coin—are you sure that you have perfect judgment as to what is and what is not weird? Is it possible that you or I might be limiting the Spirit's working based on our limited experience? I'm not talking about people disrobing and slashing their wrists in a service. You don't need discernment to figure that out! But how can you be so sure that one kind of shaking is "biblical" while another is "unbiblical"? (Have you noticed that we're making progress? At least you recognize now that there is such a thing as "scriptural shaking"!)

Of course, there's something else we haven't really touched on yet: *God can do what He wants to do.* (Remember: It is not simply a matter of *people* choosing to shake; often, *God* is shaking them.) He doesn't need our permission. If He wants to shake someone up—saved or unsaved—He can do it. To quote verses on "order in public worship" from 1 Corinthians 14 is hardly relevant here. Those Scriptures have to do with the orderliness of what *we* do in a service. They do *not* have anything to do with the orderliness of what

God does. They limit us. They don't limit Him! (Anyway, they primarily have to do with delivering public messages in an orderly and edifying way. You'll notice, for example, that nowhere does Paul teach us when and how the gifts of healing should function.)[16]

In fact, quite often, as people are overpowered by His Spirit, their shaking and trembling is a sign that He is there. This, for example, is quite common in the weekly baptismal services at the Brownsville Revival, although physical manifestations are absolutely *not* central to the overall thrust and spirit of the revival. As the new believers share wonderful testimonies of the life-changing power of the blood of Jesus, testifying to being instantly delivered from every kind of addiction, declaring that their appetite for sinful lusts has disappeared, the power of God often falls on them—to their great surprise—and they shake or become weak in the light of His presence, as frequently happened in the Word. As they are helped out of the water (or, sometimes, carried out), the congregants clap and shout for joy. It truly is wondrous, Christ-exalting, and God-glorifying—not to mention scriptural. Many a skeptic has wept his or her way through a baptismal service, crying out, "This is the hand of God!" He is alive and He is active.

One night my wife and I were coming home from a meeting in the revival. It was almost 12:30, and I stopped at a convenience store to get a bottle of soda. When I walked in (still wearing my jacket and tie) the clerk said, "Did Brownsville get out early tonight?" (Remember: It was well past midnight!) I asked him, "Have you ever attended the revival?" He replied, "My wife, daughter, and I were early converts of the revival," and he proceeded to tell me his story.

He had known the Lord earlier in life but completely fell away. His wife and 19-year-old daughter were unsaved and decided to go and watch the "holy rollers." During the time of worship, the daughter suddenly twitched, as if a strong breeze had just blown through the room. "Did you feel that?" she asked her mother. "Feel what?" Then, the daughter began to shake, to the point that her mother, feeling somewhat embarrassed, grabbed hold of her. But the more tightly she held her, the more the girl shook. Something was happening, and they knew it.

At this time, the husband was in the balcony, sitting separately from his family, but at the end of the message, when the altar call came, they went down to the altar together. The husband was convicted that it was time to get right with God. Still, his wife and daughter did not believe, although the Lord certainly had their attention by then. When it was time to receive prayer, the wife fell to the ground under God's power and couldn't get up. Her husband said to her, "Now do you believe this is real?" Still, she did not yield her life to God.

The next morning, as she was putting her coat on, her husband noticed that she was lifting her left arm up and moving it freely, something she had been unable to do because of a torn rotator cuff. He said to her, "Look at your shoulder! Move your arm!" She had been completely healed.

Over the next few days, both she and her daughter surrendered their lives to Jesus, committing themselves to a local church. All this had happened about one year before I met this exuberant believer.[17]

Did the devil shake the daughter? Did demons knock the mother over and heal her shoulder? Was it the powers of darkness that supernaturally confirmed the message of the blood, the cross, and salvation through Jesus? Now that this family is committed to a gospel-preaching church—and the husband and father is an active, overt witness for Jesus—would anyone dare argue that their conversions were counterfeit? Yet it all started with a little shaking, and God didn't ask if it was okay before He did it, no more than He asked Saul of Tarsus if it was all right to knock him to the ground and blind him with His blazing light for three days. Our Sovereign Lord does sovereign things, and I for one am thrilled that He does.

"But doesn't Paul teach against 'confusing practices' in public worship?" Yes, he does. But where does the Word say that shaking brings confusion or, for that matter, is "out of order"? Paul makes perfectly clear what practices are "out of order" (as we mentioned earlier with reference to 1 Corinthians 14).[18]

"But shaking is a distraction!" you object. Granted, you might be distracted because the person next to you is shaking during a time of praise and worship, but that person might be distracted because you are standing there as stiff and lifeless as a corpse! Really now, is aimless staring better than ardent shaking? Is it better to look like a zombie than a zealot? Is deadness a sign of devotion?

Anyway, you need to look beyond the mere physical appearance of things. What if the man next to you is a lost sinner who suddenly begins to sob under conviction? Would that be a distraction? Or what if he was instantly healed of 20 years of constant pain and begins to quietly laugh for joy? Would that be a distraction? Or what if a teenage girl who had been molested by her father as a child catches a revelation of the love of the heavenly Father and becomes overcome to the point of shaking? Would that be a distraction? Is it illogical or unscriptural to think that there will be *some* signs of life in a service that is supposedly devoted to meeting with the living God?

Let's be honest. Genuine biblical worship and scriptural responses to the presence of God are enough to scandalize plenty of our brothers and sisters in Christ. In fact, as I have often said, what the world calls fanaticism and most of the Church in the West calls extremism, God calls normal. This applies, not only to lifestyle, but sometimes also to forms of worship.

To a non-charismatic, speaking in tongues with interpretation seems out of order in a church service. Prophesying seems confusing. The very order prescribed by Paul in the Word would strike many a church-goer as odd (including many "charismatics"). Look at Paul's directives:

> What then shall we say, brothers? When you come together, everyone has a hymn, or a word of instruction, a revelation, a tongue or an interpretation. All of these must be done for the strengthening of the church. (1 Cor. 14:26)

A meeting like *that* would be a whole lot harder for the critics to swallow than one in which a few people tremble or fall. "How disorderly!" they would exclaim—about the very thing Paul called orderly.

Well might the prayer of Charles Spurgeon be prayed again in our day. (Ironically, those most willing to pray this kind of prayer are probably the ones who need to pray it the least—in fact, an opposite prayer might be best for them—while those who would disdain the scriptural soundness of this petition are probably the very ones who need to pray it the most!)

> God, send us a season of glorious disorder. Oh, for a sweep of the wind that will set the seas in motion, and make our ironclad brethren, now lying so quietly at anchor, to roll from stem to stern! Oh, for the fire to fall again—fire which shall affect the most solid! Oh, that such fire might first sit upon the disciples, and then fall on all around! O God, Thou art ready to work with us today even as Thou didst then. Stay not, we beseech Thee, but work at once. Break down every barrier that hinders the incoming of Thy might! Give us now both hearts of flame and tongues of fire to preach Thy reconciling word, for Jesus' sake! Amen![19]

And do we completely ignore the experience of the Old Testament prophets? What do you think they were trying to express when they spoke of the gut-wrenching, soul-tearing burden they carried? What did they mean when they spoke of being shattered and overcome by the word of the Lord? What do verses like these convey?[20]

> My heart falters, fear makes me tremble; the twilight I longed for has become a horror to me. (Is. 21:4)

> Oh, my anguish, my anguish! I writhe in pain. Oh, the agony of my heart! My heart pounds within me, I cannot keep silent. For I have heard the sound of the trumpet; I have heard the battle cry. (Jer. 4:19)

> Concerning the prophets: My heart is broken within me; all my bones tremble. I am like a drunken man, like a man overcome by wine, because of the LORD and His holy words. (Jer. 23:9)

> The word of the LORD came to me: "Son of man, tremble as you eat your food, and shudder in fear as you drink your water. Say to the people of the land: 'This is what the Sovereign LORD says about those living in Jerusalem and in the land of Israel: They will eat their food in anxiety and drink their water in despair, for their land will be stripped of everything in it because of the violence of all who live

there. The inhabited towns will be laid waste and the land will be desolate. Then you will know that I am the LORD.' " (Ezek. 12:17-20)

Is there nothing to be taken literally in these descriptions? Does the strong language used have no meaning? And, to take an example from the New Testament, what did Paul mean when he spoke of wrestling in prayer (Col. 4:12), or, even more vividly, when he referred to being in "the pains of childbirth" for the Galatians (Gal. 4:19)? Was there no anguish of heart that he felt when he knelt down to pray for these misled people?[21] (Of course, Paul's words in Galatians 4:19 might not be limited exclusively to prayer, but they certainly *include* that deep intercessory burden that he carried within.) Mothers, would you use an expression like "pains of childbirth" lightly? Would it not describe an experience of intense pain and effort? And who goes through the pangs of childbirth without emotion?

Abel Clary, a man who spent years interceding for Charles Finney's ministry, could tell us much about this. Listen to Finney's description:

And here I must introduce the name of a man, whom I shall have occasion to mention frequently, Mr. Abel Clary. He was the son of a very excellent man, and an elder of the church where I was converted. He was converted in the same revival in which I was. He had been licensed to preach; but his spirit of prayer was such, he was so burdened with the souls of men, that he was not able to preach much, his whole time and strength being given to prayer. The burden of his soul would frequently be so great that he was unable to stand, and he would writhe and groan in agony. I was well acquainted with him, and knew something of the wonderful spirit of prayer that was upon him. He was a very silent man, as almost all are who have that powerful spirit of prayer.[22]

Yes, the very burden of prayer can be overwhelming and exhausting, even to the point of writhing and groaning in agony, and it is not without merit that many have spoken of the *agonies* of intercession. I believe the prophets of Israel would have had no problem at all with many of the most common manifestations in revival, including shaking and prostrations, not to mention being *consumed* with the burden of the Lord or being *undone* through an encounter with Him. In fact, they might say to us, "That's nothing! Did you ever read what happened to *me*?[23]

Listen to Habakkuk the prophet describe his reaction to the revelation of the glory of God: "I heard and my heart pounded, my lips quivered at the sound; decay crept into my bones, and my legs trembled" (Hab. 3:16a). What would the critics do with a testimony like that in a revival service today?

"Tell me, sir, what happened to you in the meeting last night?"

"Well, I heard the Word of the Lord thundering in my ears, and I felt like my insides were ready to burst. My heart felt like it was about to pound out of my chest. Then, I felt something like decay creep into my bones and I started to shake and quake all over. In fact, even as I speak of it now, my insides are trembling."

"That's not God!" cries the critic. "That's an altered state of consciousness at best and a demonic spirit at worst. The Holy Spirit doesn't cause things like that!"

"Sorry," says the prophet. "It's written in the Word!" (Please don't try to argue that things like that only happened during Bible days—which, by the way, is about as historically accurate as saying that people only got saved during Bible days. Has human nature changed since the canon of Scripture was completed? Can an encounter with God through His Word no longer shake us up?)

Actually, Daniel and John would say to Habakkuk, "Hey brother, you think *you* had a heavy experience. You haven't seen anything yet!" Let's hear Daniel's testimony first:

> I, Daniel, was the only one who saw the vision; the men with me did not see it, but such terror overwhelmed them that they fled and hid themselves. So I was left alone, gazing at this great vision; I had no strength left, my face turned deathly pale and I was helpless. Then I heard him speaking, and as I listened to him, I fell into a deep sleep, my face to the ground. A hand touched me and set me trembling on my hands and knees. (Dan. 10:7-10)

And Daniel lay there speechless, until the angel touched his lips and opened his mouth (see Dan. 10:15-16).[24]

As for John, the disciple who was so intimate with the Master that he laid his head on Jesus' breast, when he saw his risen Lord, he "fell at His feet as though dead" (Rev. 1:17a). That's a bit heavier than shaking, don't you think? Ezekiel knew all about this too (see Ezek. 1:28; 3:23; 43:3; 44:4). The fact is, it is the *denial* of outward manifestations and emotional responses that is contrary to the Word. The critics have it backwards, and remember, I'm using Scripture to make my point. Who is following the Word and who is rejecting the Word here?

You might say to me (as a skeptic once did): "All your biblical examples about people falling to the ground have no third person involved. They fell because of an encounter with God, not because someone laid hands on them or prayed for them."

But arguments like this are a smoke screen. Why? First, the skeptic fails to recognize that people often *do* have an encounter with God when hands are laid on them. (For more on this specific point, see Chapter Twelve, "A Lot of Fall Out Over a Little Falling Out.") Second—and this is the bigger issue here—when someone today falls under God's power *without anyone touching them* and, in some cases, *without ever having heard of such a thing*, whether it be during a time of worship, or while being baptized, or after leaving a revival meeting, or upon entering a house where people have been praying (these are all real-life examples), the so-called "biblical purist" *still* rejects the phenomenon as unscriptural. He just has a problem with shaking or falling. (Do you?) He has a problem really believing all the things the Bible describes.

If that's you, why not admit it? Why not say, "Lord, I struggle with skepticism" (or, maybe, by now, cynicism)? Or, "Lord, I think I may be just a little bit stiff and narrow in my thinking." At least you're beginning to deal with some of the roots of the problem instead of merely striking out at the manifestations. And you might be interested to know that many a skeptic has had the skepticism shaken right out of him. It sure is an effective method!

Of course, the issue is not whether you shake or fall. (Some of the most committed Pentecostal/charismatic believers I know have never once fallen or shaken or even twitched "under the power" in their entire lives.) The issue is whether, in your own thinking, there is room for God to be God. The issue is whether you really believe that He can do as He pleases, even when it's different than anything you may have experienced. And you must ask yourself if His touch can ever be so real that it evokes a real response, even if the response be intensely emotional or overtly physical.

My truth-seeking friend, I urge you not to be so small-minded and petty that a great move of God passes right before your eyes and you miss the whole thing because of a little shaking. What a pity that would be! What a shameful thing it would be to look into the Savior's face and say, "Lord, I didn't recognize the powerful presence of Your Holy Spirit because I was offended by that man who always shook in church. I feel so stupid now. I failed to see Your glory—even when this man proved to be a true convert, a sound and solid believer, a man of the Word, a soul-winning saint. Instead, I tried to keep You cramped in my own little religious box. I'm so sorry, Lord!"

Why not repent before it's too late? Why not say, "Father, I'm certainly not looking for manifestations, and You know I'm not asking You to prove Yourself to me. But from here on, I repent of my premature and rash judgmentalism, and I ask You to do whatever You want to do however You want to do it."

Get ready, fellow worker in the Lord. He might just take you at your word.

There are Christians and churches that boast of being mature when really they are spiritually frostbitten. We have developed a prejudice against feeling and emotion until amens would be no scarcer if they cost a hundred dollars apiece—and the real truth is, we have lost our first love....

This accounts for a lot of church troubles. When we love the Lord we love the brethren. When we break up the fallow ground of our hearts we uncover roots of bitterness....There is a reckless enthusiasm about first love. It is not cold and calculating.

Vance Havner
Messages on Revival

True religion consists so much in the affections that there can be no true religion without them. He who has no religious affection is in a state of spiritual death, and is wholly destitute of the powerful, quickening, saving influences of the Spirit of God upon his heart. As there is no true religion where there is nothing else but affection, so there is no true religion where there is no religious affection.

Jonathan Edwards
A Treatise on Religious Affections

With regard to the Author of faith and salvation, abundance of objections have been made; it being a current opinion, that Christians are not now to receive the Holy Ghost.

Accordingly, whenever we speak of the Spirit of God, of his operations on the souls of men, of his revealing unto us the things of God, or inspiring us with good desires or tempers; whenever we mention the feeling his mighty power "working in us" according to his good pleasure; the general answer we have to expect is, "This is rank enthusiasm [i.e., religious fanaticism]. So it was with the Apostles and first Christians. But only enthusiasts pretend to this now."

Thus all the Scriptures, abundance of which might be produced, are set aside at one stroke. And whoever cites them, as belonging to all Christians, is set down for an enthusiast.

John Wesley
A Farther Appeal to Men of Reason and Religion

It is filled with a divine enthusiasm which it once rejected as fanatical.

Charles H. Spurgeon
from his sermon "A New Creation,"
speaking of the born-again soul

Nobody, I suppose, will accuse the author of "Grace Abounding" of being ashamed of his feelings.

G.K. Chesterton, *Heretics*

Chapter Eleven

Now Don't Get Too Emotional!

Have you read the Scriptures from cover to cover? Once? Twice? Ten times? Twenty times? Stop and think for a moment. Jar your memory. Take out a concordance or topical Bible. Make a careful, fresh study if you need to. How often does the Word of God warn us about emotionalism? How many times does it tell us to beware of being too enthusiastic in our worship or too fervent in the service of our Lord? How frequently does it call for dispassionate and restrained adoration of the King of all kings?

You might reply, "That's an interesting point, but I don't think words like *emotionalism* or *enthusiasm* are even found in the Scriptures. That seems to invalidate your whole argument."

Not in the least. The fact is, we are *commanded* to worship, love, and serve God with *everything* within us—heart and soul, body and spirit, passions and will, emotions and reason—and we are rarely, if ever, cautioned against worshiping, loving, or serving Him with *too* much intensity or devotion.

Of course, intense fervor or emotional display are no proof of godliness or spirituality, and many people are deceived into thinking that the more hyped-up and super-charged the meeting, the more the Spirit is moving. To the contrary, this can be evidence of the flesh, not the Spirit.[1] *But to draw the opposite conclusion—that is, that loud praise, upbeat music, clapping, dancing, shouting, or weeping exclude, obstruct, or disallow the working of the Spirit—is to be completely wrong.* In fact, from a consistent biblical viewpoint, the absence of emotion in worship and service is the exception, not the rule.

Still, lest I be misunderstood, I want to make some things perfectly clear. (Of course, some critics will misunderstand me no matter what I say, but for the honest and open reader, I want to be crystal-clear.) First, I am *not* saying that we base our relationship with God on feelings. Absolutely not! We believe God and His Word no matter what we feel or do not feel. Second, I am *not* saying that all true worship must be loud, outward, or "emotional." Often, quiet reflection and silent meditation can be deep, genuine forms of worship. Third, I am *not* saying that the biblical usage of words like *heart* always refers to emotion as opposed to will. In fact, the Hebrew word *lebh*, generally rendered as "heart," often includes concepts such as mind and will.[2] Fourth, I am *not* saying that there is no need to discern between "soul" and "spirit." The New Testament speaks of distinctions between these aspects of the inner man. What *I am saying* is this: Emotional, fervent, outward, and demonstrative singing, preaching, praying, and responding is thoroughly scriptural, logical, and appropriate, *especially in times of revival.* When God is moving powerfully, you will more often encounter the *presence* of shouts of joy, cries of deliverance, and sobs of repentance than the *absence* of such moving sounds.[3]

Of course, I need to emphasize again that the presence of these types of responses and releases does not *prove* that God is working or that true revival is at hand. But—let me emphasize this even more clearly—the fact that these types of things are found in a meeting in no way disproves the Spirit's working or diminishes the reality of the revival. To the contrary, such strong reactions to such powerful divine actions are both fitting and right. As John Wesley asked, "Who will prove that it is enthusiasm [religious fanaticism] to love God, even though we love him with all our heart? to rejoice in the sense of his love to us? to praise him, even with all our strength?" And Wesley reproved those who wanted to take all experience out of their relationship with God, writing: "You even revile that 'life which is hid with Christ in God;' all seeing, tasting, hearing, feeling God. These things are foolishness unto you. No marvel; 'for they are spiritually discerned.' "[4]

Really, it is impossible to read the Bible without seeing that emotions play a vital part in our worship of God and walk with

God—unless it is possible to rejoice, exult, cry out, weep, or wail without any emotion. In this case, wouldn't such "emotionless" words and actions smack of hypocrisy? The prophets and the Savior deplored such "heartless" divine service. Through the prophet Isaiah the Lord said: "...These people come near to Me with their mouth and honor Me with their lips, but their hearts are far from Me. Their worship of Me is made up only of rules taught by men" (Is. 29:13). And Jesus quoted these very words with reference to the hypocritical leaders of His day. As He put it, "They worship Me in vain" (see Matt. 15:7-9; Mark 7:6-7).

How ironic it is that what some critics call "emotionalism" and others call "mysticism" is in fact the expected biblical norm, while the very thing that many critics call sober and sane service is actually a poor excuse for lack of fervor! I believe that John Bunyan had it right when he wrote, "When thou prayest, rather let thy heart be without words, than thy words without a heart."[5]

Yes, it is true that there is such a thing as zeal without knowledge (see Rom. 10:2), but there is also such a thing as knowledge without zeal. Where is the passion of the prophets in today's preachers? Where is the cry of compassion in today's clergy? Where is the longing for the lost in today's leaders?

Of course, you could rightly argue that *both* extremes are common in Christian circles today—from hyped-up emotionalism to cooled-down intellectualism—and I would fully agree with this. Why then do I take so much time to demonstrate that strong emotional displays are quite often appropriate in revival? There are two reasons: first, this is often where the critics attack, making the very strange (as well as illogical and historically inaccurate) claim that the presence of strong emotional displays militates against the reality of the revival; second, *the Bible itself* emphasizes the place of emotion in our walk with God. After all, He made us completely—body, soul, and spirit—and He wants us to serve Him completely—body, soul, and spirit. In fact, when our whole person is involved in worship and service— our bodies set apart to the Lord, our minds engaged with His Word, and our hearts overflowing with gratitude—it is very difficult for Satan to sidetrack us.

Can we go wrong in following the example of Jesus, a man especially anointed with the oil of joy (Heb. 1:9), a man who sometimes prayed with anguish (Luke 22:44), loud cries, and tears (Heb. 5:7), a man who commonly expressed His feelings? (For His deep sighs see Mark 7:34; 8:12; for His weeping see John 11:35 and Luke 19:41; for His burdens and desires see Mark 14:34 and Luke 12:49-50; 22:15. Take a few minutes to look up this representative sampling of verses. What kind of picture does it paint?)[6]

It is hard to argue with the clear teaching of the Word. Sometimes the Bible exhorts us to celebrate our God with great joy:

> Come, let us sing for joy to the LORD; let us shout aloud to the Rock of our salvation. Let us come before Him with thanksgiving and extol Him with music and song. (Ps. 95:1-2)

> Shout for joy to the LORD, all the earth, burst into jubilant song with music; make music to the LORD with the harp, with the harp and the sound of singing, with trumpets and the blast of the ram's horn— shout for joy before the LORD, the King. (Psalm 98:4-6)

> Shout for joy to the LORD, all the earth. Worship the LORD with gladness; come before Him with joyful songs. (Ps. 100:1-2)

> Let the word of Christ dwell in you richly as you teach and admonish one another with all wisdom, and as you sing psalms, hymns and spiritual songs with gratitude in your hearts to God. (Col. 3:16)

At the risk of begging the question (the answer is just too obvious), is there to be no feeling in our rejoicing and being glad before the Lord? Is there no valid emotional response to our meditations on His goodness and thoughts about His love? (Actually, it is these mental exercises that often spark our emotions! Look back to Colossians 3:16, just cited, where teaching and admonishing with all wisdom go hand in hand with joyful singing and praise.) Does the psalmist somehow *exclude* the emotions when he stirs himself to bless God with *all that is within him* (Ps. 103:1-2, KJV)? Of course, we do not have to feel joyful to rejoice, but when our rejoicing is heartfelt and real, we will certainly feel it. Is there anything strange in this position?

But joy is just one small aspect of the place of emotion in our relationship with God. Sometimes the Word commands us to mourn with great sorrow because of coming calamity or current crisis:

> This is what the LORD Almighty says: "Consider now! Call for the wailing women to come; send for the most skillful of them. Let them come quickly and wail over us till our eyes overflow with tears and water streams from our eyelids. The sound of wailing is heard from Zion: 'How ruined we are! How great is our shame! We must leave our land because our houses are in ruins.' " Now, O women, hear the word of the LORD; open your ears to the words of His mouth. Teach your daughters how to wail; teach one another a lament. Death has climbed in through our windows and has entered our fortresses; it has cut off the children from the streets and the young men from the public squares. (Jer. 9:17-21)[7]

> Put on sackcloth, O priests, and mourn; wail, you who minister before the altar. Come, spend the night in sackcloth, you who minister before my God; for the grain offerings and drink offerings are withheld from the house of your God. (Joel 1:13)

> Submit yourselves, then, to God. Resist the devil, and he will flee from you. Come near to God and He will come near to you. Wash your hands, you sinners, and purify your hearts, you double-minded. Grieve, mourn and wail. Change your laughter to mourning and your joy to gloom. Humble yourselves before the Lord, and He will lift you up. (Jas. 4:7-10)

Is there no emotion in all this (what a question!)? Rather, the prophets urged the people not to simply go through the motions of an outward display of grief (rending the garment), but to truly grieve and repent from deep within:

> "Even now," declares the LORD, "return to Me with all your heart, with fasting and weeping and mourning." Rend your heart and not your garments. Return to the Lord your God, for He is gracious and compassionate, slow to anger and abounding in love, and He relents from sending calamity. (Joel 2:12-13)

I can just hear the critics branding Joel's call to repentance a classic example of emotional manipulation: "I can repent just fine without all the weeping and wailing. You're just trying to work the people into a frenzy!" Tell it to the Lord, friend.[8]

Was it emotionalism when the Israelites shouted aloud and fell on their faces after fire came from the Lord and consumed Aaron's sacrifices?

> Then Aaron lifted his hands toward the people and blessed them. And having sacrificed the sin offering, the burnt offering and the fellowship offering, he stepped down. Moses and Aaron then went into the Tent of Meeting. When they came out, they blessed the people; and the glory of the LORD appeared to all the people. Fire came out from the presence of the LORD and consumed the burnt offering and the fat portions on the altar. And when all the people saw it, they shouted for joy and fell facedown. (Lev. 9:22-24)

If this was not emotionalism, then why is it emotionalism when we shout or drop to our knees or fall to our faces when God's holy presence fills the very room where we are meeting?

Was it Israelite emotionalism that caused the walls of Jericho to fall? (After all, Joshua probably caused the people to enter into an altered state of consciousness— or was it the walls that were brought into an altered state of consciousness?)

> The seventh time around, when the priests sounded the trumpet blast, Joshua commanded the people, "Shout! For the LORD has given you the city!" ... When the trumpets sounded, the people shouted, and at the sound of the trumpet, when the people gave a loud shout, the wall collapsed; so every man charged straight in, and they took the city. (Josh. 6:16-20)

If this was not emotionalism (or "socio-psychological manipulation"—how people love to throw around these sophisticated sounding terms!), then why are our shouts of victory emotionalism (or worse)? What makes one outward display different from the other?

Was it emotionalism when Peter urged and exhorted his hearers to repent and get right with God on the day of Pentecost?

> With many other words he warned them; and he pleaded with them [the King James Version reads: "And with many other words did he testify and exhort"], "Save yourselves from this corrupt generation." (Acts 2:40)

If this was not emotionalism, then why is it emotionalism if an evangelist today takes time to warn his hearers of the consequences of rejecting the Lord Jesus, urging them to repent and believe before it is too late? Didn't Jesus Himself use the strongest possible terms when He warned the crowds to flee from the coming wrath, speaking of being cut off or cut to pieces, of perishing and being destroyed, describing a place of total darkness where there is weeping and gnashing of teeth, a place of endless pain? Such images are designed to make an impact, and for those who grasp the weight of the message, emotions will be stirred. Who can possibly glimpse the horrors of hell (or the glories of Heaven) without being moved? Is this wrong?

Was it emotionalism when the just-healed lame man came joyously jumping into the sacred Temple courts?

> Then Peter said, "Silver or gold I do not have, but what I have I give you. In the name of Jesus Christ of Nazareth, walk." Taking him by the right hand, he helped him up, and instantly the man's feet and ankles became strong. He jumped to his feet and began to walk. Then he went with them into the temple courts, walking and jumping, and praising God. When all the people saw him walking and praising God, they recognized him as the same man who used to sit begging at the temple gate called Beautiful, and they were filled with wonder and amazement at what had happened to him. (Acts 3:6-10)

If this was not emotionalism, then why is it considered emotionalism when people who have been dramatically saved or healed or delivered through a revival leap, jump, dance, and run? Does God frown upon such outward displays of overflowing inner joy? To the contrary, if someone who was born blind was instantly healed, would they simply say, in a cool, collected, and calm voice, "This is really quite extraordinary. I was not aware that there was such a wide spectrum of colors and images. Fascinating indeed"? I don't think so! No, the person would be crying or laughing or awestruck or praising God. He would be touching and looking and gazing and wondering at everything around him. It would be hard to contain his enthusiasm. In fact, it would be *wrong* to put a damper on it.

And this is the state that many of the newly redeemed find themselves in: It is difficult for them to hold back their exuberant praises, to suppress the joyful shouts, to stop the flow of tears. After all, the darkness is gone! The depression has lifted! The suicidal thoughts have vanished! The sense of hopelessness has disappeared! Satan no longer rules them. Sin no longer dominates them. They are children of God! They are serving a new Master! They are free—and free indeed. Ought they to be stifled?

> The blind and the lame came to Him at the temple, and He healed them. But when the chief priests and the teachers of the law saw the wonderful things He did and the children shouting in the temple area, "Hosanna to the Son of David," they were indignant. "Do You hear what these children are saying?" they asked Him. "Yes," replied Jesus, "have you never read, 'From the lips of children and infants You have ordained praise'?" (Matt. 21:14-16)

Whose response was right? That of the children or that of the chief priests and teachers of the law? And why should it only be the children, the recently converted, or the newly healed who are overflowing with thanksgiving and praise? Why should we grow stale with the passage of time? Aren't the Lord's mercies new every morning (Lam. 3:22-23)? Doesn't Jesus grow "sweeter and sweeter" as the days go by? Actually, the reason that some of us have such a problem with any kind of emotional demonstration in church (or even when we are alone with God) is that we have barely known His touch or experienced His reality for years—and our walk with God is something we do experience.

These words may hurt, but God often wounds us before He heals us. Ask yourself honestly: Is your walk with God vibrant? What kind of *relationship* do you have with Him?

At this point some critic may suddenly say, "Aha! I knew you were going somewhere with all of this, and it's a dead end, plain and simple. You're deceived! You see, you're basing your relationship with God on an experience. I'm basing mine on the Word. I see that you are very clever. You know that no serious student of the Scriptures can deny that we are commanded and exhorted to worship and serve God with both heart and mind, emotions and will. But you have made a fatal leap of logic. You—and emotionally based, experience-oriented believers like you—have set yourselves up for a fall. The Bible is our foundation, not experience. This is why your position is so dangerous."[9]

Poor critic! Experiencing the Lord and basing one's relationship with Him on the Bible go hand in hand. In fact, from a biblical standpoint, it's difficult to think of believing the Word and living by the Word *without* having an experience with God as well. As one theologian once asked his anti-experience colleague, "Did you experience salvation?"

Somehow, to many critics, experiencing *anything* in the Lord—even during times of worship or prayer—is somehow deemed dangerous, while anyone whose emotions are stirred by the preaching of the Word or by testimonies of His grace is somehow viewed as unstable. *That mentality is totally unscriptural.*

During a Chapel of the Air radio interview some years ago, David Mains asked Alan Redpath whether emotional displays might be expected in revival. The distinguished preacher and author replied, "When God breaks a man's heart, there will be emotion." This should cause no surprise!

It is here that we must make an interesting observation. No God-fearing Christian leader thinks of himself as a "revival critic." Rather, he see himself as a critic of false revival and a champion of truth. In the same way, no serious believer fashions himself to be a proponent of spurious revival. Rather, he sees himself as someone completely open to the real move of the Spirit. Yet it is not hard to see who the critics really are, since the charges they level against true revival today are the same as those leveled by the past critics against true revivals in their day. (In the words of one critic, who actually dismisses virtually *all* revivals, past and present: "In fact, what is commonly called 'revival' today, is not at all different from the revivals of yesteryear—a religious carnival show steeped in mysticism and rampant emotionalism.")[10]

This is not to say that every point that the critic makes is wrong or that everything called revival today is really revival (something that I have stressed for years). Nor is this to say that past revivalists would have endorsed every aspect of contemporary revival. (Anyway, God's endorsement—not that of any person, past or present—is ultimately what we need.) Still, it's interesting to see how the great opponent of the Great Awakening, Charles Chauncy, a pastor in Boston, whose anti-revival books were best-sellers in his day, described revival meetings in the Awakening:

> 'Tis scarce imaginable what Excesses and Extravagancies People were running into, and even encouraged in; being told such Things were Arguments of the *extraordinary Presence of the Holy Ghost* with them. The same houses of Worship were scarce emptied Night nor Day for a Week together, and unheard of Instances of supposed Religion were carried on in them, some would be *praying*, some *exhorting*, some *singing*, some *clapping their Hands*, some *laughing*, some *crying*, some *shrieking and roaring out*; and so invincibly set were they in these Ways, especially when encouraged by any Ministers (as was too often the Case), that it was a vain Thing to argue with them, to shew them the Indecency of such Behavior; and whoever indeed made an Attempt this Way, might be sure aforehand of being called an *Opposer* of the *Spirit*, and a *Child of the Devil.*[11]

Sound familiar? In fact, John Wesley in his day noted that, the moment people were confronted with a genuine experience with the Lord, they would try to dismiss it all by simply crying out, "Emotionalism! Fanaticism! Extremism!"

> Every proposition which I have anywhere advanced concerning those operations of the Holy Ghost, which, I believe, are common to all Christians in all ages, is here clearly maintained by our own Church.

> Under a full sense of this, I could not well understand, for many years, how it was, that on the mentioning any of these great truths, even among men of education, the cry immediately arose, "An enthusiast! An enthusiast!" But I now plainly perceive this is only an old fallacy in a new shape. To object enthusiasm to any person or doctrine is but a decent method of begging the question. It generally spares the objector the trouble of reasoning, and is a shorter and easier way of carrying his cause.

> For instance, I assert that "till a man 'receives the Holy Ghost,' he is without God in the world; that he cannot know the things of God, unless God reveal them unto him by the Spirit; no, nor have even one holy or heavenly temper, without the inspiration

of the Holy One." Now, should one who is conscious to himself that he has experienced none of these things, attempt to confute these propositions, either from Scripture or antiquity, it might prove a difficult task. What then shall he do? Why, cry out, "Enthusiasm! Enthusiasm!" and the work is done.[12]

And yet, the truth be told, charges of "enthusiasm" were completely out of place with the intensely logical Wesley and his disciplined Methodists. In fact, he instructed his followers to "carefully avoid all enthusiasm" and noted that:

Fanaticism, if it means anything at all, means the same with enthusiasm, or religious madness, from which (as was observed before) these doctrines [to which we hold] are distant as far as the east from the west. However, it is a convenient word to be thrown out upon anything we do not like; because scarce one reader in a thousand has any idea of what it means.[13]

Yet, rather than deal with the truth content of Wesley's message, he was libelously labeled an enthusiast. Yes, there is nothing new under the sun. Critics still cry out, "There's just too much emotional display! It's irreverent, extreme, and dangerous." In this, they sound like Chauncy who exclaimed, "How heated are the imaginations of a great many, and into what excesses do they betray them?"[14] He, like today's critics, seem unable (or, unwilling) to distinguish between an emotion-filled encounter with God and an empty exhibition of emotionalism. There is quite a difference between the two! And just as the Word of God has no place for hypocritical displays of worship and service (shedding enough tears to fill a bucket while the heart is hard and cold; shouting to the Lord with uplifted hands while the life is filled with sin), it gives ample space to describe dramatic encounters that frail human beings had with an awesome God. And these encounters were certainly experienced! They touched the whole being, within and without.

Let's look again to the Word, a book that is certainly *not* anti-experience.

Jesus taught that His Father was "not the God of the dead but of the living" (Matt. 22:32). What did He mean? In context, He meant that "all live to Him"—in other words, there is life beyond the grave.

But there is a further truth to His words. They also indicate that the God of the past is also the God of the present, and therefore we don't have to serve Him based on the experience and testimony of former generations alone. We can know Him too! We can experience Him firsthand, just as our forefathers in the faith did.[15] As I wrote in a previous book on revival:

> Moses made it clear: "It was not with our fathers that the LORD made this covenant, but with us, with all of us who are alive here today" (Deut. 5:3). And, "your children were not the ones who saw and experienced the discipline of the LORD your God...but it was your own eyes that saw all these great things the LORD has done" (Deut. 11:2-7).
>
> Every generation in Israel must have a personal encounter with the living God. This holds true for all peoples and nations. Grandpa's stories won't do. There is no such thing as a "second generation Pentecost." "He is not the God of the dead, but of the living" (Mt. 22:32). Are you experiencing Him today?[16]

Consider the testimony of Saul of Tarsus, best known as Paul the apostle. His conversion experience is one of the most famous accounts recorded in the Word. It is repeated—at great length—three times in Acts: first, in the actual description of his dramatic (and to him, shocking) encounter with *the Lord* Jesus (Acts 9:1-28); second, in Paul's public testimony before his Jewish people in Jerusalem (Acts 22:1-22); and third, in his testimony before Herod Agrippa and Festus (Acts 26:1-23). This was the experience that changed his life, the experience that caused him to know that Jesus was the One whose coming was predicted by the prophets of old, the experience that he powerfully and shamelessly declared. And Paul made no apologies for it! Jesus made Himself known to Saul of Tarsus personally and dramatically, and this was something he never lost sight of to his dying day. (In fact, he died a martyr for that very same Jesus.) I think Paul would have agreed with the wise adage of Leonard Ravenhill: "A man with an experience is never at the mercy of a man with an argument."[17]

We must never forget that this man Paul was a careful student of the Scriptures, and he made it his practice to go into the synagogues of every city, preaching, reasoning, and debating with the

Jewish leaders there, proving from the Word that Jesus was the Messiah (see, for example, Acts 9:22; 18:4; 28:23; note also 18:28, with reference to Apollos). It was not a matter of either the Word *or* personal experience. He had a supernatural encounter with God, and it was this encounter that brought him to know who Jesus really was. Then as he went back to the Bible, he found Him spoken of by the prophets everywhere. Therefore he could say to Agrippa and Festus, "I was not disobedient to the vision from heaven" (Acts 26:19), proceeding then to explain, "I am saying nothing beyond what the prophets and Moses said would happen" (Acts 26:22). He preached from the Word, using arguments of Messianic prophecy and fulfillment (see Acts 13:32-41), but he also shared the story of his encounter with the Lord, his "conversion" experience.

In the same way, Peter used the Hebrew Scriptures to preach Jesus the Messiah (see Acts 2:22-36), but he also pointed to the reality of the supernatural experience of the believers in the upper room on the day of Pentecost (Acts 2:14-21,32-33). And a short time later, he pointed to the miraculous healing of the lame man, coupled with biblical prophecies, to demonstrate that Jesus was indeed the promised Messiah, once dead but now alive forever more (see Acts 3:12-26). (For more on this, see Chapter Twelve, "A Lot of Fall Out Over a Little Falling Out.")

To repeat: The Bible is not anti-experience (and the Bible is our guide!). Wasn't it an experience—a personal encounter with the living God—that changed the lives of Abram, Jacob, Moses, Gideon, Samuel, Isaiah, Jeremiah, Ezekiel, and many other Old Testament saints? And wasn't it an experience—a Heaven-sent word, revelation, or visitation—that changed the lives of Peter, Philip, the Ethiopian eunuch, and others in the New Testament? Let us also not neglect to mention that all the apostles were transformed through their encounter with the Lord Jesus Himself (see 1 John 1:1-3!). Having a vibrant personal experience is in keeping with serving a personal, living God. It is also in keeping with faithfulness to the written Word, our final source of truth, even bringing confirmation to the biblical message:

We did not follow cleverly invented stories when we told you about the power and coming of our Lord Jesus Christ, but we were eyewitnesses of His majesty. For He received honor and glory from God the Father when the voice came to Him from the Majestic Glory, saying, "This is My Son, whom I love; with Him I am well pleased." We ourselves heard this voice that came from heaven when we were with Him on the sacred mountain. And we have the word of the prophets made more certain [cf. NRSV: "So we have the prophetic message more fully confirmed"], and you will do well to pay attention to it, as to a light shining in a dark place, until the day dawns and the morning star rises in your hearts. (2 Pet. 1:16-19)[18]

The truth is that the vast majority of believers around the world today did *not* repent of their sins and put their trust in the Lord Jesus through rational arguments or intellectual reasoning—and I say this as one who has devoted years of my life to Jewish apologetics (i.e., answering Jewish objections to Jesus), having spent countless hours in debate and dialogue with rabbis and anti-missionaries, even writing the first, full-length Jewish apologetics manual.[19] I believe in fully using the intellect in the service of God! Still, I am totally aware that the Spirit must open every heart and mind to receive the truth of the gospel, and ultimately, it is the Spirit who reveals Jesus in a saving way. This is how it always has been throughout the history of the Church.

With all his study and religious pursuits, it was when John Wesley felt his heart to be "strangely warmed" on May 24, 1738, that he was wonderfully born anew. For Augustine, his conversion came suddenly when the Word supernaturally came alive to him. For Martin Luther, it was conviction of the truth of justification by faith, coupled with a deep personal experience, that made him into the great reformer that he was. And the account of Charles Finney's dramatic conversion and baptism in the Spirit has become a Christian classic. It is certainly quite common—in fact, it is the norm in evangelism around the world to this day—that sinners see the light of God's grace and are saved from their sins *before* they comprehend the gospel message in totality. Wasn't this the case with you?[20]

Think back to your conversion. Did you know somehow that you were guilty in God's sight and that Jesus really was the Savior, leading you to salvation, before you understood all the in's and out's of the gospel? This, in fact, is the rule, not the exception. Even for someone like Charles Spurgeon, a man raised in the Scriptures and Christian classics from his childhood, the "light needed to go on." In his case, it was not until he heard a simple Methodist minister's simple message on, "Look to the Lord and be saved"—preached in a little meeting that the teenage Spurgeon only attended because of a snowstorm—that he was born again.[21]

And who will forget Blaise Pascal's "night of fire," the landmark event of his life? Pascal, who lived in seventeenth century France, was one of the greatest intellects ever to walk this earth, a man credited with the invention of the computer (350 years ago!). Although deeply religious, it was an awesome divine encounter that changed him forever. To his last breathing moment, he wore pinned to his garment the piece of paper he inscribed that extraordinary night (Nov. 23, 1654): "From about half-past ten in the evening until about half-past twelve...FIRE...God of Abraham, God of Isaac, God of Jacob, not of the philosophers and savants. Certitude. Certitude. Feeling. Joy. Peace. God of Jesus Christ. My God and Thy God. 'Thy God shall be my God'...." It is altogether fitting that a recent compendium of his writings was entitled, *The Mind on Fire*.[22] His whole being was ablaze for God.

Friends, I make no apology for saying emphatically that the Bible is a book of glorious experiences, and as we follow the God of that book, we too will experience Him. And just as the ancient Jewish rabbis allegorically interpreted the Song of Solomon as a love song between God and Israel, so the Church Fathers interpreted it allegorically as a love song between Jesus and the Church, His Bride. We still call out to our Lord, the Lover of our souls, "Take me away with you—let us hurry!" (Song 1:4a). And He in turn calls out to us: "Come away, my lover, and be like a gazelle or like a young stag on the spice-laden mountains" (Song 8:14).[23]

It was this same Jesus who said to His disciples, "I have eagerly desired to eat this Passover with you before I suffer" (Luke 22:15), and it was this same Jesus who called us His friends, saying, "Greater love has no one than this, that he lay down his life for his friends. You are My friends if you do what I command" (John 15:13-14). And it was our best Friend Jesus who said to the backslidden church of Laodicea, "Here I am! I stand at the door and knock. If anyone hears My voice and opens the door, I will come in and eat with him, and he with Me" (Rev. 3:20). On these verses, William Law wrote:

> Again, Christ, after his glorification in heaven, says, "Behold I STAND at the DOOR and KNOCK." He does not say, Behold ye have me in the scriptures. Now what is the DOOR at which Christ, at the right-hand of God in heaven, KNOCKS? Surely it is the heart, to which Christ is always present. He goes on, IF ANY MAN HEARS MY VOICE; how hears, but by the hearing of the heart, or what voice, but that which is the speaking or sounding of Christ within him; he adds, AND OPENS THE DOOR, that is, will be a living holy nature, and spirit born within him, AND SUP WITH HIM, and HE WITH ME. Behold the last finishing work of a redeeming Jesus, entered into the heart that opens to him, bringing forth the joy, the blessing, and perfection of that first life of God in the soul, which was lost by the fall, set forth as a supper, or feast of the heavenly Jesus with the soul, and the soul with him. Can anyone justly call it enthusiasm to say, that this supping of the soul with this glorified Christ within it, must mean something more heavenly transacted in the soul than that last supper which he celebrated with his disciples, whilst he was with them in flesh. For that supper of bread and wine was such, as a Judas could partake of, and could only be an outward type or signification of that inward and blessed nourishment, with which the believing soul should be feasted, when the glorified Son of God should as a creating Spirit enter into us, quickening, and raising up his own heavenly nature and life within us.[24]

Our living Lord still calls us to sup with Him.

I leave you with the words of Spurgeon, the Baptist leader called the Prince of Preachers, thoroughly Calvinistic in his faith, and hardly given to impressionism or flightiness:

> Call it fanaticism if you will, but I trust that there are some of us who know what it is to be always, or generally, under the influence of the Holy Spirit—always in one sense, generally in another...

The unregenerate world of sinners despises the Holy Ghost, "because it seeth him not." Yes, I believe this is the great secret why many laugh at the idea of the existence of the Holy Ghost—because they see him not. You tell the worldling, "I have the Holy Ghost within me." He says, "I cannot see it." He wants it to be something tangible—a thing he can recognize with his senses. Have you ever heard the argument used by a good old Christian against an infidel doctor? The doctor said there was no soul, and asked, "Did you ever see a soul?" "No," said the Christian. "Did you ever hear a soul?" "No." "Did you ever smell a soul?" "No." "Did you ever taste a soul?" "No." "Did you ever feel a soul?" "Yes," said the man—"I feel I have one within me." "Well," said the doctor, "there are four senses against one; you only have one on your side." "Very well," said the Christian, "Did you ever see a pain?" "No." "Did you ever hear a pain?" "No." "Did you ever smell a pain?" "No." "Did you ever taste a pain?" "No." "Did you ever feel a pain?" "Yes." "And that is quite enough, I suppose, to prove there is a pain?" "Yes." So the worldling says there is no Holy Ghost, because he cannot see it. Well, but we feel it. You say that is fanaticism, and that we never felt it. Suppose you tell me that honey is bitter, I reply, "No, I am sure you cannot have tasted it; taste it and try." So with the Holy Ghost; if you did but feel his influence, you would no longer say there is no Holy Spirit, because you cannot see it. Are there not many things, even in nature, which we cannot see? Did you ever see the wind? No; but ye know there is wind, when you behold the hurricane tossing the waves about, and rending down the habitations of men; or when, in the soft evening zephyr, it kisses the flowers, and maketh dew-drops hang in pearly coronets around the rose. Did ye ever see electricity? No; but ye know there is such a thing, for it travels along the wires for thousands of miles, and carries our messages; though you cannot see the thing itself, you know there is such a thing. So you must believe there is a Holy Ghost working in us, both to will and to do, even though it is beyond our senses.[25]

I invite you—no, the Lord Himself invites you—to come and experience Him afresh. Just remember not to check your mind—or your emotions!—at the door.

Not too loud and not too long;
We want a nice revival.
Nothing heavy, weird or wild;
Our first goal is survival.

Make our church grow big, dear Lord;
Give us souls galore!
And bless our new faith budget, God;
That's what revival's for!

We're praying and we're fasting, Lord;
Please send Your Spirit in power.
And do whatever You see fit—
Just keep it to an hour!

Send the river, send the flood,
Send Your mighty rain.
Send Your glory down, O God:
It will be to our gain.

And now we close with this request;
We pray with heart and soul:
Send a great revival, Lord—
But leave us in control!

Prayer for a 'Nice' Revival
MLB

Lord, if it please thee, work the same work again, without the blemishes. But if that may not be, though it be with all the blemishes, work the same work.

John Wesley, repeating the prayer of a Scottish believer

If they wait to see a work of God without difficulties and stumbling-blocks, it will be like the fool's waiting at the river side to have all the water all run by. A work of God without stumbling-blocks is never to be expected. "It must needs be that offences come." There never yet was any great manifestation that God made of himself to the world, without many difficulties attending it. It is with the works of God as with his word: they seem at first full of things that are strange, inconsistent, and difficult to the carnal unbelieving hearts of men. Christ aned his work always was, and always will be a stone of stumbling, and rock of offence, a gin and snare to many.

Jonathan Edwards
The Distinguishing Marks of a Work of the Spirit of God

Chapter Twelve

A Lot of Fall Out
Over a Little Falling Out

Did you hear about the controversial miracle that took place in Detroit late last year? There was a notorious, demonized man who roamed the streets of the city for months, screaming and crying out, foaming at the mouth, slashing himself with razor blades, and even disrobing. He was locked up several times, but within a few days, he was back on the streets—matted hair, disheveled clothing, disgusting stench, and all.

One Sunday morning, he wandered into the plush sanctuary of First Assembly, letting out a blood-curdling shriek as soon as he cracked the doors. Immediately, the pastor, a real man of God who knew all about this poor demoniac, looked him in the eyes and spoke directly to the spirits that so horribly tormented him: "I command you in the name of Jesus to leave him now!"

And then—what a sight!—the man bolted, ran straight down the center aisle heading right towards the pulpit, and suddenly fell to the ground in a heap. Barely raising his head, he said (actually, it was the demons who spoke through him), "Please! Don't cast us into the pit! Let us go into the used cars!" And the pastor said, "Go!"

And then—who can describe it?—there was a sound of hundreds of engines revving up, and to the astonishment of the people who happened to be walking by, these driverless cars began to pull out of the huge, used car dealership, making their way to the bridge, where each of them, at the very highest point of the bridge's suspension, suddenly veered right, careening down into the watery depths below. It was incredible! What power there is in the name of Jesus!

"That's totally absurd!" you say. "Absolutely preposterous. Pentecostal fiction if I ever heard it."

Well, you've caught me this time. I made the whole story up. I confess! (Of course, you knew that already, or, at least by the time I got to the lemming-like cars.) But I think you got the point too. The miraculous deliverance of the demoniac in Mark 5 was no less incredible, controversial, and to some religious leaders, preposterous. All I did was couch the biblical story in contemporary terms. Now a story like *that* would be something for the critics to attack. That would be fuel for their fodder. (For thoughts on this, see Chapter Six, "Was Jesus a False Prophet?")

Naturally, I already hear the repetitive refrain of the critics, "But that was for Bible days, not for today." (Of course, as I have pointed out already, these same critics often ask, with reference to a particular manifestation or phenomenon in revival, "Where's *that* in the Bible?" Yet when we *do* show them where "that" is in the Bible, they reject it as being only for the Bible!) The fact is—and this is what I want to emphasize—*Jesus chose to perform unusual, controversial, and highly disruptive acts while He was here on the earth.* What makes our critical friends so sure that He has changed since then? Isn't it the critics who are guilty of *not* following Scripture when they think it impossible or unlikely that He will do such things again today? Yet it is they who claim to be loyalists to the Word, while in their opinion, the revivalists are unsteady, emotionally based, Word-distorting (or, Word-ignoring!) misleaders. Is this really the case?[1]

Once more I appeal to my fellow leaders who oppose the present revival: Are you sure you are not limiting the Lord? Are you sure you are completely open to the outpouring of the Spirit, as *He* wills?

Now, I said all that to say this. There has been all too much fall out over the subject of "falling out in the Spirit." Similar to the issue of shaking, it has been blown completely out of proportion, and just because some believers have a hard time with people "going down under the power," they completely reject the current revival. (For those of you who might not be aware of this, while laying on of hands is not central to the present evangelistically driven outpouring, in many circles, there is time set aside in nightly services to lay hands on hungry believers for a fresh touch from God, which often results in testimonies of miraculous impartation. That's why we're spending some time on this subject now.)[2]

Maybe if we take a few minutes to look at the Word it will help us to sort things out. But let me make it clear that I have viewed the subject of people being "slain in the Spirit" from several different angles, having been for it and against it and having seen foolish abuses as well as awesome fruit. Therefore it's easy for me to relate to those who are concerned with superficiality and extremism as well as to understand the skepticism that exists in some circles. On the other hand, I don't have the least problem participating in revival services where people are laid out under God's power for hours.[3]

In any case, I'm not married to this particular phenomenon, and I have seen God move powerfully with and without laying on of hands or falling. So, I have no axe to grind, and, to repeat, the question of falling is simply not a central issue when it comes to the foundations of revival. But, because so much fuss has been made about it, we need to study it out. Can we look at the Scriptures and think through the relevant issues without either of us getting worked up? Let's give it a try!

We'll start with the subject of laying on of hands in general. Did you know that the Bible speaks of this as one of the foundational, elementary doctrines of the Church?

> Therefore let us leave the elementary teachings about Christ and go on to maturity, not laying again the foundation of repentance from acts that lead to death, and of faith in God, instruction about baptisms, the laying on of hands, the resurrection of the dead, and eternal judgment. (Heb. 6:1-2)[4]

Notice again this list: repentance; faith; baptisms; laying on of hands; resurrection of the dead; eternal judgment. How in the world did laying on of hands get included here? Obviously, it is a subject of importance, something basic which was recognized to be of great significance in the early Church. Yet, in most Bible schools, semiaries, and churches today, it receives little or no emphasis, and it is rarely taught on. Something is wrong here.[5]

Going through some relevant Scriptures (and this will be the briefest of surveys), we see that something was *imparted* through the laying on of hands. For example, the one pronouncing a blessing would often lay his hands on the heads of those being blessed (see Genesis 48, where great importance was attached to which hand was laid on which son), while on the Day of Atonement the high priest was given instructions to lay his hands on the so-called scapegoat, and "...confess over it all the wickedness and rebellion of the Israelites—all their sins—and put them on the goat's head. He shall send the goat away into the desert in the care of a man appointed for the task. The goat will carry on itself all their sins to a solitary place..." (Lev. 16:21-22). So Israel's sins were symbolically transferred to a substitute through the laying on of hands (see also Lev. 1:1-9).[6]

According to Numbers 27:18-23, Moses was to lay his hand on Joshua and commission him before the people of Israel, giving him some of his authority. Thus Deuteronomy 34:9 states, "Now Joshua son of Nun was filled with the spirit of wisdom because Moses had laid his hands on him. So the Israelites listened to him and did what the LORD had commanded Moses." Something happened to Joshua when Moses laid hands on him! He received something tangible. So also in Acts 8:14-17, the Samaritan believers received the Holy Spirit when Peter and John laid hands on them, and this fact was so obvious that Simon the Sorcerer actually offered them money and said, "Give me also this ability so that everyone on whom I lay my hands may receive the Holy Spirit" (Acts 8:19). Yes, it was clear that the Spirit was imparted through the laying on of hands. This is found also in Acts 19:6 with the Ephesian believers: "When Paul placed his hands on them, the Holy Spirit came on them, and they spoke in tongues and prophesied."

If you think back to our brief study of the word *dunamis* (power) in Luke and Acts, you will recall that on some occasions, it is recorded this miracle-healing power actually *went out* of Jesus into the sick, making them completely whole (see Luke 6:17-19; 8:43-48). And when Jesus commissioned His disciples in Matthew 10, He told them, "Freely you have received, freely give" (Matt. 10:8b). What is one means by which they were to "give away" this healing power? According to Mark 16:18b, Jesus said "they will place their hands on sick people, and they will get well."[7] Healing can be imparted through the laying on of hands! And this is exactly what we see in Acts 28:8, where the father of a man named Publius, the chief official of the island of Malta, "...was sick in bed, suffering from fever and dysentery. Paul went in to see him and, after prayer, placed his hands on him and healed him."

Notice also Luke 13:10-13:

On a Sabbath Jesus was teaching in one of the synagogues, and a woman was there who had been crippled by a spirit for eighteen years. She was bent over and could not straighten up at all. When Jesus saw her, He called her forward and said to her, "Woman, you are set free from your infirmity." Then He put His hands on her, and immediately she straightened up and praised God.

Did you read the text carefully? Jesus made the pronouncement, "Woman, you are set free from your infirmity." But it was not until He laid His hands on her that she straightened up. That's when the healing power was imparted.

Now, it is quite true that the laying of on hands was also the central rite in the act of public "ordination" or "commissioning," as seen in Acts 13:3 or 1 Timothy 5:22. (By the way, Paul's exhortation to Timothy in 1 Timothy 5:22 to "lay hands suddenly on no man"—in the familiar language of the King James—does *not* mean, "Don't come up on someone unexpectedly on a prayer line" [although that may be good "ministry etiquette"]; rather, it means, "Don't be hasty in ordaining someone into a leadership position.").[8] But we must remember that this was not merely a formal ceremony signifying public recognition (although that is what it has become in many modern church circles); instead, it was also understood to be an act of impartation (as with Moses and Joshua). That's why Paul instructed Timothy: "Do not neglect your gift, which was given you through a prophetic message when the body of elders laid their hands on you" (1 Tim. 4:14; see also 2 Tim. 1:6, "For this reason I remind you to fan into flame the gift of God, which is in you through the laying on of my hands.")

It is perfectly clear then that the Scriptures teach that there can be supernatural, divine impartation through the laying on of hands. In fact, in light of the verses we have examined, it is certainly plausible that when Paul wrote to the Romans, "I long to see you so that I may impart to you some spiritual gift to make you strong" (Rom. 1:11), he planned to minister to them through the laying on of hands.[9] (Note that the Greek word *metadidomai*, translated here as "impart," normally means "share" in the New Testament; see Luke 3:11 and Ephesians 4:28. This in itself is an interesting semantic concept to explore.)[10]

Now I ask you, having just reviewed some very clear biblical evidence for the practice of the laying on of hands, how much emphasis is placed upon it by your church or ministry? According to the Word, through the laying on of hands the Holy Spirit can be given, spiritual gifts can be imparted (often in conjunction with ordination and/or commissioning), and sickness can be healed. This is hardly an unimportant issue! It is for good reason, then, that Hebrews 6 speaks of this as one of the basic teachings of the faith, and it is for good reason that current renewal movements have emphasized the impartation of divine blessing through the laying on of hands. That is a primary way that the baptism of the Spirit was conferred in the early Church, and it is thoroughly biblical.

There is something else that should be noted. It is a common criticism of the current revival movements that, for example, Bro. A. (whose ministry the critics disdain) laid hands on Bro. B. (whose style is not liked by the critics) who then laid hands on Bro. C., after which unusual manifestations started occurring in his meetings. Then, Bro. C. laid hands on Bro. D., who is now in the midst of a powerful revival. Therefore, according to some critics, the revival is to be rejected for this reason alone![11] The problem with this approach is that when Bro. A. lays hands on someone, *his* spirit is not imparted to those for whom he is praying anymore than the spirit of Peter and John was imparted to the Samaritans or the spirit of Paul imparted to Timothy. Rather, it was the Holy Spirit (or, a gift of the Spirit) that was transmitted. In other words, through laying on of hands, the Spirit (not a human spirit) is imparted.

If someone with imperfect doctrine lays hands on me (does anyone have perfect doctrine?), does that mean I too will become doctrinally unbalanced? If someone who does not handle money well lay hands on me, does that mean that I too will become financially irresponsible? Obviously not. Of course, I wouldn't want a demonized man to pray for me and say, "Such as I have, I give you," nor would I want someone who was enslaved to perversion or pornography to "impart" what he has to me. In these cases, what these people have to impart is from the pit. But, unless you believe that people who are being prayed for in the current revival are receiving a *demonic* impartation (careful, careful!), then you have no right to dismiss outright a mighty move of God because you don't like some of the people who have prayed for some of the leaders involved.[12]

Simply stated, if Bro. A. lays hands on Bro. B., that does *not* change the history of Bro. B.'s whole walk with God through the years. It does not change who he is in the Lord, nor does it make him like Bro. A. Yet critics will write off the salvation of tens of thousands of sinners, questioning the genuineness of their conversion experience, primarily because Bro. B. was prayed for by Bro. A. and the critics have some differences with Bro. A. This is without scriptural foundation.

What about the issue of people "falling under the power" after the laying on of hands? Is that explicitly taught in the Scriptures, or are there examples of this in the Word? Certainly not. But, as we have seen already (see especially Chapter Six, "Was Jesus a False Prophet?"), these are not the right questions to ask. Instead, the right questions are, Is this practice or phenomenon contrary to the Scriptures? Is it *un*biblical (as opposed to *extra*-biblical)? The answer to these questions is emphatically no. There is nothing unbiblical about it at all. In fact, this phenomenon actually follows logically from what the Word teaches.

How so? Well, just follow this line of reasoning with me. Since, 1) there can be divine impartation through the laying on of hands; and 2) the Bible records instances of God's presence overwhelming people, causing them to fall to the ground; then 3) it should not be thought impossible or unlikely that His powerful touch, coming through the laying on of hands, could knock someone over. Is that unreasonable? And is it unreasonable to think that God could *demonstrate* His power (or get someone's attention) by knocking him to the ground—especially skeptics and mockers?

Of course, this does not mean that everyone who falls over is genuinely being touched by the Lord, nor does it mean that we should put special emphasis on people falling. (In other words, we shouldn't lay hands on people with the goal of seeing them fall, nor should we judge people's spirituality by their falling or lack thereof. And, just for the record, I should note that my wife has never once "fallen under the power" in more than 23 years in the Lord.) But what this discussion *does* mean is that there is certainly nothing unscriptural about people "falling under the power," in spite of the fact that one vocal critic repeatedly refers to this as "completely unbiblical" without any genuine support for his position.[13]

"But what about this business of having catchers standing behind the people? Doesn't this create an expectation in their minds about falling?" Maybe so. That's why it's good to always emphasize that, "This is not about falling (or shaking). This is about receiving a fresh touch from the Lord. You receive from God by faith, whether or not you feel anything or fall." On the other hand, having catchers might also help people take their minds *off* falling, since they will not be worried about what will happen if they fall and instead will simply concentrate on receiving from the Lord.

In any case, I find it interesting that one of the most common objections of the critics is that revival services are chaotic and out of order, yet when we try to do things in an orderly way, with prayer lines and catchers, the critics ridicule us for this "unbiblical, assembly line" practice. Ironic, isn't it?

And this leads to another point. The critics often hail past revivals as models of decency and order, when, in fact, some of the meetings described in these classic accounts follow *anything but* the order prescribed in 1 Corinthians 14. Take this example from John Wesley's *Journal*, June 14, 1759:

> While Mr. B. preached in the church, I stood with many in the church yard, to make room for those who came from far; therefore I saw little, but heard the agonizing of many, panting and gasping after eternal life. In the afternoon, Mr. B. was constrained, by the multitude of people, to come out of the church, and preach in his own close. Some of those who were here pricked to the heart, were affected in an astonishing manner. The first man I saw wounded would have dropped, but others, catching him in their arms, did, indeed, prop him up, but were so far from keeping him still, that he caused all of them to totter and tremble. His own shaking exceeded that of a cloth in the wind. It seemed as if the Lord came upon him like a giant, taking him by the neck, and shaking all his bones in pieces. One woman tore up the ground with her hands, filling them with dust and with the hard trodden grass, on which I saw her lie, with her hands clinched, as one dead, when the multitude dispersed. Another roared and screamed in a more dreadful agony than ever I heard before. I omitted the rejoicing of believers, because of their number, and the frequency thereof, though the manner was strange; some of them being quite overpowered with divine love, and only showing enough of natural life to let us know they were overwhelmed with joy and life eternal. Some continued long as if they were dead, but with a calm sweetness in their looks. I saw one who lay two or three hours in the open air, and being then carried into the house, continued insensible another hour, as if actually dead. The first sign of life she showed was a rapture of praise intermixed with a small joyous laughter.

This sounds like quite a meeting! And though Wesley's whole ministry was devoted to leading sinners to Christ through the preaching of the cross, he recognized that God's Spirit, *in conjunction with* the message (not *in opposition to* the message), often moved in unusual ways:

> It is the preaching of remission of sins through Jesus Christ, which alone answers the true ends of devotion. And this will always be accompanied with the co-operation of the Holy Spirit; though not always with sudden agonies, roarings, screaming, tremblings, or droppings down. Indeed, if God is pleased at any

time to permit any of these, I cannot hinder it. Neither can this hinder the work of his Spirit in the soul; which may be carried on either with or without them. But...I cannot apprehend it to be any reasonable proof, that "this is not the work of God," that a convinced sinner should "fall into an extreme agony, both of body and soul;" ...that another should "roar for the disquietness of her heart;" that others should scream or "cry with a loud and bitter cry, 'What must we do to be saved?' " that others should "exceedingly tremble and quake;" and others, in a deep sense of the majesty of God, "should fall prostrate upon the ground."[14]

This, of course, also highlights the fact that most critics do not speak against the phenomenon of people falling to the ground under conviction when the Word was preached by Finney or Whitefield, even though there is no explicit scriptural support for this phenomenon.

"But of course!" the critic responds. "That case it totally different. You see, the preachers of the Word were not doing this to the people. They were merely bringing the message. The Spirit brought the conviction, and the people fell on their own."

But that's similar to what happens to people who are "slain in the Spirit." The ministers are not knocking the people over; they are merely laying hands on them. The Spirit then touches the people, and they fall on their own. (Of course, there is a difference between "falling under the power" and falling under conviction, although in the current revival, it is not uncommon to see *both* of these phenomena. The point I am making here is that in neither case are the people ministering producing the results. Also, although some people make a big deal about people falling backwards instead of forwards, the Bible makes no issue out of this, and it is very common to see people in revival meetings falling on their faces under conviction or falling forward after hands are laid on them. Does this mean that *they*, in contrast to those who fall backwards, are genuinely being touched by the Lord?)[15]

"Now hold on there," someone says. "Aren't there times when the prayer ministers unintentionally push people over?" I'm sure there are! And I'm also sure that in times past, some revival preachers have unintentionally pushed their listeners into an emotionally super charged state, causing some of them to overreact with humanly induced faintings and prostrations. (I wonder what the critics would have thought about Jonathan Edward's historic sermon, "Sinners in the Hands of an Angry God," if they had actually *been there* when he preached it in Enfield, New England, in June of 1741....)[16]

"But," the critic continues, "there are people who fall down—and they would claim it was supernatural—without being changed. How can this be the work of the Spirit?" I'll answer your question with a question. What about the men on the road to Damascus with Saul of Tarsus? According to Acts 26:12-14, Saul (Paul) said that he "saw a light from heaven, brighter than the sun, blazing around me and my companions," as a result of which, *"We all fell to the ground."* Yet the other men did not have an encounter with the Lord, nor did they understand the voice that spoke, nor is there any record of them being changed. In other words, God's presence can overwhelm and overpower without being redemptive (i.e., saving) in its effect.[17]

The same phenomenon is found in John 18:3-12. According to verse 3, Judas guided a "detachment of soldiers and some officials from the chief priests and Pharisees" to the garden to arrest Jesus. "They were carrying torches, lanterns and weapons," obviously ready for action. Yet when they said they were seeking Jesus of Nazareth and He said, "I am He," John records that "they drew back and fell to the ground." They were overpowered by His presence, yet they proceeded to arrest and bind Him! So, a person can be overcome by the glorious presence of the Lord without being affected on the inside. (Before anyone takes me wrong, I'm not using these verses to prove that the Bible speaks of people being "slain in the Spirit." I'm simply pointing out that people can be literally "floored" by the Lord's power without being changed.)

And what of King Saul in the Old Testament? He was on his way to kill David when "...the Spirit of God came even upon him, and he walked along prophesying until he came to Naioth. He stripped off his robes and also prophesied in Samuel's presence. He lay that way all that day and night..." (1 Sam 19:23-24), and this was without changing! When he returned home he was still bent on killing David. Think what you will, but God is not a cookie-cutter

God, and the Spirit doesn't always do things according to our understanding.

It's one thing to say, "This whole 'falling under the power thing' is just so much nonsense. No one ever changes or receives anything tangible from God." If that were the case, the whole thing would not be a truly wonderful phenomenon but rather a phenomenal waste of time. It would be foolish, futile, and fruitless. But that is not the case! Tens of thousands of people can attest to remarkable spiritual impartation through the laying on of hands in recent revival services (and I'm not even talking about healings here). In fact, it is commonly reported today by pastors that, after being prayed for in a revival service, they returned to their churches and, without making any kind of announcement or doing anything different in their services (in other words, without "raising anyone's expectations"), people began to weep and repent (spontaneously, without prompting), others began to shake or fall under God's power (without anyone touching them), and—this is perhaps the most amazing thing of all—*unsaved visitors* came forward asking what they needed to do to be saved. It's happening across America and around the world.[18]

My critical friend, you may not believe that such things are actually taking place, and you may always be trying to find a natural, rational answer for the supernatural things God is doing or trying to write them off as exaggerated or even fabricated reports, but the rationalizing and denying won't change the truth. Miraculous, inexplicable things are happening now in churches (and individual lives) everywhere, often through the laying of on hands (including cases of skeptics and mockers being floored by God's power and getting radically converted before they arise!),[19] and you will either have to bow down and worship or say that it is the work of the devil. But I caution you in the fear of the Lord: Before you say that it is from below, you had better be ready to stake your salvation on it. If you are not 100 percent sure that it is the work of the devil, without any possible doubt in your position, hold your peace.

"But over the years, I've seen so many abuses in this whole 'slain in the Spirit' thing. It just troubles me." Therefore you are willing to reject an international, Jesus-exalting outpouring of the Spirit touching millions of lives and resulting in a glorious harvest of souls because of some abuses you have seen in the past? You are willing to speak against the current revival because you don't like the style?

Can you honestly reject something genuine happening today because of something not genuine that you previously witnessed? Please! Every revival has had its abuses and extremes, and the critics have always majored on these aspects of the work.[20] Why not embrace what *God* is doing (just as Paul did with the Corinthians; see 1 Corinthians 1:1-9) and, as a laborer in the revival harvest, help to bring correction to any extremes you may see (again, following Paul's example in 1 Corinthians)? This is constructive; so much of the critics' work is destructive.[21]

"But I've heard of some *really* wild abuses in the current revival. I just can't get involved." First, I'd like to ask you if you are *sure* about the accuracy of the reports you have heard. It's amazing to see just how many false *negative* reports are being repeated and spread. (Remember Proverbs 18:8: "The words of a gossip are like choice morsels; they go down to a man's inmost parts." How some people love to receive and spread these nasty little rumors!) Many of the scandalous reports have no foundation in truth; others are gross exaggerations. Second, even the greatest revivals of the past have had wild abuses, some even accompanied with tragic consequences.

One may think immediately of the extremist ministry of Rev. James Davenport during the Great Awakening. His unbalanced preaching and actions—which the critics of the day considered to be *representative* of the Awakening—scandalized many ministers, driving them *away* from the revival, and helped to quench the revival's fires. Preachers like this, the critics argued, are the natural fruit of this so-called "outpouring of the Spirit." And then there was the tragic suicide in Northampton, Jonathan Edwards' hometown, when a depression-prone man went over the deep end with feelings of guilt and remorse, becoming hopeless and ultimately taking his own life. This is something the critics of today, who launch a holy war over a single abuse or bad report, don't tell you. (I stagger to think of what some of them would do if such a tragic event took place in alleged conjunction with the current revival!) Yet these critics laud the Great Awakening and lament the current, growing awakening. (And mark these words: It is already an incipient awakening.)

"But wasn't it Jonathan Edwards who claimed that it was the unusual manifestations that helped bring the Great Awakening to a premature end?" To say the least, that certainly is a serious overstatement, and it ignores the damage done to the Awakening by its critics.[22] The fact is, Edwards never reversed the earlier works he had written which documented the saving reality of some of these experiences and offered practical guidelines for judging the work. (For a non-technical discussion of Edwards' *The Distinguishing Marks of the Work of the Spirit of God* in connection with the present move of God, see my book *From Holy Laughter to Holy Fire: America on the Edge of Revival,* Chapter Fourteen, "The Proof of the Revival is in the Living").[23]

In either case, regardless of what Edwards did or did not believe, the fact is that physical manifestations and emotional reactions will not be uncommon when God moves powerfully (see Chapters Ten and Eleven, "All Shook Up Over a Little Shaking" and "Now Don't Get Too Emotional!"), but they should not be exalted as signs of spirituality or magnified as indisputable proof that the Lord is moving. And when they draw attention away from the message of the Word and the ministry of the Spirit, they should be checked. The goal in revival ministry must always be to major on the majors and not make the manifestations central. Still, when *God Himself* chooses to move in exceptional ways—beyond human instrumentality—we do best to let God be God and get out of His way.[24]

For example, during the Hebrides Revival in 1949–1952 (a staunchly Presbyterian, non-charismatic move of God), Duncan Campbell reported that at one meeting, while he was speaking, half of the congregants suddenly threw their hands in the air while the other half suddenly fell to one side as they were seated in their pews—all of them staying frozen like that for the next few hours!

How would the critics explain away *that* manifestation? And what should Campbell have done? Tried to get the people "unstuck"?[25]

But, returning to the decline of the Great Awakening, it is rare that today's revival critics talk about how *criticism* of the Awakening was a major factor responsible for the revival's decline. In point of fact, a widely read book published during the Awakening was written by Charles Chauncy, the arch-critic of Edwards, and it was his writing that helped breed and feed suspicion, confusion, and division. And what did he major on? The extremes! He pointed to the alleged lack of order in the meetings, the emotional displays, and the methods used by some of the preachers. His work also denied the reality of most of the fruit. History is repeating itself! The difference this time is that, by God's grace, the critics will *not succeed* in putting out the Spirit's fire. It's too widespread for that to happen, and, I believe, the hour is too urgent to allow for another rejection of a Heaven-sent, national (actually, international) visitation.

Iain H. Murray, the fine (non-charismatic) biographer of Edwards notes, "After a cautious survey of the differences which emerged between men as a result of the Great Awakening, Archibald Alexander conclude[d]: 'I cannot doubt that, in a good degree, the contest between the parties was between the friends and enemies of true religion.' "[26] Will the same conclusion be drawn after the dust settles with regard to the contemporary revival?

Interestingly enough, while many critics point to the "perilous" nature of the last days (based on 2 Timothy 3; see Chapter Nine, "Are We Living in the Last Days?" for discussion), arguing that there will be widespread spiritual *decline*, as opposed to restoration or revival, at the end of the age, they fail to note that Paul concludes his list of the sinful conditions that will abound "in the last days," by describing people who *have a form of godliness but deny its power* (2 Tim. 3:5a). Yes, dead religion—not just counterfeit miracles and false christs—is also to be expected "in the last days"![27]

Now, I am not saying that the critics are spiritually dead or suggesting for a moment that they are not brothers or sisters in the Lord or that they are not doing many fine things for the Lord. But I *am* saying that: 1) there is just as much danger with empty forms as with extreme forms; 2) the critics often claim that false power (i.e., fleshly or demonic) is at work in the current revival without demonstrating true power (i.e., Holy Spirit) in their own circles; 3) for every "casualty" of revival that the critics claim they can point to, there are thousands of believers dying on the vine in spiritually starved churches. In fact, it is these very people who often come flocking to revival meetings, hungry for the Lord.[28]

The fact is, revival, by its very nature, can be loud, intense, confrontational, and emotional. When and if there is an abuse or extreme, it can be quite noticeable. In contrast, the abuses of traditional, powerless religion—preaching about a living God in a lifeless way; praising His acts in the past while denying their validity for today; giving little hope for healing to the sick or for deliverance to the bound—tend to be more quiet and less noticeable. (Plus, the critics are hardly "monitoring" the services in these kinds of churches!)

A collision between horses and buggies would be less dangerous than a collision between two speeding cars, but that does not mean that we should go back to horses and buggies. It means that we should teach driver safety, wear seat belts, and develop effective air bag systems. In the same way, the antidote for occasional revival extremes is *not* a return to stale, staid, predictable, powerless services but rather pastoral wisdom to help keep focused and on track.

"But you yourself just mentioned believers who 'come flocking' to revival services, wanting to receive some kind of fresh touch from the Lord. Isn't this an abuse of revival in and of itself?" Of course not. The New Testament is full of examples of "come and see" faith (see, for example, John 1:35-45; 4:1-42; in other words, "I just met someone who changed my life; come and see for yourself!"), and there is nothing illogical or unscriptural about going to a place where the Lord is moving in a special way. Would it have been wrong 1,900 years ago for the congregants in Laodicea to visit Smyrna and learn from the believers there? Is it wrong for people today who long to see many souls saved in their own city ("Lord, could it ever happen here?") to go to a city where thousands *are* being saved?

"But Jesus taught us that we would no longer have to go a sacred city like Jerusalem to receive from Him. Rather, the 'true worshipers' would worship the Father 'in spirit and truth, for they are the kind of worshipers the Father seeks' (see John 4:23-24). That's what I believe!" Well, I certainly agree with Jesus (of course!), but He was not saying what you're saying. His point was that we would not need to go to special places to offer acceptable worship to His Father.[29] But He was *not* discouraging us from going to a specific place to receive from Him when His Spirit was doing special things. Doesn't this type of seeking Him honor Him, rather than dishonor Him?

What if believers in a particular fellowship have fasted and prayed for years, humbling themselves in God's sight and preaching a clear word of repentance, leading to a powerful spiritual outpouring. Why *not* visit there and be challenged, refreshed, and encouraged, especially if the believers and leaders in your fellowship have *not* been praying, fasting, and holding to the Word? What's the problem with this? Why can't God move in a particular place in a particular way? And why is it okay to visit a church across town but not okay to visit a church across the country? What's the difference? And what if the Lord was moving mightily in your own midst? Would you tell hungry or discouraged believers *not* to come to your meetings? Would you keep the blessing to yourself?

And if it is wrong to sometimes make "pilgrimages" to a special place to receive a special blessing, then why have special conferences or retreat centers? And why advertise special meetings at your own church (or, even list your church in the yellow pages or put a sign in front of your building)? If we need nothing more than a good walk with the Lord and a good, healthy church home (of course, these essential elements are far more important for long-term spiritual health than any number of "pilgrimages"), why listen to national Christian teachers on radio or TV and why even read their printed messages or books? And remember, in spite of John 4:23-24 (cited above), the Samaritans still didn't receive the Spirit until Peter and John came from Jerusalem and laid hands on them. There's something in all of this that joins us together and shows us our interdependence.

That's why Saul (Paul) did not receive his sight until Ananias came and laid hands on him, confirming to this soon-to-be-apostle what the Lord had shown him in a vision (see Acts 9:10-19). In this way, Saul not only had an encounter with Jesus, the Lord of those he had been persecuting, but he was also immediately joined together with—and, to a very real extent was made dependent on—the rest of the Body. And so, though he had an independent and isolated conversion experience, he immediately became united with the believers (see Acts 9:19b; after he received his sight, "Saul spent several days with the disciples in Damascus"). Similarly today, someone might be critical of a particular revival movement, but when one of his or her friends attends one of the services, is prayed for, and returns transformed for the glory of God, there can be no denying the clear connection to the revival. Neither can anyone deny that "pilgrimages" can sometimes be effective.

The modern Pentecostal movement (which accounts for the largest single group of believers in the world today) can trace its *international* roots to Azusa Street, as hungry, inquisitive, and seeking saints came there from around the globe to receive an impartation of the Spirit's power.[30] Charles Finney notes that when God began moving powerfully in Rochester in 1830,

> ...persons wrote letters from Rochester, to their friends abroad, giving an account of the work, which were read in different churches throughout several states, and were instrumental in producing great revision of religion. Many persons came in from abroad to witness the great work of God, and were converted. I recollect that a physician was so attracted by what he heard of the work that he came from Newark, New Jersey, to Rochester, to see what the Lord was doing, and was himself converted there.[31]

And Cynddylan Jones, a leader in the Welsh Revival, had this to say in December of 1904:

> Is the revival likely to continue? Yes, till it has done its work...We do not want it to last any longer—the tension is too great...Will it extend? Through Wales, yes; through England, doubtful. However, it depends upon England itself. Given the necessary conditions, the Spirit will descend. The Saxon race

works by mechanics, the Celts by dynamics—that makes all the difference in the world....And here precisely lies the danger of the present movement. Wales has never had professional missioners [i.e., formal churchmen, possibly the equivalent of institutionalized church boards today]—we have no equivalent word in our language, because the thing is alien to our nature and habits. Here is the peril: that Evan Roberts will fall in to the hands of the religious showmen, who are always on the look-out for new lions...The other danger is that the professional missioners will try to capture the movement. They are already gathered like eagles ready for their prey. To all these I say, in the name of Wales: Hands off! Come and see and get the blessing, return home, and pass the blessing on. "I want to learn the secret," said one of these missioners to Mr. Evan Roberts, as though there was a trick or secret spring to be touched by the operator. "I have no secret," replied the young preacher, "ask and ye shall receive."[32]

And to all critics who are "already gathered like eagles ready for their prey," poised to pounce on the next negative report relating to the current revival, I say with Cynddylan Jones: Hands off! Come and receive for yourself, then take the blessing home when you leave. And don't forget to have someone lay hands on you when you visit. It just might change your life!

Far from being an expert on revivals, it nevertheless seems rather strange to me that modern-day revivalists proclaim that "God is going to be bringing a great revival in these last days, characterized by a new and powerful working of the Holy Spirit." Yet the Bible says that God's plan for the last days is the Great Apostasy, characterized by all kinds of counterfeit miracles, signs, and wonders (2 Thes. 2:3, 6-10). Is God really bringing revival, or is what we see happening now that which will culminate in the greatest delusion of all time (vs. 11)?

Discernment Ministries
"Revival and the Revival Mentality"

Are we who profess to be His disciples covering our unbelief about the possibility of revival by murmurings about "a day of small things", "the end times", or "the Laodicean age"? Let us search our hearts, lest He should say of us, "Ye do err…not knowing the power of God."

Arthur Wallis, *In the Day of Thy Power*

Across the centuries, Bible-believing Christians have become an ever-larger proportion of world population. In AD 1430 only one in one hundred was a Bible-believing Christian. Today, one in nine is.

U.S. Center for World Mission

Chapter Thirteen

Is Good News Bad News for the Gloomers and Doomers?
Exposing the Laodicean Lie

A seriously flawed teaching has infiltrated the Church in recent decades. It is based on an interesting but incorrect interpretation of the Word. And though it *seems* innocent enough, it is downright dangerous. I call it the Laodicean Lie.

Every student of the Word knows Jesus' messages to the seven churches in Asia Minor in Revelation 2–3, where the Lord brings words of rebuke, correction, and encouragement to these congregations located in Ephesus, Smyrna, Pergamum, Thyatira, Sardis, Philadelphia, and Laodicea. The biblical text seems straightforward. There were seven groups of believers in seven different cities, and there was a distinct message delivered to each of them.[1] And, just as holds true with the rest of the Bible, there was a definite message for the original readers and a definite application for readers living in every subsequent age. That is to say that even though Jesus brought direct words to these original churches, to whatever extent that any of these seven words apply to a church or individual believer living at any time in history, His words can be applied to that situation as well.

And so, we read these chapters in Revelation just as we would read the Epistles to the Corinthians, Romans, or Colossians. We learn from the general truths set forth in each Epistle or message, and to the degree that the specific "shoe" fits, we wear it. Simple enough, right?

Not quite. For some time now, there has been a popular interpretation stating that the seven churches represent seven Church ages, from New Testament times until today. In other words, although the messages to the churches may have applied to seven real congregations in Asia Minor in John's day, they are interpreted to ultimately point to seven different eras of Church history. So, for example, Jesus first addresses Ephesus, which represents the Church at the end of the apostolic age, backsliding from its first love. Next is Smyrna, representing the next few centuries of the Church as it underwent intense persecution and suffering. Last on the list of seven is the church of Laodicea, representing the Church at the end of the age—and this church is almost completely apostate![2]

> To the angel of the church in Laodicea write: These are the words of the Amen, the faithful and true witness, the ruler of God's creation. I know your deeds, that you are neither cold nor hot. I wish you were either one or the other! So, because you are lukewarm—neither hot nor cold—I am about to spit you out of My mouth. You say, "I am rich; I have acquired wealth and do not need a thing." But you do not realize that you are wretched, pitiful, poor, blind and naked. I counsel you to buy from Me gold refined in the fire, so you can become rich; and white clothes to wear, so you can cover your shameful nakedness; and salve to put on your eyes, so you can see. Those whom I love I rebuke and discipline. So be earnest, and repent. Here I am! I stand at the door and knock. If anyone hears My voice and opens the door, I will come in and eat with him, and he with Me. To him who overcomes, I will give the right to sit with Me on My throne, just as I overcame and sat down with My Father on His throne. He who has an ear, let him hear what the Spirit says to the churches. (Rev. 3:14-22)

Now, how much hope would you have for revival today if you were convinced that we were living in "the Laodicean age," an age in which Jesus described the Church as being completely unaware of its "wretched, pitiful, poor, blind and naked" condition? If this desperate and dire state was all you had to look forward to, how fervently would you be praying for a national revival, or an international revival? Would you be anticipating a mighty, end-time outpouring of the Spirit, or would you be awaiting a general spiritual decline? As we approach the Lord's return, would you be expecting the Church to grow healthier or sicker? What would you be looking forward to? Would you be a pessimist or an optimist? And would you receive reports of contemporary great awakenings and visitations with excitement or with suspicion? The answers, I think, are obvious.

Unfortunately for these "gloomers and doomers" who expect nothing better than ever-increasing darkness until the Lord returns— yet fortunately for the rest of us—there is no scriptural support for this Laodicean Lie. Read the Book of Revelation through 100 times, and you will still not find a hint of any kind that chapters 2–3 are to be read as "prophetic history." Not only so (although the point just made is enough in and of itself), but such an interpretation is a logical impossibility. This is because in every century, the seven so-called Church ages would have to be adjusted! In other words, using Christians living in the year AD 1000 as an example, since these believers felt the end of the world was near, they would have considered *themselves* to be the Laodicean church. Thus they would have split up these seven eras over a 1,000-year period, whereas believers today split up the eras over a 2,000-year period. And this changes everything! In fact, the only generation that could ever get the whole interpretation right would be the last generation, and no one will know with *total* certainty that they are part of that final generation until Jesus comes back.

So, not only does the "Church age" interpretation make it impossible for believers throughout the centuries to interpret Revelation 2–3 correctly (do you think for a split second that believers living in the year 300 understood that there would be at least 1,700 years of history after them, and if they didn't, how then could they have rightly understood the remaining messages to the churches?), it also means that only in the very last of the last days will the correct interpretation of these chapters be revealed. This is hardly an enviable position to take! It requires that the truth of certain portions of the Bible to be hidden from the eyes of Bible believers until the time came for the real interpretation to be revealed. Shades of cult-like esoteric knowledge and secret revelation! It is one thing to say that as prophecy unfolds, the prophetic Scriptures will become clearer. It is another thing to say that the true meaning of whole chapters of the Bible will be withheld from the Church for almost all of its history!

But there are further interpretive problems with the Church-age theory. One difficulty is that either historical truths have to be distorted or specific verses stretched in order to make everything fit into a neat package (again, that's accepting the presupposition that we or our children are now in the final generation).[3] The descriptions are far from perfect and hardly obvious. A second difficulty—and this has to do specifically with the "Laodicean lie"—is that Jesus exhorts the church of Laodicea to "buy from Me gold refined in the fire, so you can become rich; and white clothes to wear, so you can cover your shameful nakedness; and salve to put on your eyes, so you can see." Even Laodicea can be restored! In fact, Laodicea has the greatest "revival" promise of any of the seven churches, culminating with a personal invitation from the Lord Himself to answer His call and eat with Him. What a glorious word!

So we see that the church most soundly reproved in the Book of Revelation is given the most special promise. Restored fellowship is being offered. Jesus stands at the door, ready and willing to bless. This is hardly a guarantee of apostasy! Rather, it is an earnest, expectant, and hopeful call to repent. So, even if the Church-age theory were true (and it is not) and even if we were living in the Laodicean age (which, in fact, does not exist), there would be every reason to pray for revival, preach revival (i.e., the message of repentance with the promise of restoration), and believe for revival. There would be every reason for great hope!

But there is another, even bigger problem with the Laodicean lie. *The description doesn't fit.* It is a North American and/or European projection of the state of the Church, and it is completely inapplicable to the Body of Christ in most of the world today. In other words, although the message to Laodicea most definitely applies to much of the complacent, rich, self-sufficient, and lukewarm Western Church as it has existed over the last few decades ("You say, 'I am rich; I have acquired wealth and do not need a thing.' But you do not realize that you are wretched, pitiful, poor, blind and naked"), it does not apply in the least to most of the Church in China, Africa, India, Vietnam, Iran, Indonesia, etc.[4] Instead, it is the message to Smyrna that so aptly describes these impoverished, persecuted, yet thriving believers who actually make up the bulk of the Body today:

> I know your afflictions and your poverty—yet you are rich!... Do not be afraid of what you are about to suffer. I tell you, the devil will put some of you in prison to test you, and you will suffer persecution for ten days. Be faithful, even to the point of death, and I will give you the crown of life. (Rev. 2:9-10)

Stop for a moment and think. How absurd it is to apply the words, "You say, 'I am rich; I have acquired wealth and do not need a thing,' " to the persecuted house churches in China, where Bibles are as scarce as precious jewels, or to the grass-hut churches in the villages of India, where one family in 10,000 has running water and electricity. And how ignorant and self-centered it is to project the state of a small-but-influential part of the Body (i.e., the Church of the West) on the rest of the Body (i.e., the Church of the Third World, better called "the Two-Thirds World").

Right now, more Christians are dying for their faith every year than at any other time in history, "being faithful to the point of death, that they may receive the crown of life" (in the words of Jesus to Smyrna; see Rev. 2:10). In contrast with this, we sit in our luxurious homes in North America, drive our air-conditioned cars to our multi-million dollar sanctuaries, and spend more money on new carpeting than on foreign missions. For many of us today, sacrifice is defined as, "The remote control on the VCR is not functioning"— in which case we actually have to *get up* and change channels! And from this overstuffed vantage point, we look at our backslidden, compromised, comfortable condition and say, "How Laodicean we are!" And I agree! The messages to Laodicea, as well as to Sardis, really do apply to most of us in the West today.[5] But they don't apply to most of the Church worldwide by any stretch of the imagination. (And, thank God, they are applying less and less even to those of us in the West these days, since, contrary to the congregations in Laodicea and Sardis, we are becoming fully aware of our naked, shameful, sleeping state.)

The bottom line is that there is no scriptural support for the notion that there will be an end-time, apostate Laodicean Church-age. The Bible simply doesn't teach it. Tragically, those who buy into this erroneous concept become enemies of revival, expecting gross apostasy and not great awakening, sinful regress and not spiritual progress, a deteriorating virus and not a divine visitation. How morbid!

Could you see the Father talking to the Son and saying, "As a result of Your sacrifice, as a fruit of Your blood being shed, I will close out the Church age with the greatest apostasy the world has ever seen! It will declare to all humanity just how powerful Your death and resurrection really are. It will demonstrate Your keeping power. It will show Your detractors that I have truly given all authority to You and that Your name is higher than any other name. Yes, the people whom You have purchased will be falling like flies and fading like flowers, growing weaker and wearier by the hour until You come to take them home. Yes, My Son, this is what I have planned for You!"[6]

Somehow, I have a hard time reconciling this scenario with verses like Ephesians 5:27 where it is stated that Jesus will present His people "to Himself as a radiant church, without stain or wrinkle or any other blemish, but holy and blameless." Does this sound like an apostate Church? And what of the Lord's promise that He would build His Church and the gates of Hades would not prevail against it (Matt. 16:18)?[7] Is this a promise of victory or defeat? And what of the ministry of the Holy Spirit? Will it be a grand failure too, just like the Jesus of the gloomers and doomers? (By the way, lest you think the word *failure* is too strong, proponents of what I have been calling the Laodicean lie have sometimes spoken of "the failure of Christianity."[8] Can you believe this?)

·"But didn't Jesus Himself say that there would be a great defection from the faith before His return? Didn't *He* say that the love of many would grow cold?" Well, let's look at His words, reading them as if they applied directly to us (that is, not even addressing the issues of the original context or potential future application), just as the critics do:

...Watch out that no one deceives you. For many will come in My name, claiming, "I am the Christ," and will deceive many. You will hear of wars and rumors of wars, but see to it that you are not alarmed. Such things must happen, but the end is still to come. Nation will rise against nation, and kingdom against kingdom. There will be famines and earthquakes in various places. All these are the beginning of birth pains. Then you will be handed over to be persecuted and put to death, and you will be hated by all nations because of Me. At that time many will turn away from the faith and will betray and hate each other, and many false prophets will appear and deceive many people. Because of the increase of wickedness, the love of [many (note: NIV's "most" is an incorrect translation")] will grow cold, but he who stands firm to the end will be saved. And this gospel of the kingdom will be preached in the whole world as a testimony to all nations, and then the end will come. (Matt. 24:4-14)

Since we have already dealt with some of the other verses in this passage (see Chapter Five) and since Matthew 24:12 is commonly quoted by the critics as proof that there will be no end-time revival, let's zero in on this one verse: "Because of the increase of wickedness, the love of [many] will grow cold." The big problem with this interpretation of the critics is that what is happening to Christians in today's revival describes the exact *opposite* of the situation described in this verse. Rather than the love of many growing cold, the love of many is growing hotter by the day! Rather than wickedness causing people to turn away from the faith, revival fires are causing them to turn away from wickedness. How can anyone possibly apply this verse to the current visitation?[9]

"Aha!" says the critic. "Even by the end of your book, you still haven't figured it out. You see, this false revival is paving the way for the great apostasy spoken of here. That's the great deception!"

But that's not what the Word of God says. Because you don't agree that this is a real move of God, and because the Scriptures warn us about end-time deception, you're concluding that this "revival" must actually be part of the "deception"—especially since so many are buying into it. (After all, Jesus said that many would be deceived and fall away!)

Friend, that's just ludicrous. You must have some kind of biblical support for an extreme position like that, and you have none. I
might just as well say that all those who differ with me are part of
the great deception because Jesus said that great deception was
coming. The fact is, Matthew 24:12 is perfectly clear in its meaning:
Because iniquity will abound, the love of many will grow cold.
That's pretty forthright, isn't it? Because wickedness will be on the
increase—meaning it will be widespread, ugly, and readily available—
many people will become compromised and cold, all of which has no
possible application to the current revival. Also, the surrounding verses
that speak of martyrdom and betrayal, etc., make it clear that Jesus
is talking about something very different than what the critics are
talking about.[10] (And may I say again to all pretribulational critics:
Most dispensational scholars—in other words, most pre-tribulation
scholars—apply this whole passage to the *tribulation period*, believing that Jesus was only addressing His Jewish disciples who
would be on the earth after the Church was raptured [see, for example, the verses that immediately follow the section we just quoted,
Matt. 24:15-23]. Therefore, according to this view, Matthew 24:12,
just like the other warnings about deception and false prophets and
false messiahs, does not even apply to the Church!)

Let's also look carefully at this word *many* (Greek *pollos*) in
Matthew 24. Verse 5 states, "For many will come in My name,
claiming, 'I am the Christ [Messiah],' and will deceive many." How
many false messiahs will be there? Does the word have to mean
millions and millions? Obviously not. In any case, the "many" who
will be deceived will be those who follow some man who claims to
be the Messiah (as we saw earlier, this would refer to a David
Koresh type of figure) and do not wait for the true Messiah who is
coming in the clouds. *This, quite obviously, has absolutely nothing
to do with the current revival.* In fact, you could more plausibly argue that those who listen to the critics are following false messiahs
than you could claim that those who are worshiping the crucified,
risen, and soon-coming King are following a false messiah.

In Matthew 24:10, Jesus said, "At that time *many* will turn
away from the faith and will betray and hate each other." Once more
we must ask, How can anyone possibly apply this to a revival

through which multitudes of sinners have turned *to the faith* and been gloriously converted from darkness to light, from sin to salvation, and from the clutches of Satan to the embrace of the Savior, now walking in love and loyalty? What a gross misapplication of the Word!

"But what about Matthew 24:11?" says the critic. "I've got you there! Jesus warned us that, '*many* false prophets will appear and deceive *many* people.' So that proves it." Proves what? Really, if I hadn't heard these kinds of arguments, I would never have believed that people could possibly use them. I would think that interpretations like this weren't even worthy of some cult somewhere. But coming from sincere, children of God, it's absolutely tragic.[11]

To repeat: Just because Jesus said that many people will be deceived by many false prophets at a certain time in history does *not* give anyone the right to claim that those who are part of a movement or group with which they differ are therefore "the deceived." If anything, that is a *self-deceived* position. Jesus told us what kind of deception to watch out for, as we have stressed throughout this book. He warned us about false christs (like some powerful Hindu "holy man" who claims to be the current "incarnation" of Christ) backed by false prophets working false miracles (this could well become rampant in the New Age movement).[12] He also predicted that an increase in persecution would cause many to turn away from the faith while an increase in wickedness would cause the hearts of many to grow cold. And this cannot be applied to red-hot, doctrinally sound, Jesus-centered, clean-hearted children of God. The shoe just doesn't fit.

In light of this, I say to every critic: Back off! Not a syllable of this description can possibly be related to the current revival, except to say that, as God is moving powerfully around the world and the blood of martyrs is being spilled in unprecedented measure, some are yielding to the pressure of persecution and turning from the faith. (Interestingly, it is in the midst of real moves of God—like that in Sudan, for example, where Muslim extremists have wreaked havoc on whole Christian families, putting out the eyes of the men and cutting off their right hands, chopping off one breast of the nursing mothers so their babies starve, putting the boys into Islamic schools and selling the girls into slavery and prostitution—that some believers have succumbed to the pressure and turned from the faith. Is this part of the great deception too?)[13]

Note also that Jesus declared in Mark 10:45 that He would give His life as a "ransom for *many*" and that Revelation 7:9-14 speaks of "...a *great multitude* that no one could count, from every nation, tribe, people and language...who have come out of the great tribulation...[and] have washed their robes and made them white in the blood of the Lamb." So it is not just "many" who will be deceived but "many" who will be redeemed! And, even in the midst of "great tribulation," an innumerable multitude will be saved. (For the pre-tribulationist, this means that in spite of the false prophet with his false miracles supporting the antichrist during the period of the "great tribulation," and in spite of widespread deception, apostasy, and persecution, multiplied millions of souls will be saved. For those who do not hold to a pre-tribulation rapture, these verses in Revelation could well be applied to the vast harvest of souls taking place today in the midst of terrible suffering and a worldwide increase in wickedness.)[14]

I would also encourage the careful student of Matthew 24 (again, continuing to read the whole chapter as if it were directly relevant to us, either warning us of events that will occur immediately before and after the "rapture," or speaking of events that will all take place in our day) to notice that throughout the chapter, Jesus speaks to "you"—that is, to His disciples whom He addresses directly—as those who will hold fast to the end. In other words, there is no reason for His own to turn away! Even Matthew 24:24, where Jesus warned that "false Christs and false prophets will appear and perform great signs and miracles to deceive even the elect—if that were possible," is a subject of hot debate. Can the elect be deceived?[15]

But putting this aside (who needs to add more controversy at this point!), there is something of real importance we should focus on in Jesus' words in Matthew 24:14. There He said that "this gospel of the kingdom will be preached in the whole world as a testimony to all nations" before the end will come, and, all praise and glory to God, the gospel is being preached to the nations like never before.[16] The message is getting out!

Consider the following facts: In the year AD 100, the Bible had been translated into six languages; by AD 200 (100 years later) the number had only grown to seven; by AD 500 it had only increased to 13 and by AD 1000 to just 17. Nine hundred years passed with only 11 new translations! By AD 1500 the number of languages with the Word of God had grown to 34 (still pretty slow going), then, picking up a little speed, by AD 1800 to 67, and then—get this!—by the year AD 1900 the number had swelled to 537, and by the year 2000, the number will go over the 2,000 mark.[17]

Isn't this incredible? From AD 200 to 1500, only 27 new language translations of the Bible were made (despite the fact that there were several thousand languages and dialects being used around the world). From AD 1500 to 1800, there were 33 new translations; from AD 1800 to 1900 there were 504 new translations (glory!), and in this century alone, 1,500 new translations. This doesn't sound like worldwide apostasy to me! It sounds like harvest time!

Missiologists tell us that roughly 70 percent of all Church growth in world history has taken place in *this century*. And of that phenomenal growth, 70 percent has taken place since World War II. And—brace yourself— of that incredible increase, 70 percent has taken place since the late 1980's![18] Did you get that? These overwhelming statistics mean that *one-third* of 20 centuries of Church growth has taken place *in the last ten years*—and most of it is occurring among the most impoverished, oppressed, and persecuted peoples of the world. I tell you again, it's harvest time!

Writing in the November, 1990, issue of *Missions Frontiers*, Ralph D. Winter stated that in the year AD 100, after the glorious period of the Acts and the early Church, there was approximately one true, gospel-believing Christian for every 360 people on the earth; by AD 1900, there was one believer for every 27 people; by 1989, one for every seven; and at the present rate of growth, by the year 2000 there will be *one in three*! Even if you differ with these statistics, claiming, for example, that by 1989 more realistic numbers would indicate that there was one believer for every 15 people on the planet (and I'm not aware of many missiologists who would share such a pessimistic outlook), or that by the year 2000, there will be one believer for every ten people on earth, that still would represent an absolutely supernatural and exponential increase in the spread of the gospel and the growth of the Church. Yes, it's harvest time!

Or, to look at this from another angle and with a small variation in statistics, here is a chart supplying "Milestone Dates in the Growth of True Christianity." According to the compilers, it offers "at the dates indicated, a comparison of 1) the number of Bible-believing Christians and 2) the total number of people in the world." Examine this carefully and begin to rejoice!

One per hundred (1%)	by AD 1430	(One to 99 after 1430 years)
Two per hundred (2%)	by AD 1790	(One to 49 after 360 years)
Three per hundred (3%)	by AD 1940	(One to 32 after 150 years)
Four per hundred (4%)	by AD 1960	(One to 24 after 20 years)
Five per hundred (5%)	by AD 1970	(One to 19 after 10 years)
Six per hundred (6%)	by AD 1980	(One to 16 after 10 years)
Seven per hundred (7%)	by AD 1983	(One to 13 after 3 years)
Eight per hundred (8%)	by AD 1986	(One to 11 after 3 years)
Nine per hundred (9%)	by AD 1989	(One to 10 after 3 years)
Ten per hundred (10%)	by AD 1993	(One to 9 after 4 years)
Eleven per hundred (11%)	by AD 1995	(One to 8 after 2 years)[19]

What this means in practical, down-to-earth terms—and it really is staggering—is that "there are 78,000 conversions each day and 16,000 new churches planted each week."[20] Stand up and shout for joy, my friend. It's harvest time!

Zechariah 10:1 reads, "Ask the LORD for rain in the springtime [literally, in the time of the spring rains]; it is the LORD who makes the storm clouds. He gives showers of rain to men, and plants of the field to everyone."[21] You see, there is a time for sowing and a time for reaping, a time for the fall rains and a time for the spring rains, and just as surely as there are agricultural times and seasons established by God, there are spiritual times and seasons established by God. And the unprecedented, worldwide influx of souls into God's Kingdom in these last few years means, without doubt, that it is spiritual harvest time. And if it's harvest time it must be springtime (in Israel, a time for the maturity of the harvest),[22] and if it's springtime then it's time for rain, and if it's time for rain, it's time to ask the Lord for the showers. Let the rains come down! (And remember also Joshua 3:15, "Now the Jordan is at flood stage all during harvest..."; in other words, that's when the river is ready to overflow!)[23]

At an urgent hour in Israel's history, Hosea cried out to his backslidden people, "Sow for yourselves righteousness, reap the fruit of unfailing love, and break up your unplowed ground; for it is time to seek the LORD, until He comes and showers righteousness on you" (Hos. 10:12). There was a divine window of opportunity, a moment that had to be maximized, a *kairos* (the Greek word often used for a special or appointed time) that had to be seized. But that generation missed its moment! We dare not follow their example. *Now* is the time to seek the Lord. *Now* is the time for the outpouring of heavenly rain. *Now* is the time for revival. *Now* is the time to break up the unplowed, fallow ground of our own hearts, to sow the seed of the gospel in new fields where it has never been sown and to reap from the fields where much seed has already been sown. It's time!

The prophet Isaiah also spoke of a special time of God's favor, a time when He was especially near: "Seek the LORD while He may be found; call on Him while He is near. Let the wicked forsake his way and the evil man his thoughts. Let him turn to the LORD, and He will have mercy on him, and to our God, for He will freely pardon" (Is. 55:6-7). When God is knocking at the door, we must open to Him at once. When He says, "I am near! I may be found right now!" we must respond that very moment.

What if, after decades of praying that He would visit us, we deny that it is really Him when He *does* visit us? (After all, if we have been without His supernatural visitation for so long, what makes us so sure we will recognize Him when He comes in power—and, that means coming His way, doing His thing, and on His terms.) What if we decide that it is *not* His voice calling and *not* His Spirit moving and we choose not to answer the door? What if He stops calling and knocking? What if we forfeit the opportunity of a lifetime? May it not be! As Leonard Ravenhill said just a few months before his death, "The opportunity of a lifetime must be seized during the lifetime of the opportunity."[24] The lifetime of that opportunity is *now*.

Friends, I tell you with my heart aflame: This is the hour we have been waiting for! This is the day of visitation. As Jonathan Edwards wrote many years ago:

> God hath had it much on his heart, from all eternity, to glorify his dear and only Son, and there are some special seasons he appoints to that end, wherein he comes forth with omnipotent power to fulfil his promise and oath to him: and these are times of remarkable pouring out of his Spirit, to advance his kingdom; such a day is a day of his power.[25]

This is such a time! This is a day of God's power.

You might say, "But I believe that only a few will be saved, since the Word teaches that only a remnant will come to the Lord."[26] But even if you're right, how big is a remnant? Throughout the vast majority of human history, only a tiny handful of people have truly known the Lord. Therefore, even if *half* of this present generation repented and believed—and that would be absolutely extraordinary— that would still only represent a remnant of the totality of humanity. It took almost 2,000 years of Church history just to reach the point that *one-tenth* of the world's current population was saved, and that represented a huge leap forward as far as the advance of the gospel is concerned. So you've got nothing to worry about. You can have your "tiny remnant" theology and *still* believe for end-time revival!

And, if you *must* have something pessimistic to look forward to, consider the fact that *many* will have to be saved before *many* can turn away, so there will have to be some kind of great revival before the great deception.[27] (Once again I ask you to forgive my sarcasm.) This much is indisputably clear: There is a glorious harvest of souls being gathered around the world through the power of the gospel, and it would be criminal not to throw in the sickle and reap. Jesus is beginning to receive the reward of His labor, the Spirit is being poured out on all flesh, the darkness is growing darker while the Light shines brighter still, and the Lord of the harvest says of His great prophetic plans, "I am the LORD; in its time I will do this swiftly" (Is. 60:22b). Once more I say, it's time!

There are some who find no biblical hint of end-time victory for the Church, even claiming that those who hold to such triumphant views are heretics.[28] Of course, there has been all too much worldly triumphalism in the Church in our day, as if human power and might could bring about God's will. But there is a biblical side to the triumph of God's people, and it is important to remember that some of the greatest revival leaders of the past (including men like Jonathan Edwards and Charles Finney) believed that the Church itself would usher in the millennium in their lifetime, in particular through the awakenings that were sweeping the land. Were these men therefore heretical? If not, then how can believers today be looked at with scorn when they say, "We could be at the beginning of the last great awakening, the final revival that will usher in the return of the Lord"? In light of the worldwide outpouring taking place today, what is so farfetched about this view? Is there no chance that it is absolutely right?

I know that some of you fashion yourselves to be among the "elite troops of God's holy remnant," but I would rather see myself as part of that multitude that no one can number! And though some of you can only foresee great apostasy on the horizon, praying only that the Lord would keep you free from deception, I would rather echo the inspired prayer of a passionate prophet of the Lord:

> Oh, that You would rend the heavens and come down, that the mountains would tremble before You! As when fire sets twigs ablaze and causes water to boil, come down to make Your name known to Your enemies and cause the nations to quake before You! For when You did awesome things that we did not expect, You came down, and the mountains trembled before You. Since ancient times no one has heard, no ear has perceived, no eye has seen any God besides You, who acts on behalf of those who wait for Him. (Is. 64:1-4)

That prayer ignites my soul!

Rend the heavens, O Lord! Come down and make Your name known! Cause the nations to quake and the mountains to shake! Act, O God, on behalf of those who wait for You. If not now, when?

Some of you may be eagerly awaiting the day when Jesus will descend and rescue you from certain doom, but I would rather remember that, as we eagerly await the great day of His return, we also have a glorious promise: Times of refreshing must come first! As I wrote in 1990:

> Peter was an eye-witness of the glory of the Lord. He saw Jesus heal the sick and raise the dead. He saw Him drive out demons and feed the hungry. He saw Him as He suffered and he saw Him when He rose. He saw Him ascend to heaven.
>
> Then, on the day of Pentecost, Peter experienced the glory—he was immersed in the Spirit on fire. His own being became supercharged with God. He preached with authority and thousands were saved. He spoke with power and cripples danced for joy. He was soaked with a deluge from on high.
>
> But Peter didn't stop there. In fact, he said there was more. There was a promise from God to the people: The times of refreshing must come! "Repent, then, and turn to God, so that your sins may be wiped out, that times of refreshing may come from the [presence of the] Lord, and that He may send the Messiah, who has been appointed for you—even Jesus. He must remain in heaven until the time comes for God to restore everything, as He promised long ago through His holy prophets" (Acts 3:19-21).
>
> Repentance…Refreshing…Return…Restoration: This is the program of God. Repentance unlocks the door, and then the Refreshing comes. And after the Refreshing, the Lord will Return. And then He will fully Restore. Until then, "He must remain in heaven." First the Showers, then the Son; first the Rain, then the Return; first the Outpouring, then the Appearing. We will be Drenched before He Descends. Even now, there are rain clouds in sight….[29]

—and now those same clouds have burst!

Yes, heavenly showers are falling and the hour we have dreamed of is here. Isn't it time you came into the rain?

If you have much of the Spirit of God, you must make up your mind to have much opposition, both in the Church and the world. Very likely the leading men in the Church will oppose you. There has always been opposition in the Church. So it was when Christ was on earth. If you are far above their state of feeling, Church members will oppose you. If any man will live godly in Christ Jesus, he must expect persecution (2 Timothy 3:12). Often the elders and even the minister will oppose you, if you are filled with the Spirit of God.

Charles Finney
Lectures on the Revival of Religion

We were everywhere represented as mad dogs, and treated accordingly. In sermons, newspapers, and pamphlets of all kinds we were painted as unheard-of-monsters. But this moved us not; we went on testifying salvation by faith, both to small and great, and not counting our lives dear unto ourselves, so we might finish our course with peace.

John Wesley, as cited by Bill Gothard

Our Lord meant, next, "Go in peace" in reference to all the criticisms of all these people who have looked at you. Do not mind them. Do not trouble about them. What have they to do with you? It is enough for a servant if his master accepts him: he need not mind what others have to say about his service. Thy faith hath saved thee. Forget all the unkind things they have said, and do not trouble thy heart about the cruel speeches they may yet make. Go in peace, and be under no alarm as to upbraiding tongues.

Charles H. Spurgeon, commenting on Luke 7:50

I am coming soon. Hold on to what you have, so that no one will take your crown.

The Lord Jesus, Revelation 3:11

Chapter Fourteen

Let No One Take Your Crown

When Charles Spurgeon began pastoring at the tender age of 18, the skeptics said it would never last. After all, he was only a boy. Years later, preaching to a congregation of thousands, he declared:

> The critics said—and I must quote this because this sermon is very much a personal one—the critics said, when the lad commenced his preaching, that it was a nine days' wonder, and would soon come to an end. When the people joined the church in great numbers, they were "a parcel of boys and girls." Many of those "boys and girls" are here to-night, faithful to God unto this hour—[1]

and "this hour" has lived on and on. In fact, Spurgeon's ministry has outlived its critics by more than 100 years!

His ministry also outlived disaster and difficulty, including the tragic stampede that broke out in a crowded meeting when someone yelled, "Fire!" causing serious injury and death. Still, even a terrible accident could not dampen the holy flames that burned in his heart, and so he marched on with confidence, never backing down or letting up. And, in spite of all hell coming against him, he could boast in the Lord, because:

> ...the testimony for God in this place, by the same voice, has not ceased, nor lost its power. Still the people throng to hear the gospel after these thirty years and more, and still the doctrines of grace are to the front, not-withstanding the opposition. In the darkest hour of my ministry I might have declared, "I shall not die, but live, and declare the works of the Lord." If you have been set on fire by a divine truth, the world cannot put

an extinguisher upon you. That candle which God has lighted, the devils of hell cannot blow out. If you are commissioned of God to do a good work, give your whole heart to it, trust in the Lord, and you will not fail. I bear my joyful witness to the power of God to work mightily by the most insignificant of instruments.[2]

And in this day and hour, when our Lord, through thousands of insignificant instruments, has chosen to pour out His Spirit around the world, when He has set His servants ablaze with revival fire, when He has ignited a holy torch that cannot be extinguished, now more than ever He is calling us to go for it—come opposition, come misunderstanding, come criticism, come death. As Spurgeon so powerfully said, "That candle which God has lighted, the devils of hell cannot blow out."

So fear not and press on. This is what you were made for! This is why you were redeemed: So you could shine brightly and boldly for your Master; so you could serve Him with heart and soul; so you could make an everlasting impact on this generation in Jesus' mighty name; so the Father could say, "Well done!"; so you would run your race with perseverance, "and all the more as you see the Day approaching" (Heb. 10:25b).

When George Whitefield came to America, not everyone welcomed him. In fact, he was hotly opposed by some, with church leaders in Georgia even bringing charges against him in court. Not surprisingly, because he was so mightily used by God and therefore could not be easily ignored, his critics painted him out to be a rank heretic. He wrote:

> Had some infernal spirit been sent to draw my picture, I think it scarcely possible that he could paint me in more horrid colors. I think, if ever, then was the time that all manner of evil was spoke against me falsely for Christ's sake. The Commissary seemed to ransack church history for instances of enthusiasm [i.e., religious fanaticism] and abused grace. He drew a parallel between me and all the Oliverians, Ranters, Quakers, French Prophets, till he came to a family of Dutartes, who lived not many years ago in South Carolina, and were guilty of the most notorious incests and murders.[3]

Yes, the greatest preacher of the eighteenth century was grouped together with every extremist faction and heretical group, even being associated with sexual perverts and murderers. (When this happens to you, dear fellow worker in revival, remember: There's nothing new under the sun! And are you noticing a pattern here? Those Christian leaders who have been most wonderfully used by the Lord have suffered the most abuse from their fellow leaders!) Of course, the charges against Whitefield were dismissed and forgotten, but it is interesting to see how the opposition and hostility he experienced through the years never caused him to slacken his pace even for a moment, nor did it seem to steal his peace.

When Whitefield returned to New England in 1745, after touching many lives during his previous visits there, Jonathan Edwards noted that antagonism to his ministry had greatly increased, in particular on the part of the clergy. Writing to a friend in Scotland he said:

> Many ministers were more alarmed at his coming than they would have been by the arrival of a fleet from France, and they began soon to preach and write against him....I question whether history affords any instance paralleled with this, as so much pains taken in writing to blacken a man's character and render him odious....Many that when he was here before durst as soon eat fire as speak reproachfully of him, the regard of the people in general was so great to him, now have taken liberty of opposing him most openly and without restraint....It was kind of miracle that Mr. Whitefield should appear so little moved by all that he met with, and should in the midst of all possess himself with so much courage and calmness....[4]

We too should follow Whitefield's lead: If the Lord is with us and we are doing His work, if our hearts are not haughty and our hands are not unclean, if we are grounded in the Word and intimate with our Savior, we must let nothing move or deter us. We must be true to our God! We must not retreat when the going gets rough. After all, anyone can stand tall in times of favor and esteem. It is when opposition rises that the flesh wants to run. So my friend, hold your ground! No one should be able to apply Proverbs 24:10 to you: "If you falter in times of trouble, how small is your strength!" May *your* strength prove great in times of trouble. May the battle bring out the best in you.

Listen again to Spurgeon, the eighteenth century's Prince of Preachers:

> When they see that God is with you, and that he has given you the triumph, you shall have honour, even in the eyes of those who now ridicule you. I think sometimes the Christian should have very much the same bravado against the judgment of men as David had when Michal, the daughter of Saul, came out and said, "How glorious was the king of Israel today, who uncovered himself today in the eyes of the handmaids of his servants," and he said, "It was before the Lord, and I will yet be more vile than thus." Let your eye be to God, and forget the eyes of men. Live so that, whether they know what you do, or do not know, you will not care, for your conduct will bear the blaze of the great Judgment Day, and, therefore, the criticisms of earth do not affect you. Let no man domineer over you.[5]

All too often, we react to criticism, sometimes withdrawing from practices and positions that we once held dear. After all, we don't want to seem arrogant and unteachable! But what if the criticism was fleshly and carnal, having its origin in the sinful heart of man? Or what if it flowed from the devil, having its origin in the pit? What then if we dishonored God so as to honor Satan or the flesh? What then if we quenched God's Spirit under the guise of being sensitive to His Spirit? What then if we feared the face of man more than the face of our Father? Or, as W.E. Sangster asked many years ago, "How shall I feel at the judgment, if multitudes of missed opportunities pass before me in full review, and all my excuses prove to be disguises of my cowardice and pride?"[6] Have we simply learned to cover our compromise with the banner of "balance"?

Every one of us must ask: Do I want to be accepted by people or by the Lord? Whose approval do I seek? Whose favor do I desire? Or, to put it more bluntly, who do I really serve? That is the ultimate question.

For some leaders—let the truth be told!—the issue is not one of popularity or acceptance. Instead, the crux of the matter is money.

(Sometimes we are so reluctant to admit the obvious!) What happens if a few of the "big givers" leave? What happens if the budget goes down? What happens if staff members have to be dismissed because of lack of funds, or if the building drive temporarily stalls? To all those who struggle in this area I have one thing to say: If you deny Jesus and quench the Spirit for the sake of money, you are no better than Judas Iscariot who betrayed the Lord for 30 pieces of silver. Will you betray Him too? God forbid!

Instead, you must hold your ground for the sake of the truth and the glory of God. Don't cave in now! Souls are at stake and lives are on the line. Now is the time to take your stand—with meekness, with graciousness, and with gentleness, but without any taint of compromise at all. Hold your ground and steer your course. Don't be easily moved.

We must all determine not to compromise because of criticism and controversy or retreat because of ridicule and rejection, no matter what the cost. And we must make sure we know which Spirit/spirit we are following. Is it from above or below? Does it urge you to save your life or to lose it? Does it focus on what is best for you and yours, or does it concentrate on the reputation of Jesus and the good of His Kingdom? You must respond to the right voice and reject the wrong one. And you must always remember that a destructive critical spirit paralyzes, poisons, cripples, and crushes. Don't let it handicap you!

Just think: If Jesus had listened to His critics, He would not have healed anyone on the Sabbath—including the man with the withered hand, the man who had been crippled for 38 years, the woman who had been bent over for 18 years, and the man who had been born blind—all because His opponents said that it was in violation of Sabbath law to heal on that sacred day.[7] But they were wrong! Jesus—the Truth Himself—kept marching on, His face set like a flint, His heart unmoved. Thank God He didn't listen to His detractors!

If He had listened to them He never would have transformed men like Zaccheus or women like Mary Magdalene, since His opponents ridiculed Him for eating with tax collectors and sinners.

I'm glad He knew whose voice to listen to! And if He had heeded His critics, He would not have died for us on the cross, since He was mockingly challenged by the people and the leaders alike to come down from the cross, some speaking *to* Him and others speaking *about* Him (isn't this the norm too?): "...You who are going to destroy the temple and build it in three days, save yourself! Come down from the cross, if you are the Son of God!...He's the King of Israel! Let Him come down now from the cross, and we will believe in Him" (Matt. 27:40-42).[8] But He didn't get off that cross! He knew that His death was the only way to redemption and that resurrection was near. He knew that one day the tongues of those who cursed Him as a liar would have to confess Him as Lord of all.

We too must follow His pattern: Let those who oppose revival say what they will (remember, they are our brothers and sisters in the Lord, washed in the same blood and redeemed by the same Savior), and let them heap reproaches on us if they must. We dare not cower or draw back. Soon enough the reality and fruit of revival will be known to all, and those who discounted it will either be standing on the front lines with us, or else discounted themselves. The Lord will sort it all out!

And we can listen again to Spurgeon, a man who was no stranger to controversy throughout his entire ministry: "If you get fellowship with Christ, I care little for the merits of my sermon, or the perils of your criticism. One thing alone I crave, 'Let him kiss us with the kisses of his mouth'; then shall my soul be well content, and so will yours be also."[9]

Give yourself to the service of the Lord. If people are touched—whether they like you or not—rejoice. If they reject the word and ministry you bring, bless them and move on. As Jesus said with regard to the blind guides of His day, "Leave them alone" (see Matt. 15:14)!

Of course, as I have stated before (see Chapter Four, "Characteristics of a Critical Spirit"), the religious leaders who opposed Jesus were unbelieving unbelievers while the critics who oppose revival today are unbelieving believers. Still, the principle holds true: If they do not see the glorious, heavenly nature of the outpouring, let them be. There's just too much work to be done! If there is something constructive in their criticism, learn from it and move on. If not, don't even stop for minute. Just keep on running your race! As expressed in the famous words of the American statesman and poet, Ralph Waldo Emerson,

> Life is too short to waste
> In critic peep or cynic bark,
> Quarrel or reprimand:
> 'Twill soon be dark;
> Up! mind thine own aim,
> and God speed the mark!

Each of us must give account before God—individually and for our lives alone. And, since no one will stand beside us on that great day and no one's opinions about us will count in the least, we do well not to give them too much attention now. If rumors and innuendoes, opinions and accusations will be of no consequence then, why should we make them of any consequence now? Really, the most powerful criticism we face today will seem utterly puny when we face the Lord. "Is *that* what was holding me back, Lord?" May that future perspective help govern our present!

Of course, there are times when the critics must be addressed (Jesus certainly knew this well!), and this too is for the glory of God and the strengthening of the Body. When we refute the critics, we help those who have become discouraged because of destructive criticism, and we strengthen those who do not have the ammunition to reply to erroneous—but seemingly formidable—attacks. We provide clarity in the midst of controversy and direction in the midst of disorder. We magnify what the Lord is doing while so many others choose to minimize the work. And—this is something for which the critics must be thanked—responding to criticism helps revival leaders to sharpen their theological swords and fine tune their ministry tools, causing them to provide the "whys" and "wherefores" of what they do.[10]

It was in response to the critics that Jonathan Edwards wrote some of his classic works (most notably, *The Distinguishing Marks of a Work of the Spirit of God. Applied to that uncommon Operation*

*that has lately appeared on the Minds of many of the People of this
Land*, published in 1741; *Some Thoughts concerning the present
Revival of Religion in New-England, and the Way in which it ought
to be acknowledged and promoted*, published in 1742; and *A Treatise concerning Religious Affections*, published in 1746).[11] And it is
in response to the critics today that ministry leaders have once again
addressed subjects like the nature and purpose of revival, the theology of the last days, constructive correction versus destructive
criticism, the place of emotion in worship, and the question of
manifestations. For this, we can thank God for the critics!

But whatever we do, we must not get sidetracked. (And remember: Not everyone is called to address the critics, neither is it
the average believer's responsibility, nor even the average minister's responsibility, to respond to *everything* the critics say. In time,
the truth will make itself plain.) What would happen to an athlete
who focused on the hecklers instead of the finish line? He would be
miserably defeated, and the thing for which he trained so hard
would escape him, and for quite a foolish reason at that. How he
would wish he could run that race again. And what would happen to
a political candidate who spent all his time responding to his opponent's smear campaign instead of articulating his own agenda for
office? His opponent would win and he would lose, because he
failed to be true to his vision and goals. And what would happen *to
us* if we got our eyes on the critics and off the Christ, on the slander
being spread and off the souls being saved, on the junk and off the
genuine? The enemy would laugh in glee as God's soldiers started
shooting at each other just when his infernal troops were ready to be
routed. Fellow soldiers in this end-time battle, can't we move on?

To the critics I make this appeal: If you are so convinced that
the current revival is really a great deception, why not give yourself
unceasingly to prayer and fasting for the real visitation you claim is
still to come? Why not point out the things that you feel are wrong
in the present move of God and then go out and do His work the
right way? And why not spend your time seeking out the lost and
dying and going after the backslidden saints and the straying sheep?
Wouldn't the Lord be pleased with this?[12]

And to those of you who find yourselves in the thick of true revival in our day, I urge you to pursue the things the Lord has called you to pursue and to make sure you finish your race. If you have addressed the critics, move on! (For my part, I don't plan on writing three or four sequels to this book called *Let No One Deceive You II, III, IV,* and *V.* I don't plan on spending the rest of my life responding to those who differ with me. It was necessary for me to take the time to answer and refute the critics, and when needed, important issues will still be addressed. But we're in the midst of revival, and it is to this great visitation that we must devote ourselves!)

Friends, the needs of the hour are just too great for us to be distracted and, since the Lord has been gracious enough to send us rain in abundance, we must jealously utilize every drop. Otherwise the showers might cease! So let's roll up our sleeves and get to work. Have you anything better to do?[13]

Of course, no matter how hard we try, there will be no way to avoid controversy during times of visitation. Revival, by definition and nature, will always be too loud for the lukewarm and too heavy for the halfhearted. It will be too convicting for the complacent, too cutting for the comfortable, and too challenging for the compromised. And since revival means radical change, there will always be those who say, "Oh, for the good old days!" But the good old days weren't always so good! In fact, what some people really mean is, "Oh, for nonconfrontational sermons! Oh, for predictable, packaged services! Oh, to be able to slumber in serious sin and sleep in spiritual stupor! Oh, for the days when church was acceptable to the rebellious and acclaimed by the religious! Oh, for the days when the Holy Spirit didn't unexpectedly disrupt our orderly meetings and when God showed at least a little respect for our schedule. Oh, for the days when we talked about the Lord and sang about the Lord and even prayed to the Lord—but never had to encounter the Lord. Oh, for the good old days!"

Frankly, if you want the "good old days," you can have them. As for me, give me revival or I die. Yes, come, Lord—however, wherever, and whenever You want, regardless of the consequences. We can live without anything but You.

Isn't that your heart too?

And as we ask God to come and move according to His pleasure and will, let us not try to put Him into the little box of our own spiritual upbringing and background, acting as if anything that deviates from what we are used to is not from above. John Wesley once again gives us wise counsel and caution, reminding us that bigotry "is too strong an attachment to, or fondness for, one's own party, opinion, church and religion."[14] May none of us turn out to be spiritual bigots—be it for the cause of revival or in the name of criticism. Both are a stench in God's nostrils. *Both* divide and destroy. Instead, we must walk in broad-hearted love. We must pursue the Lord in a way that honors Him.

And we must never lose our sense of excitement in the Lord. Constant negative talk pollutes the very atmosphere, stealing joy and freedom, making us more oriented towards failure than faith, helping us to be more devil-conscious than God-conscious, and glorifying the power of the enemy while minimizing the power of the Lord. What an unbiblical mentality! This is not the mentality that will take the gospel to the nations. This is not the mindset that will experience revival. This is not the attitude of a Spirit-filled saint. So don't let the devil steal from you!

Oh yes, there will always be those who seem to have unlimited time and energy to devote to attacking God's latest move. Every little manifestation will disturb them and the slightest trace of something new will trouble them. And, of course, they will expect you to spend all *your* time explaining every shudder and shake.[15] But rather than get frustrated with them—or, far worse, embarrassed by them—ask yourself a question: *Is the Lord* disturbed by the emotional or physical responses of those He touches? If not, then why should you be so caught up with them? Maybe He does certain controversial things on purpose (that's right, *God Himself sometimes does controversial things on purpose*) in order to expose what is in people's hearts.

If you object to this concept, I suggest you carefully read the Gospels, where, for example, Jesus often went out of His way to heal people on the Sabbath, sometimes doing specific things designed to exasperate His opponents—thereby exposing what was really in their hearts—and prove that they were more interested in human traditions than in heavenly truth, in the praises of men more than the person of the Messiah. As Simeon said of the divine babe in the Temple courts, "This child is destined to cause the falling and rising of many in Israel, and to be a sign that will be spoken against, so that the thoughts of many hearts will be revealed" (Luke 2:34b-35a). Yes, it is as He is spoken against that the thoughts of many hearts are revealed, and many may fall before they rise. Revival will reveal the true condition of people's hearts, and the hidden things will come to light.[16]

Of course, we must fully understand that it is not our job to intentionally do controversial things so as to infuriate those who differ with us or to draw attention to unusual manifestations or the like. And, as much as it depends on us, we should exercise pastoral sensitivity towards those who have honest questions and concerns. But if the Lord chooses to come down and shake things up, if He decides to move in an unexpected way at an unexpected time, then it behooves us to quit making excuses for what God Himself is doing or apologizing for the Spirit's work in our midst. If people are offended they are offended. Revival fire always brings the impurities to the surface. It separates those who really want God to move any way He chooses from those who already have everything figured out, as well as carefully packaged and sealed. It's time to break the seals!

No doubt, revival will bring division no matter how careful and pastoral we try to be. In fact, looking back at the Great Awakening, Archibald Alexander observed:

> Revivals of religion were nowhere heard of, and an orthodox creed and a decent external conduct were the only points on which inquiry was made when persons were admitted to the communion of the church. The habit of preachers was to address their people as though they were all pious, and only needed instruction and confirmation....Under such a state of things, it is easy to conceive that in a short time vital piety may have almost deserted the church. And nothing is more certain, than that when people have sunk into this deplorable state, they will be

disposed to manifest strong opposition to faithful, pointed preaching; and will be apt to view every appearance of revival with an unfavourable eye. Accordingly, when God raised up preachers, animated with a burning zeal, who laboured faithfully to convince their hearers of their ruined condition, and of the necessity of a thorough conversion from sin, the opposition to them was violent. The gospel, among people in such a condition, is sure to produce strife and division between those who fall under its influence and those whose carnal minds urge them to oppose it.[17]

Let the strife come if it must. We must hold to our course!

Charles Finney, often called America's greatest evangelist, assured his hearers that trouble and opposition would arise in the wake of personal and corporate revival, stating clearly:

[If you have much of the Spirit of God] you will be called eccentric; and probably you will deserve it. Probably you will really be eccentric. I never knew a person who was filled with the Spirit that was not called eccentric. And the reason is that such people are unlike other folk. There is therefore the best of reasons why such persons should appear eccentric. They act under different influences, take different views, are moved by different motives, led by a different spirit. You are to expect such remarks. How often I have heard the remark respecting such-and-such persons: "He is a good man—but he is rather eccentric." I have sometimes asked for the particulars; in what does his eccentricity consist? I hear the catalogue, and it amounts to this, that he is spiritual. Make up your mind for this, to be "eccentric." There is such a thing as affected eccentricity. Horrible! But there is such a thing as being so deeply imbued with the Spirit of God that you must and will act so as to appear strange and eccentric, to those who cannot understand the reasons of your conduct.[18]

So walk with God and be faithful to His voice. Misunderstanding is nothing new for faithful servants of the Lord.

Of course, if you want to be an independent, unaccountable, unteachable, unreliable flake, there's nothing anyone can do to stop you. Just don't quote Finney for support! But if you are determined to walk closely with the Master no matter what people may think, be prepared for criticism. Be prepared to be hurt.

Finney continued:

> If you have much of the Spirit of God, it is not unlikely you will be thought deranged, by many. We judge men to be deranged when they act differently from what we think to be according to prudence and common sense, and when they come to conclusions for which we can see no good reasons. Paul was accused of being deranged by those who did not understand the views of things under which he acted. No doubt Festus thought the man was crazy, that "much learning had made him mad." But Paul said: "I am not mad, most noble Festus" (Acts 26:24, 25). His conduct was so strange, so novel, that Festus thought it must be insanity. But the truth simply was, he saw the subject so clearly that he threw his whole soul into it. Festus and the rest were entirely in the dark in respect to the motive by which he was actuated. This is by no means uncommon. Multitudes have appeared, to those who had no spirituality, as if they were deranged. Yet they saw good reasons for doing as they did. God was leading their minds to act in such a way that those who were not spiritual could not see the reasons. You must make up your mind to this, and so much the more, as you live the more above the world and walk with God.[19]

Have you ever wondered why the opponents of Jesus said He was demon-possessed? Why didn't they simply say that He was a false teacher or a deceived leader? Why didn't they claim He was using sleight of hand or trickery? Why did they have to speak of Him in such extreme terms? It was because what He was doing was *too* supernatural to be explained in natural, human terms. It was either from above or from below. There was no middle ground.

The same is true of revival. The results are too supernatural to be easily dismissed or superficially discounted. (Those who do try to attribute the fruit of the current revival to fleshly means like "socio-psychological manipulation" betray their ignorance of what is really happening throughout the world. There simply is no human explanation!)[20] And as it was with Jesus, so it will be with the outpouring of the Spirit: The visitation will either be welcomed as coming from above or warned against as coming from below, and as the revival intensifies and spreads, there will be no middle ground to take. Where will *you* stand?

Finney's warnings are strikingly prophetic:

If you have not the Spirit, you will be very apt to stumble at those who have. You will doubt the propriety of their conduct. If they seem to feel a good deal more than yourself, you will be likely to call it "animal feeling." You will perhaps doubt their sincerity when they say they have such feelings. You will say: "I don't know what to make of Brother Such-a-one; he seems to be very pious, but I do not understand him, I think he has a great deal of animal feeling." Thus you will be trying to censure them, for the purpose of justifying yourself.

(My critical friends, does this apply to you even in the least?)

[If you have not the Spirit,] you will be much troubled with fears about fanaticism. Whenever there are revivals, you will see in them "a strong tendency to fanaticism," and will be full of fears and anxiety.

Oh, how familiar this sounds. But there's more!

[If you have not the Spirit,] you will be much disturbed by the measures that are used in revivals. If any measures are adopted, that are decided and direct, you will think they are all "new," and will stumble at them just in proportion to your want of spirituality. You do not see their appropriateness. You will stand and cavil at the measures, because you are so blind that you cannot see their adaptedness, while all heaven is rejoicing in them as the means of saving souls.[21]

Doesn't it seem as if this was written for this very day? Then let us listen to Finney's words and follow His example! Like Wesley and Whitefield, Spurgeon and Edwards, Finney refused to stop. He preached and the fire fell. He fulfilled the call of God. And we too must fulfill His call. We must strike while the irons are hot and dive in while the waters are deep. We must seize this glorious hour of revival while it is here, and we must let no one seize our crown. The finish line is near!

The fact is, the critics who oppose us are not shedding our blood, nor are they calling us demon-possessed, at least for the most part.[22] (We haven't done enough to be worthy of such honors, be it in the eyes of the world or in the eyes of our fellow-believers.) And if our Master never flinched in the face of hellish resistance, who are we to recoil before the mild opposition we meet? If whips, fists, nails, and a cross didn't slow His gait, how dare we draw back because of a few wagging tongues, especially at harvest time.[23]

This is not the hour to shrink back, stagnate, or stall. This is the time to shift into high-gear. This is the time to sprint!

The critics challenged us to look inside and be honest with ourselves, to turn yet again to the Word, to question whether we were sure this was a real revival, whether we knew that our path was right and whether God indeed was the author of this move. We can answer without the slightest hesitation or fear: This is the revival we have prayed for! This is the day of visitation for our nation. We will march on and not be deterred. At last, the hour has come.

How long these days will last, no one knows, and how deep the work will go is yet to be determined. Of this much I am sure: No critic will stop me from giving my heart and mind and body and soul—to my very last ounce of strength and my very last breath—to fully participating in this holy, Heaven-sent day of God's power. I have waited and prayed and fasted and wept and labored for too many years to miss this opportunity now that it is here.

What about you?

Appendix

Counterfeit Criticism
A Review of
Hank Hanegraaff's
Counterfeit Revival[1]

Word Publishers, which has distinguished itself over the years through the publication of many important evangelical works, including the comprehensive *Word Biblical Commentary* series and popular books by authors such as Billy Graham, has disgraced itself with the publication of Hank Hanegraaff's *Counterfeit Revival*.[2] The result of three years of research by the author (this according to his own claims on his nationally syndicated "Bible Answer Man" show), *Counterfeit Revival* is actually an unscholarly, often inaccurate, highly judgmental, and at times, even slanderous work that barely touches on the subject of revival.

Moreover, because of the book's malicious and exaggerated tone, it is of little value in helping critique some of the failings and shortcomings of the recent renewal movements it attacks. This is an especially serious flaw, seeing that Hanegraaff's ministry has been of help to the Body in dealing with the cults as well as in pointing out some extremes in the Word of Faith movement. Thus, theoretically, he could have raised some important issues and concerns in terms of renewal-revival excesses and errors. Such a constructive study would have made for a welcome contribution to the growing body of renewal-revival literature and could have served as a fit challenge for those who tend to neglect the Word for the sake of experience. As one involved in revival-related ministry since 1982, I too have often addressed some of these issues and had hoped that *Counterfeit Revival* would have helped fine-tune and deepen the present move of the Spirit.

Instead, Hanegraaff has produced a volume that is almost completely destructive in tone and content, rejecting all of the current renewal movements in their entirety. And although I have little desire to defend many of the practices and teachings which are ridiculed in *Counterfeit Revival*,[3] and though I actually agree with much of Hanegraaff's scriptural exegesis, it is important that the serious flaws of his book be exposed, hence this review.

To Hanegraaff's credit, he has produced a highly readable volume, aided throughout by the use of alliterations and acronyms. Unfortunately, the acronym forming the general outline for the book is "FLESH" (!), standing for, "Fabrications, Fantasies and Frauds; Lying Signs and Wonders; Endtime Restorationism; Slain in the Spirit; and Hypnotism." Subsumed under the last heading is the acronym "APES," short for "The Altered State of Consciousness; The Psychology of Peer Pressure; The Exploitation of Expectations; The Subtle Power of Suggestion." There can be no doubt, therefore, as to Hanegraaff's views concerning current "renewal" movements: They are fleshly at best (and this ranges from willful lying and deception on the part of the leaders to hypnotism and ashram-like techniques) and demonic at worst (17: "these techniques are fertile soil for satanic and spiritual deception"; 193: "[John] Wimber would do better to attribute the manifestations in his sensational stories to Satan," with reference to 2 Thessalonians 2:9-10).

The fact is, Hanegraaff does not say one positive word about any of the leaders or movements he criticizes. Not one! Needless to say, this is absolutely astounding. Have John and Carol Arnott, Mike Bickle, Paul Cain, Wes and Stacey Campbell, Guy and Janis Chevreau, Randy Clark, Gerald Coates, Paul Crouch, Kenneth Copeland, William DeArteaga, Jack Deere, Jesse Duplantis, David du Plessis, Marc Dupont, Colin Dye, Claudio Freidzon, Kenneth

Hagin, Marilyn Hickey, Benny Hinn, Rodney Howard-Browne, Charles and Frances Hunter, Todd Hunter, Rick Joyner, Bill Ligon, Francis MacNutt, Bill McCartney, Larry Randolph, Richard and Kathryn Riss, Oral and Richard Roberts, James Ryle, Karl Strader, John White, and John and Carol Wimber done nothing good or praiseworthy for the Church? Readers drawing all their information from *Counterfeit Revival* might actually think that the answer is yes!

This entirely negative tone, however, is in keeping with Hanegraaff's outlook on virtually the entire contemporary Pentecostal movement: Its origins at Azusa Street in 1906 are scorned (rarely have Charles Parham and William Seymour been described in more disparaging terms; see 125-129);[4] the so-called healing revival of the 1940's and 1950's is completely dismissed by singling out the abuses of its more controversial leaders (131-139);[5] and the charismatic renewal is painted in quite negative terms (141-144). Indeed, even the phenomenon of being "slain in the Spirit" (to which considerable space is given; see 165-205) is thoroughly vilified: "While Counterfeit Revival leaders like Wimber attribute the slain in the spirit phenomenon to the Holy Ghost, in truth it is better attributed to Hindu gurus, hucksters, and hypnotists" (194). The "Counterfeit Revival," then, is simply the culmination of these misguided movements, manifestations, and messengers.[6] Strikingly, while Hanegraaff scorns Todd Hunter's statement that from "Azusa Street to today, the Pentecostals have been *the* largest, most dynamic force of Christians on the earth" (131), Pentecostals and charismatics today *are* the "largest, most dynamic force of Christians on the earth"— like it or not (see Chapter Thirteen of this book, "Is Good News Bad News for the Gloomers and Doomers? Exposing the Laodicean Lie").

According to Hanegraaff, "Christianity is undergoing a paradigm shift of major proportions—a shift from faith to feelings, from fact to fantasy, and from reason to esoteric revelation. This paradigm shift is what I call the Counterfeit Revival" (9). Indeed, it is nothing less than "a great apostasy," where "Sardonic laughter, spasmodic jerks, signs and wonders, super apostles and prophets, and people being 'slain in the Spirit' are pointed to as empirical evidence of the power and presence of the Holy Spirit" (9). And this apostasy is spreading at an alarming rate: "Some of the most recognizable names in the Christian community are endorsing this paradigm shift with little or no reservation....It is now estimated that seven thousand churches in England alone have embraced the Counterfeit Revival....As secular television cameras demonstrate to a watching world, the essence of our faith is being systematically subverted" (10). To Hanegraaff has fallen the task of being a voice of sanity in the midst of this terrible deception: "With sadness I have had to point out to [newscaster Peter] Jennings and others that what they are being told is 'great awakening' is, in reality, a great apostasy" (10-11).

What then are the consequences of this widespread falling away? "Many of the followers who at first flooded into Counterfeit Revival 'power centers' have become disillusioned and have now slipped through the cracks into the kingdom of the cults" (14). And what proof does Hanegraaff offer for this startling claim? Absolutely none.[7]

Tragically, these kinds of sweeping, serious, but unproved allegations pepper the entire book (as noted elsewhere in this review). Moreover, Hanegraaff makes it perfectly clear that the leaders of the "Counterfeit Revival" are not merely misled; they are willful deceivers and charlatans who perpetrate hoaxes and manufacture lies. Thus he writes, "Today's hypnotists not only operate in carnivals and communes, they also operate in churches. What was once relegated to the ashrams of cults is now replicated at the altars of churches. Whether they are referred to as Hindu gurus or Holy Ghost bartenders, the methods they employ have much in common. They all work subjects into altered states of consciousness, use peer pressure to conform them to predictable patterns, depend heavily on arousing people's expectations, and abuse the power of suggestion to make subjects willing to accept virtually anything that enters their minds" (17). Yes, "...leaders of the Counterfeit Revival enslave devotees through hypnotic schemes" (17).

To give two examples of many, Hanegraaff informs us that John Arnott told "his unsuspecting audience" of an alleged miraculous healing that took place during a service in the "Toronto Blessing," playing "fast and loose with the truth" and "wildly" embellishing the story (59-60; see below, for the facts concerning this healing). On another occasion, Arnott "tried to dupe devotees by denouncing the theology of Calvin while in the same breath affirming the theology of Jonathan Edwards," doing this because, although he himself knew that Edwards was a Calvinist, "he apparently banked on the fact that his followers did not" (81-82)! And, Hanegraaff hastens to add, Arnott "is not alone in this deception." The other duplicitous leaders of what Hanegraaff continually calls the Counterfeit Revival are experts in fraud and deceit. In fact, he can even speak of "the mythology of the Counterfeit Revival" (15). Thus all reports of unusual miracles and manifestations that have not been caught on camera or cannot be fully documented are assumed to be outright lies, exaggerations, or fantasies.[8]

Moreover, men like Paul Cain, Rick Joyner, and Bob Jones are flatly labeled "pretenders" and "false prophets," who according to Hanegraaff are aptly described in 2 Peter 2:18-19: "they mouth empty, boastful words and, by appealing to the lustful desires of sinful human nature, they entice people who are just escaping from those who live in error. They promise them freedom, while they themselves are slaves of depravity—for a man is a slave to whatever has mastered him." Indeed, not only do they fail the test of a true prophet according to Deuteronomy 18:19-21 (i.e., their words do not always come to pass), but they also fail the test of Deuteronomy 13:1-10—meaning that they are telling God's people to follow other gods! (See 160 for these specific charges; more broadly, see 155-62.) So, these men not only prophesy out of their own minds (cf. the similar accusation brought against James Ryle on 77-78), but they "are slaves of depravity" who seduce God's people into idolatry.

Again, I am neither a defender nor a spokesman for any of these men. However, severe accusations such as these, which at the very least border on libelous, should have been enough to stop a major Christian publisher such as Word from releasing this book, simply in the name of biblical ethics and truthful ministry. Unfortunately, there are even uglier remarks to be found within the covers of *Counterfeit Revival*. In fact, while Hanegraaff accuses Arnott of trying to dupe his unsuspecting listeners, one can only pity the unsuspecting reader of *Counterfeit Revival* who will be led to believe that numerous renewal leaders are predicting a *literal bloodbath* over revival issues. Hanegraaff writes: "Prophets of the Counterfeit Revival claim that the entire Christian community is going to be polarized by a bloody civil war. On one side will be those who embrace new revelations. On the other will be those who obstinately cling to reason....While leaders of the Counterfeit Revival predict a great battle in which those who stand against them will be eliminated, [Jonathan] Edwards warned against just such a 'holy war.' He made it clear that even in a cause as crucial as the Reformation, kindness rather than killing should be the order of the day....In place of excessive zealousness that predicts a bloodbath in which those who refuse to accept new revelations are eliminated, the life of Edwards personified the maxim 'In essentials unity; in nonessentials liberty; and in all things charity.' " (9, 95)[9] Yes, according to Hanegraaff's interpretation of these prophetic words, those who resist the revival will be slaughtered!

Of course, it is difficult to believe that even Hanegraaff thinks that the "prophets" he cites are advocating *killing* those who differ with them. But if he did, in fact, believe that they were teaching such things, how could he possibly put these charges in print without asking the leaders themselves exactly what they intended? After all, it is no light thing to make explicit declarations of a coming bloody "elimination" of those who "obstinately cling to reason." Yet there is no evidence that Hanegraaff requested clarification from any of these "civil war" leaders. (Lest someone say that he is only repeating actual quotes from these leaders, remember that: 1) he provides no full context of those quotes, thus allowing for no clarification of meaning; and 2) he explicitly interprets them in a *literal* manner.)

Not only is this inflammatory; it is highly irresponsible. But responsible scholarship does not seem to be the goal of *Counterfeit Revival*. If it were, then Hanegraaff would have interacted more fully with the serious, written works of men like John Wimber, Jack Deere, and Guy Chevreau, rather than simply lifting select quotes from their audiotapes or television interviews. Moreover, it is fair to ask whether Hanegraaff's goal was to make these men look foolish or to find out what they really believed. Unfortunately for the reader of *Counterfeit Revival*, Deere's two volumes on the power and voice of God, published by Zondervan, are not even mentioned in the bibliography, nor is the reader of *Counterfeit Revival* told that Deere formerly served as a professor of Old Testament and Hebrew at Dallas Theological Seminary.[10] And Hanegraaff fails to interact in depth with Chevreau's relevant books, also neglecting to mention that Chevreau holds a Th.D. from Wycliffe College, Toronto School of Theology, University of Toronto, in the field of historical theology. Instead, these leaders are presented in the worst possible light, and, as is paradigmatic of the book as a whole, the picture that emerges of the leaders and movements under attack is so caricatured as to be virtually unrecognizable.[11]

Thus it must be asked plainly: In a book (purportedly three years in the writing) in which extreme, damning claims are frequently made (e.g., 14: "the Counterfeit Revival is founded on fabrications, fantasies, and frauds"), is it too much to ask the author to at least treat those he attacks with fairness and honesty? If their sins are so grievous and their deceptive ways so egregious, presenting a full and fair picture of their beliefs and practices would hardly undermine the force of the book. Yet a lack of fairness, and even at times downright misrepresentation, is found throughout *Counterfeit Revival*. Three examples will illustrate this.

First, Hanegraaff explicitly claims that Arnott lied to his listeners about the miraculous healing of Sarah Lilliman, a miracle which Arnott said was "the best one so far." Refuting Arnott's claims, Hanegraaff states that "Sarah was *not* incapacitated, paralyzed, and blind" before the healing, "Jesus did *not* heal Lilliman," and "Arnott's associate (who allegedly documented the case)…confessed that he had not done any investigation." And so, "despite the broad circulation of this story by Arnott and his associates as evidence of God's power in the Toronto Blessing, *Sarah Lilliman is still, as before, legally blind.* Unfortunately, just as before, she and her family are continuing to struggle with her physical and psychosomatic disorders" (59-60)—statements for which Hanegraaff provides *no* documentation of any kind, not even a reference to a phone call to the family.

In contrast with this, Jon Ruthven, Associate Professor of Practical Theology at Regent University School of Divinity in Virginia Beach, Virginia, called Sarah's mother in April, 1997, and spoke with her at length and in meticulous detail concerning her daughter's healing. *She flatly denied Hanegraaff's version of the story and corroborated the basic version of John Arnott.*[12] In fact, when Ruthven read to Mrs. Lilliman Hanegraaff's statement that Sarah "is still, as before, legally blind," she replied by saying, "No, she certainly isn't legally blind."[13] In light of this, Hanegraaff's next words are nothing less than amazing: "As you read on, you will become painfully aware that this fabrication on the part of John Arnott is not unique. Fellow Counterfeit Revivalists pepper their appearances with fabrications, fantasies, and frauds, seemingly unaware of the disastrous consequences" (61). On what basis can such outrageous charges be made?

Second, Hanegraaff produces an extreme prosperity quote from the lips of Benny Hinn, noting that Hinn "had a profound impact on such Counterfeit Revival leaders as John Arnott" (106). Thus, by association, Arnott must also hold to such extreme teaching. Indeed, Hanegraaff alleges, for John Arnott, Rodney Howard-Browne, "and other proponents of the Counterfeit Revival," the promised land "is a utopia in which Christians will be 'the head and not the tail,' 'the lender, not the borrower' " (59). But statements like this are highly irresponsible and misleading, since John Arnott is hardly a prosperity teacher; the Benny Hinn quote comes from 1990, *before* Hinn renounced his extreme prosperity emphasis; whatever impact Hinn had on Arnott, it was not in the area of prosperity teaching; Howard-Browne and Arnott are hardly theological bedfellows; Howard-Browne's actual views on prosperity, in which he seeks to provide balance for some "Faith" extremes, are never cited.[14] Thus, Arnott is indicted for something to which he does not even hold, based on a quote of someone else who subsequently modified his position (even though Arnott was not even influenced by that position in the first place), and then grouped together with someone whose specific position he does not hold! How can such non-constructive criticism be taken seriously?

Third, David Ravenhill, a sober teacher of the Word and the son of the heralded revival author Leonard Ravenhill, is fashioned by Hanegraaff to be a "Vineyard prophet" (75),[15] despite the fact that Pastor Ravenhill has never once regarded himself a prophet, nor has he been called a prophet or looked to as a prophet in more than three decades of ministry prior to the publication of *Counterfeit Revival*. Rather, he has always been known as a teacher par excellence. So much for accuracy! Hanegraaff then quotes an audiotape of Ravenhill where the latter says, "I believe the test of a prophet is not whether his words comes to pass, it's his lifestyle. It's the character of the individual. That is how you test a prophet....It's not a matter of whether the word comes to pass or not, it's the nature of that person's life" (75). Unfortunately, Hanegraaff fails to inform his readers that a few minutes earlier, commenting on Deuteronomy 18 (vv. 18-22), Ravenhill had stated that the test of a prophet was whether his word came to pass (adding possible caveats to this based on the closing verses of the chapter), and that Ravenhill's words cited on 75 in Counterfeit Revival were spoken with reference to Deuteronomy 13:1-5, the case where a prophet spoke a word that *did* come to pass but then said, "Let's follow other gods"! Moreover, Hanegraaff ignores the fact that Jesus Himself told us that we would recognize false prophets by their fruit—not merely by their words. The bottom line is that the whole matter is far more complex than the Ravenhill quote would indicate, and the presentation of the material is hardly fair. Finally, since Hanegraaff chides other authors for not quoting their sources in full, thus giving a misleading impression (see 178-79), it would be expected that he would hold himself to that same standard. Clearly, he does not.[16]

Furthermore, if these three examples are in any way indicative of the faulty methodology of the book as a whole, then the reader of *Counterfeit Revival* has no way of knowing when a leader is being quoted out of context, when he or she is being grossly misrepresented, or when the facts themselves have been twisted. In other words, how can the reader know when the material is trustworthy and representative? Thus, when Hanegraaff states that William DeArteaga "denounces those who make essential Christian doctrine a prerequisite for unity" (96), it is difficult to determine what DeArteaga actually said and meant, since Hanegraaff bases his statement (and note that this is Hanegraaff's summary of DeArteaga's belief) on an audio teaching tape, and not on his book *Quenching the Spirit*.[17] Thus, unless the reader actually manages to purchase this particular tape and then spends the time listening to it until the alleged offensive section is found, he has no way of checking the accuracy of Hanegraaff's serious indictment. Again, we can only ask: If this is a core conviction of DeArteaga, why does he fail to stress the point in his book? And, are we really to understand that DeArteaga is willing to enter into unity with those who deny that Jesus is the Son of God or claim that He did not rise from the dead or advocate that there are many different ways to God? Yet, if Hanegraaff's portrait of DeArteaga is accurate, such would be the case.

As stated, however, the lack of serious scholarship is apparent in every section of the book, as is painfully evident in the following representative examples:[18]

1) On page 269, n. 66, Hanegraaff writes that: "The ruling sect of Jews in Jesus' day, the Pharisees were empty unprincipled religionists," a sweeping statement that is almost unthinkable in Christian scholarship at the end of the twentieth century.[19] To say that many Pharisees may have been hypocritical religionists is one thing. But to make such a blanket indictment smacks of the biased views of older Christian writings, not to mention a lack of recognition of the insensitivities prevalent in historic "Christian" anti-Semitism. (Of course, it should also be noted that the Pharisees were not the "ruling" sect of the Jews in Jesus' day. Governmental power was primarily in the hands of the Sadducees.)

2) In his denial of any differences between Old Testament and New Testament prophecy, Hanegraaff seems to be unaware of the large body of scholarly literature on the subject, citing only the *New Bible Dictionary* for support of his statement that, "An examination of the prophetic ministry in the New Testament demonstrates it

to be completely consistent with Old Testament prophecy in both character and construct" (264, n. 1).[20] In contrast with this, David E. Aune, one of the leading authorities on the subject of New Testament prophecy, finds substantial points of difference between Old Testament and early Christian prophets, while most New Testament scholars agree that there are some important distinctions to be made between those speaking prophetically before and after Pentecost, as well as before and after the close of the canon.[21] Thus, a highly nuanced, far-from-simple subject is treated in a flat and fleeting fashion, something which is all the more unfortunate in light of the fact that Hanegraaff frequently raises charges of false prophecy in *Counterfeit Revival* (as stated above).

3) In spite of his sweeping claims that many believers have been severely injured through the "Counterfeit Revival," either backsliding or falling into the cults, he offers only anecdotal "proof" consisting of a few negative testimonies that have come to his attention (see 61-64; 68-73), also failing to demonstrate that the leaders he attacks actually practice hypnosis and the like. Nonetheless, he somehow feels justified in making incredible claims: "While Kristy [a caller to his radio show] *almost* abandoned Christianity, multitudes [*sic*!] are, in fact, doing just that. Millions more [*sic*!] look on in amazement and dismiss Christianity as little more than a succession of hoaxes" (63)—and the sole proof he offers for this tremendously serious statement is one caller to his show![22] This is both completely unscientific and completely misleading, first, because leaders in the current renewal could produce scores of positive, God-glorifying testimonies for every one negative testimony supplied by Hanegraaff, and second, because scientific polling of participants in, e.g., the Toronto Blessing, produced results that were the exact opposite of the sweeping claims made by Hanegraaff.[23] Also, Patrick Dixon has provided evidence that it is simply not possible to write off various renewal manifestations and phenomena to "altered states of consciousness" and "hypnosis," observing how identical spiritual results are obtained in "meetings large, small and tiny, hyped up or low key, silent or noisy, strongly led or with an absence of clear direction, after worship or with no music at all." Therefore, "Brainwashing theories will not do. Nor

will theories that people are converted through a mass hysteria or hypnosis effect."[24]

Furthermore, those of us who have ministered in revival meetings night in and night out can supply numerous examples that defy the rationalistic explanations proffered by Hanegraaff in the last section of his book (209-42). How can he discount examples of people coming into their own homes after prayer was offered on their behalf—entirely without their knowledge—and becoming overcome with conviction (in an empty house!), leading to repentance and radical change? What is the socio-psychological explanation for conviction overtaking unbelievers in the bars, or when driving their cars past a church building that had been experiencing revival, again leading to conversion? And what hypnotic power is responsible for the instantaneous deliverance of long-term drug addicts, alcoholics, pornographers, and homosexuals in conjunction with their newfound faith in the Lord Jesus and their turning from sin by His grace? As suggested elsewhere in *Let No One Deceive You*, the critics have no answer for sound, biblical fruit, fruit which is the norm, not the exception, to the current revival.[25]

Of course, no one disputes the fact that there have been extremes in the current renewal movement, but there have also been extremes in the modern Pentecostal movement in general, and there have been extremes in the contemporary evangelical movement as a whole, all of which have resulted in some kind of casualties.[26] Moreover, it is no secret that some pastors have called Hanegraaff "the most divisive man in America," even blaming church splits on his broadcast.[27] Does this therefore prove, in and of itself, that Hanegraaff's "Bible Answer Man" radio broadcast is of no value (or that is he is the "Counterfeit Bible Answer Man")? Obviously, anecdotal evidence can be used both for and against any ministry or church in the spotlight, since every prominent minister will have his detractors and his friends. In any case, Hanegraaff fails to demonstrate that modern renewal leaders "ape" the practices of Hindu ashrams and devilish cults. In fact, since he has often claimed that "repetitive movements" can induce altered states of consciousness, it would seem that Orthodox Jews praying at the Wailing Wall (or anywhere else, for that matter, during their thrice-daily prayer times) work themselves into altered states of consciousness with their rapid, repeated bowing and swaying (which often goes on for hours at a time, especially during some all-day study sessions) and that Black gospel leaders must also cause their congregants to lose touch with reality, since their churches are famous for repetitive singing of the same choruses (often with intense rhythmic swaying and clapping).[28]

This, of course, is not to discount that people may, in some settings, get emotionally worked up or that there may, in fact, be some degree of raised expectations in certain meetings. But, again, Hanegraaff has failed to prove his case (simply stating one's case does not prove it!),[29] and, as Dixon writes, "I can accept...that the style of worship in some Vineyard meetings could slightly predispose some to a very mild hypnotic effect. The music is often gentle, almost soporific. But then so is Gregorian chanting in an ancient cathedral, or the chanting of a long metricated psalm."[30]

Also, one is tempted to ask if there is any intentional psychological manipulation on the part of Hanegraaff in his book. After all, the phrase "Counterfeit Revival" is practically a mantra throughout the chapters, sometimes occurring five times on a single page (e.g., 14). Is there nothing manipulative about this perpetual repeating of a carefully chosen, negative term? And can Hanegraaff's continual use (or, overuse) of alliterations subtly (and subconsciously) drill into the minds of the hearers the very thoughts he wants them to retain?[31] Finally, does Hanegraaff prey on the fears of his readers by presenting extreme (and often out of context) examples coupled with warnings of cult-like techniques, seductive deceptions, and satanic traps? Doesn't this hinder, rather than help, the reader's ability to think clearly and rationally?[32]

4) Hanegraaff's section on true revival (forming the acronym "WOW"—"Worship, Oneness, Witness") is so sketchy that it is not even skeletal. And, in keeping with *Counterfeit Revival* as a whole, it fails to interact with the vast body of popular and scholarly literature on the subject of revival. So, not only does Hanegraaff fail to adequately define true revival and delineate a full picture of its main characteristics, he fails to point the interested reader to

any important revival literature. Thus, there is not even a mention of the numerous scholarly writings on revival by James Edwin Orr, or the compendious works of Richard Owen Roberts now published through his International Awakening Press (including a bibliographical volume listing 50,000 revival titles!), or modern classics such as *In the Day of Thy Power* by Arthur Wallis, or key historical works documenting any of the great revivals of the past (works which are far too numerous to even begin to list), or modern digests of revivals through the centuries (just a fraction of which are pointed to, e.g., in Wesley Deuwel's exciting recent volume, *Revival Fire* [Grand Rapids: Zondervan, 1995] or in Brian H. Edwards' important work *Revival: A People Saturated with God* [Durham, England: Evangelical Press, 1990]),[33] or seminal studies such as Richard Lovelace's *Dynamics of Spirit Life*[34] or recent constructive and cautious works like B.J. Oropeza's *Time to Laugh*.[35] So, the reader of *Counterfeit Revival* comes away with a grossly exaggerated picture of what is wrong with current "renewal" movements and little vision of what real revival should look like.[36] Moreover, there is no indication that Hanegraaff has surveyed firsthand any of the significant spiritual movements in the Church in countries like China and Africa today. This too would have caused him to enlarge his paradigm.

5) Finally, and most significantly, Hanegraaff makes the striking claim that, "The most disturbing deception of all is that the leaders of the Counterfeit Revival have co-opted one of the church's true spiritual giants [viz., Jonathan Edwards] and dishonestly claimed him for their own" (82). Yes, the Counterfeit Revival leaders are not just guilty of "visionary hoaxes"; they have even stooped to "revisionary history" as well (81).[37] This is a serious charge, and once again, according to Hanegraaff, it is willful deceit, not a matter of honest scholarly differences or unintentional misuse of sources: "In teachings, transcripts, tapes, and television appearances, men like...Guy Chevreau (*Catch the Fire*)...Patrick Dixon (*Signs of Revival*), and a host of other Counterfeit Revival proponents are actively deceiving devotees by revising history. [I single out Chevreau and Dixon because both men are scholars.] Their primary ploy is to persuade people that sardonic laughter, spasmodic jerks, slaying in

the spirit, and other 'enthusiams' were not only pervasive in the First Great Awakening but were also promoted by such historical heavyweights as Jonathan Edwards..." (81). Unfortunately, Hanegraaff is himself guilty of misrepresenting Edwards in *Counterfeit Revival* (see immediately below), and he is hardly qualified to make such a sweeping academic indictment, since, as is commonly known, he does not even possess a college degree whereas some of the men whom he brands revisionists are quite competent in their fields.

As mentioned above, Guy Chevreau holds a Th.D. in Historical Theology (his doctoral thesis, for those who might care to know, was on "John Calvin's Explication of Private Prayer"), and in a recent review of his book, *Catch the Fire*, revival historian Iain Murray commended Chevreau for his lengthy treatment of Edwards' writings. Though Murray felt that Chevreau's emphasis on physical phenomenon throughout the book was not "consistent with what he rightly quotes from Edwards," he had this to say about Chevreau's 70-page discussion of Edwards' material itself:

> It must be said that the long treatment of the thought of Jonathan Edwards is, in our judgment, well and fairly done. No one could read that chapter without profit. It is clear also that the author, who writes with an appealing sincerity, has absorbed some of Edward's main emphases and in particular the point that physical actions can never of themselves provide any proof of the power of the Holy Spirit: it is inward transformation, resulting in a closer communion with Christ and a greater knowledge of God, which alone has validity.[39]

This, of course, is Hanegraaff's contention, viz., that Edwards has been misapplied. Murray, however, recognizes the soundness of Chevreau's treatment of Edwards but simply feels that the space given by Chevreau in his book to physical manifestations was not in keeping with Edwards' emphasis.[40] This is light years away from any charge of historical revisionism! Moreover, it is somewhat ironic that Patrick Dixon is also labeled revisionist, since he himself has written books exposing modern fallacies and cover-ups regarding AIDS. More to the point, in *Signs of Revival*, he primarily cites the key sources at length with little comment (see, e.g., 126-30; and note that throughout his study, he cites opposing positions as well), also noting that, because of the charismatic renewal in recent decades, "the context for revival today is entirely different from the church situation, say, in the time of Edwards in the US, or Wesley in Britain." Thus, Dixon recognizes that the *starting point* for any comparison between mid-eighteenth century Church life and late-twentieth century Church life is somewhat different.[41] Although religious historians and biblical scholars will certainly differ at points with Dixon, he is far too sharp to be guilty of historical revisionism. Yet Hanegraaff is all too quick to hurl this charge around.

Now, lest I be misunderstood, one does not need a college or graduate degree in order to understand the Word, teach the Word, or be a great blessing to the Body of Christ. Nor does lack of formal education mean that a person has not been soundly mentored and instructed in the ways of the Lord. However, when someone who has no scholarly credentials in a given field raises charges of historical revisionism, exception must be taken.[42] And, in perhaps the most startling chapter in *Counterfeit Revival*, it is Hanegraaff who grossly misapplies Edwards (I speak here of Chapter 8, "A Great Apostasy," 81-101).

However, before discussing the misuse of Edwards in *Counterfeit Revival*, I should note several points of agreement with Hanegraaff here: I agree that there has been a failure in much of the recent renewal to keep the Word of God central, and with this Edwards certainly would find fault; I agree that the preaching in the Great Awakening was often far more sober and searching than has been the norm in many recent renewal meetings; and I agree that most of the unusual manifestations dealt with by Edwards came in response to the Word or an encounter with Jesus, as opposed to coming in response to prayer ministry (although I believe that *many* do have such an encounter through prayer ministry).[43]

What then are the problems with Hanegraaff's treatment? First, he attributes the decline of the Great Awakening in its entirety to outward manifestations and emotional excesses (quoting Iain Murray in apparent support; see 115-16), writing that, "Lying signs and wonders had felled the first great revival, but revivalism had only just begun." In point of fact, when Murray spoke of the "wildfire" and "carnal enthusiasm" that dampened the awakening, he was not simply speaking of people crying out or falling into trances. It was far more complex than that. Rather, there were several sides to the problem. On the one hand, there was the "wildfire" of a man like James Davenport, who stirred his followers to burn other Christian books (as correctly noted by Hanegraaff on 116) and, at times, even their own clothes. Such fanaticism was also made more difficult to check because of the itinerant (and somewhat unaccountable) lay preachers who moved in and out of other leaders' "territory." Related to this was the judgmentalism that arose in the hearts of some of those who had been revived, as if they were able to accurately discern those who were truly born again (along with those who were not!). Then, on the other side of the coin, there were the negative and highly divisive effects of the *critics* of revival, causing some leaders to retreat from the front lines. These then, were the principle factors contributing to the end of the Great Awakening; physical manifestations (oddly termed "lying wonders" by Hanegraaff) were *not* the primary cause.[44]

And this leads to Hanegraaff's more grave error, viz., the misuse of Edwards' material to suit his own purposes. Hanegraaff writes, "Nowhere is there a more compelling contrast between counterfeit and genuine revival than in Edwards's manuscript titled *The Distinguishing Marks of a Work of the Spirit of God*," where, according to Hanegraaff, "Edwards draws a clear line of demarcation between Great Awakening and great apostasy" (83). But that is not what *The Distinguishing Marks* is about! Rather, as Oropeza notes,

> In defense of the revival, Edwards wrote *The Distinguishing Marks of a Work of the Spirit of God* (1741) in which he gives a list of signs which are *not* evidence that a work is *not* from the Holy Spirit. He elaborates that is a work (1) is unusual, (2) is attended by bodily effects such as groanings, tremblings, and outcries, (3) occasions attention and talk about religion, (4) constitutes great impressions on the mind, (5) incorporates various means, such as good examples, for its success, (6) has imprudences or irregular conduct, (7) is intermingled with delusions

from Satan, (8) has someone who falls into errors, or (9) earnestly promotes judgment from God's law [i.e., earnestly preaches judgment], none of these signs indicates that a work is *not* from God.[45]

Amazingly, Hanegraaff correctly states that Edwards "identifies nine characteristics that critics seize upon to negate the Great Awakening as a genuine work of the Spirit" (83) and then proceeds to use these nine signs for the exact opposite purpose, viz., to prove that the current renewal is *not* a genuine work of the Spirit! This is just what the critics of the Awakening did, and it was their criticisms that Edwards was seeking to refute. In fact, in *Counterfeit Revival*, Hanegraaff seizes on almost every sign that Edwards said did *not* invalidate the work (note, e.g., signs 6-8, immediately above) in order *to* invalidate the work! And, in what could be the strangest thing of all, rather than actually quoting what Edwards said about these nine signs, he quotes from elsewhere in Edwards' writings. This is utterly misleading to the uninformed, not to mention inexplicable. Why call Edwards to the witness stand to explain his nine points and then not allow him to speak his peace about these points?

To give one clear example (out of nine), Edwards' second sign that does *not* disqualify a work from being genuine is: "A work is not to be judged of by any effects on the bodies of men; such as tears, trembling, groans, loud outcries, agonies of body, or the failing of bodily strength." He continues (and I simply excerpt representative samples):

> The influence persons are under is not to be judged of one way or other by such effects on the body; and the reason is because the Scripture nowhere gives us any such rule. We cannot conclude that persons are under the influence of the true Spirit because we see such effects upon their bodies, because this is not given as a mark of the true Spirit; nor on the other hand, have we any reason to conclude from any such outward appearances, that persons are not under the influence of the Spirit of God, because there is no rule of Scripture given us to judge of spirits by, that does either expressly or indirectly exclude such effects on the body, nor does reason exclude them....

Some object against such extraordinary appearances that we have no instances of them recorded in the New Testament, under the extraordinary effusions of the Spirit. Were this allowed, I can see no force in the objection, if neither reason nor any rule of Scripture exclude such things.... I do not know that we have any express mention in the New Testament of any person's weeping, or groaning, or sighing through fear of hell, or a sense of God's anger; but is there any body so foolish as from hence to argue that in whomsoever these things appear, their convictions are not from the Spirit of God?

...Why then should it be thought strange that persons should cry out for fear, when God appears to them, as a terrible enemy, and they see themselves in great danger of being swallowed up in the bottomless gulf of eternal misery? The spouse, once and again, speaks of herself as overpowered with the love of Christ, so as to weaken her body, and make her faint. Cant. ii. 5, "Stay me with flagons, comfort me with apples; for I am sick of love."...From whence we may at least argue that such an effect may well be supposed to arise from such a cause in the saints, in some cases, and that such effect will sometimes be seen in the church of Christ.

It is a weak objection, that the impressions of enthusiasts [fanatics] have a great effect on their bodies. That the Quakers used to tremble is no argument that Saul, afterwards Paul, and the jailer did not tremble from real convictions of conscience. [Did you catch that? Edwards is saying that just because there are abuses and imitations, that does not invalidate the genuine!] Indeed all such objections from effects on the body, let them be greater or less, seem to be exceeding frivolous; they who argue thence, proceed in the dark, they know what ground they go upon, nor by what rule they judge. The root and course of things is to be looked at, and the nature of the operations and affections are to be inquired into, and examined by the rule of God's word, and not the motions of the blood and animal spirits.[46]

Edwards has made his point with unmistakable clarity. Yet Hanegraaff neither summarizes Edwards here nor even selectively quotes from his relevant remarks (obviously, this would *not* have helped *Counterfeit Revival*'s case). Instead, after appropriately entitling this second sign "Effects on the Body," Hanegraaff uses a different Edwards quote dealing with the bodily weakness that could arise from the contemplation of hell (so far so good), but then contrasts this with a Rodney Howard-Browne meeting in which people began to laugh as he preached on hell. What in the world does this have to do with Edwards' second sign? Once again (and this must be underscored), this is a complete misuse of Edwards.

It is one thing to say that Edwards (like most of us) would have been perturbed by uproarious laughter during a sermon on the terrors of hell (although Howard-Browne states that many came forward at the end of his message in deep repentance); it is another thing to quote his second sign in the first part of *Distinguishing Marks* in this context. His whole point was that unusual physical and emotional responses were completely logical and, in and of themselves, no indication that the Spirit was not at work. Yet Hanegraaff uses the material to critique what he believes are emotional excesses!

To further illustrate just how much Hanegraaff has missed Edwards' point here, the great theologian wrote elsewhere (and this amplifies the previous lengthy quote):

> Many are guilty of not taking the holy scriptures as a sufficient and whole rule, whereby to judge of this work; whether it be the work of God, in that they judge by those things which the scripture does not give as any signs or marks whereby to judge one way or the other, and therefore do in no wise belong to the scripture rule of judging, viz. The effects that religious exercises and affections of mind have upon the body. Scripture rules respect the state of the mind, and persons' moral conduct, and voluntary behaviour, and not the physical state of the body. The design of the Scripture is to teach us divinity, and not physic and anatomy. Ministers are made the watchmen of men's souls, and not of their bodies; and therefore the great rule which God has committed into their hands, is to make them divines, and not physicians. Christ knew what instructions and rules his church would stand in need of, better than we do; and if he had seen it needful in order to the church's safety, he doubtless would have given ministers rules to judge of bodily effects, and would have told them how the pulse should beat under such and such religious exercises of mind; when men should look pale, and when they should shed tears; when they should tremble, and whether or no

they should ever be faint or cry out; or whether or no they should ever be put into convulsions. He probably would have put some book into their hands, that should have tended to make them excellent anatomists and physicians; but he has not done it, because he did not see it to be needful. He judged, that if ministers thoroughly did their duty as watchmen, and overseers of the state and frame of men's souls, and of their voluntary conduct, according to the rules he had given, his church would be well provided for, as to its safety in these matters.[47]

Simply stated, the very things on which Hanegraaff majors (outward manifestations, unusual physical phenomena, etc.) to negate the current renewal are the things that Edwards says can not be used to disprove the work. To repeat: *Edwards says that the Bible does not give us the right to make judgments based on these things.*[48] Rather, as he notes in the second part of his *Distinguishing Marks* (as summarized again by Oropeza):

> The things that *do* mark a work as being of the Spirit are that (1) it confirms the message of Christ and the gospel, (2) it operates against the kingdom of Satan by turning men away from sin, (3) it prompts a greater regard for Scripture, (4) it leads to truth instead of falsehood, and (5) it leads to a spirit of love.[49]

And these are the very points made by current renewal and revival leaders, the so-called historical revisionists! A work can *not* be judged, we emphasize, either positively or negatively based on unusual outward phenomena, nor can it be disqualified by excesses and delusions that may arise. Edwards fully realized that every work has a mixture, and that, in fact, there will always be some kind of impurities or irregularities seeing that the work of the Spirit comes through frail human beings. Moreover, the devil will always try to get his hand in the work, especially when there is a pronounced emphasis on emotion and experience (and, as Oropeza points out, there were some powerful spiritual experience during the Great Awakening, with some people even going into trances and lying motionless for 24 hours at a time!). Nonetheless, Edwards was firmly convinced that God was moving mightily. The fruit was undeniable.[50] *It is to similar fruit that revival leaders point today*, and the verdict again is undeniable: God is mightily at work! (See further Chapter Seven, "Did Satan Get Saved?")

It is also important to remember that, in spite of excesses and abuses,[51] Edwards never reversed the position he took in *Distinguishing Marks* (although the reader of *Counterfeit Revival* might actually think that Edwards later completely distanced himself from any physical or emotional responses in conjunction with the Word and the Spirit). In fact, in his most enduring and mature work relative to the subject of genuine Christian experience, *The Religious Affections* (1746):

> ...he once again confirms that in a move of God there can be a mysterious mixture of good and bad, true and counterfeit, just as the saving grace of God works within the corrupted, hypocritical heart of the saint. Satan sows tares among the wheat by mingling false affections—such as false joy, comfort, or fear—with the work of the Holy Spirit, intending to delude souls and discredit the work of God....

> Truly gracious affections (1) are confirmed by the witness of the Spirit in our spirit, (2) are concerned with divine things not self-interest, (3) are founded on moral excellency, (4) arise from an enlightened mind to understand divine things, (5) have a strong conviction for divine things, (6) are accompanied with humiliation, (7) involve true conversion, (8) follow the characteristics of Christ, (9) make one sensitive to the Lord, (10) are symmetrical and proportional, exercising a well balanced instead of an impulsive or frivolous range of emotions, (11) lead one to a stronger desire for divine things, and (12) produce fruit in Christian practice.[52]

Again, the tree is known by its fruit.

Finally, it should be noted that Hanegraaff exaggerates the differences between awakenings in the mid-eighteenth and early nineteenth centuries, claiming that, "In the First Great Awakening excesses had been the byproduct of revival; in the Second they would be the bottom line" (116).[53] In fact, one prominent Edwards' scholar to whom I read this quote (in full context) responded with one word: "Ridiculous!"[54] Actually, while there were many abuses, excesses, and even (ultimately) some heresies in the so-called frontier revivals (Cane Ridge, etc.), there was also much positive fruit that came out of them, and the Word was not as peripheral as Hanegraaff suggests (*Counterfeit Revival*, 117-21).[55] More importantly, the Second Great Awakening (ca. 1795-1830) encompassed far more than frontier revivals, and in Northeast America, the Awakening was far more tame, accompanied by tens of thousands of conversions. For example, Methodists in America grew from 15,000 in 1785 to 850,000 in 1840, many of them in the Northeast.[56]

It is also my observation as one who has been on the front lines of revival-related ministry for the past 15 years that the current outpouring is moving more and more *away* from the peripheral and *towards* the central—i.e., away from an emphasis on outward manifestations and towards an emphasis on holiness and conversion. Although I expect that God's "shaking" will intensify (in other words, we haven't seen anything yet!), I also believe that we have moved from refreshing to renewal to revival, and that the work is maturing and deepening.

Sadly, just when leaders could use all the constructive, godly, spiritual input they could get, Hanegraaff has delivered a dangerous and destructive volume that virtually disqualifies itself from any usefulness since he paints with such a broad stroke that the line between helpful correction and harmful criticism is blurred by personal attacks, harsh judgments, and exaggerated examples. Thus, while claiming to follow in the footsteps of Jonathan Edwards, he has instead distinguished himself as the Charles Chauncy of this generation, the arch-critic of revival and the staunch opponent of Edwards.[57] Of course, I am in no way claiming that the unusual phenomena and teachings ridiculed throughout *Counterfeit Revival* are good examples of true "revival."[58] Nonetheless, I am sure that the Spirit *has* been moving for some years in worldwide renewal (and now, at last, in North America, in *revival*),[59] and that the Body of Christ would have been much better served by a mature word of correction and direction than by a "take no prisoners" volume such as *Counterfeit Revival*.

And now for a bit of history. On April 20, 1653, Oliver Cromwell dismissed the Rump Parliament with words that became famous in England, especially when they were repeated on May 7, 1940.

It was then that L.S. Amery shouted these words at Neville Chamberlain from the back benches of the House of Commons, after which Chamberlain left in disgrace and Winston Churchill soon came into power.[60] Cromwell said (and Amery repeated): "You have sat here too long for any good you have been doing. Depart, I say, and let us have done with you. In the name of God, go!"

Tragically, these words may find application yet again. On the one hand, I have little doubt but that Word Publishers will soon be in the forefront of producing useful books relative to the great, worldwide revival that is spreading and deepening by the hour. And as they publish solid, edifying, and challenging revival literature, the ugly blemish of *Counterfeit Revival* will be forgotten. On the other hand, the "jury" is still out on Hank Hanegraaff. If his main focus continues to be the dissemination of destructive and divisive material such as *Counterfeit Revival*, then he will have outlived his usefulness. This, of course, would be a terrible shame, since, as stated at the outset of this review article, the Lord has used Hank and the Christian Research Institute to do much good in many lives. Thus it is my earnest prayer and hope that he would have a change of heart and recognize the error of his ways. It is true that much of what he dismisses in *Counterfeit Revival* barely resembles revival. But by focusing on the negative and the extreme he has completely missed what God *is* doing in the world today.

In conclusion, therefore, it may be safely said that it is Hanegraaff's criticism that is counterfeit. The revival is real.[61]

Endnotes

Chapter One

1. Dr. Eddie Cheong, *Deceiving the Elect: A Scriptural and Critical Analysis of the Laughter Movement* (Malacca, West Malaysia: Sanctuary Productions, 1995), 4. The author, who is a "medical specialist by profession," has promoted his book on the Internet.

2. Ibid.

3. Ibid., 5.

4. Andrew Strom, "Brownsville, Pensacola: 'Toronto' or Not?", from his New Zealand Revival Bulletin Website. My refutation of this article, "Corrections to Andrew Strom's 'Brownsville, Pensacola: "Toronto" or Not?' " is available via the Destiny Image Website, www.reapernet.com.

5. Andrew Strom, "Brownsville, Pensacola: No. 2," from his New Zealand Revival Bulletin Website; cf. my refutation of this article, "Corrections to Andrew Strom's 'Brownsville, Pensacola, No. 2,' " also available via the Destiny Image Website.

6. Commenting on this verse, Gordon D. Fee notes that, "Those who persist in pursuing *sophia* [the wisdom of this age], who are destroying, not building, the church, are self-deceived—and a fearful judgment threatens them" (*The First Epistle to the Corinthians* [New International Commentary on the New Testament; Grand Rapids: Eerdmans, 1987], 151-52).

7. Strom, "Brownsville, Pensacola: No. 2."

8. Although I would in no way make such a blanket accusation of all critics of revival, Crist's (tongue in cheek?) words are strikingly applicable to a number of revival critics. For the quote itself, cf. *The Merriam Webster Dictionary of Quotations* (from the "Infopedia" CD-ROM, Cambridge, MA: SoftKey), sub "Criticism and Critics."

9. William R. Moody, *The Life of Dwight L. Moody* (from the Sage Digital Library CD-ROM, Albany, OR: Sage Software), 198.

10. John Wesley, *Journal*, July 17, 1739.

11. Wesley, *Journal*, August 27, 1739; for "Roman Catholic," the original text had "Papist."

12. Ibid.

13. The quote is from Jean Sibelius, as cited in the *Merriam Webster Dictionary of Quotations* (from the "Infopedia" CD-ROM), sub "Criticism and Critics."

Chapter Two

1. For discussion and literature, see Robert A. Guelich, *Mark 1–8:26* (Word Biblical Commentary; Dallas: Word, 1989), 166-86; E. Lövestam, *Spiritus Blasphemia: Eine Studia zu Mk 3,28f // Mt 12,31f // Lk 12,10* (Lund: Gleerup, 1968); M. Eugene Boring, "The Unforgivable Sin Logion Mark III 28-29/ Matt XII 31-31/ Luke XII 10," *Novum Testamentum* 18 (1976), 258-79; G.H. Twelftree, "Blasphemy," in Joel B. Green and Scot McKnight, eds., *Dictionary of Jesus and the Gospels* (Downers Grove, IL: InterVarsity, 1992), 75-76; Donald A. Hagner, *Matthew 1–13* (Word Biblical Commentary; Dallas: Word, 1993), 345-48. Hagner notes (348): "The only unforgivable sin is that of deliberately denying God in a fundamental way, one which goes against plain and obvious evidence. Such hard-heartedness is the result of one's own deliberate insensitivity and cuts one off from forgiveness. However, any person who is genuinely worried about having committed the unforgivable sin against God, by virtue of this conscience, can hardly be guilty of such blasphemy or denial."

2. Cf., e.g., Robert Glen Gromacki, *The Modern Tongues Movement* (2nd ed., Nutley, NJ: Presbyterian and Reformed, 1972), for an example of a recent Christian author who rejects modern tongues as either fleshly or demonic.

3. See especially Chapter Five, "Let No One Deceive You"; Chapter Six, "Was Jesus a False Prophet?"; Chapter Eight, "Does the Devil Have a Monopoly on Miracles?"; Chapter Nine, "Are We Living in the Last Days?"; Chapter Thirteen, "Is Good News Bad News for the Gloomer and Doomers? Exposing the Laodicean Lie."

4. I myself have sought to do this in several books; cf. in particular *Whatever Happened to the Power of God: Is the Charismatic Church Slain in the Spirit or Down for the Count?* (Shippensburg, PA: Destiny Image, 1991); *From Holy Laughter to Holy Fire: America on the Edge of Revival* (Shippensburg, PA: Destiny Image, 1996). See also Art Katz, "Some Cautionary Thoughts on the Present Revival" (privately distributed), for a good example of a widely circulated article by an author who had genuine concerns with recent renewal movements but has fully embraced the current, repentance-based revival.

5. Commenting on this passage, Jacob Milgrom, *Numbers* (The JPS Torah Commentary Series; Philadelphia/New York: Jewish Publication Society, 1990), 94, makes the interesting observation that what Aaron and Miriam "were really after was a share in Moses' leadership." With reference to Numbers 12:8b (rendered in the New Jewish Version with, "How then did you not shrink from speaking against My servant Moses!"), Milgrom notes that this closing comment, "Containing sixteen syllables...balances perfectly the sixteen syllables of the opening two lines in verse 6. God's speech ends using the same vocabulary (*dibber be* [speak against] as Miriam and Aaron did in their charge (v. 2) but with boomerang effect: God speaks to Moses (2) but Miriam and Aaron speak against Moses (8, cf. v. 1)."

6. This night was especially significant to me as a father because my 18-year-old daughter Megan was deeply touched by the Lord, surrendering fully to Him with many tears as we wept and prayed arm in arm.

7. Cf. the reference to Oliver Cromwell's famous quote at the end of the Appendix, and consider this strongly worded warning from Jonathan Edwards written to the critics of the Great Awakening: "If there be any who still resolutely go on to speak contemptibly of these things, I would beg of them to take heed that they may not be guilty of the unpardonable sin. [Note here that Edwards takes his warning even farther than I have in this chapter.] When the Holy Spirit is much poured out, and men's lusts, lukewarmness, and hypocrisy are reproached by its powerful operations, then is the most likely time of any for this sin to be committed. If the work goes on, it is well if among the many that show an enmity against it some be not guilty of this sin, if none have been already. Those who maliciously oppose and reproach this work, and call it the work of the devil, want but one thing of the unpardonable sin, and that is, doing it against inward conviction. And though some are so prudent as not openly to oppose and reproach this work, yet it is to be feared—at this day when the Lord is going forth so gloriously against his enemies—that many who are silent and inactive, especially ministers, will bring that curse of the angel of the Lord upon themselves, Judg. v. 23: 'Curse ye Meroz, said the angel of the Lord, curse ye bitterly the inhabitants thereof: because they came not to the help of the Lord, to the help of the Lord against the mighty.' " See *Jonathan Edwards on Revival* (Carlisle, PA: Banner of Truth, 1984), 135, from his work *The Distinguishing Marks of a Work of the Spirit of God.*

8. When Edwards was questioned in 1741 regarding some unusual phenomena taking place during the Great Awakening, he replied that, although there may have been some fleshly mixtures and excesses mingled with the genuine, "Yet as to the work in general, and the main of what is to be observed in these extraordinary things, they have all the clear and incontestable evidences of a true divine work," adding significantly, *"If this ben't [be not] the work of God, I have all my religion to learn over again, and know not what use to make of the Bible,"* cited in Iain H. Murray, *Jonathan Edwards: A New Biography* (Carlisle, PA: Banner of Truth, 1987), 217-18, my emphasis.

9. Although it is true that we, on our part, should have mercy on those who oppose God's work out of ignorance or unbelief (cf. Henry Alford, *The Greek Testament* [rev. ed., Chicago: Moody, 1968], 3:308, to 1 Timothy 1:13), it is equally true that those who oppose God's work in the name of God must see if they, like Saul/Paul, are "kicking against the goads" (Acts 26:14). Is the Lord Himself resisting them? Note that this application here of Acts 26:14 is closer to the traditional understanding of the passage, as reflected by the well-known interpretations of Augustine and Luther, than to the reading of F.F. Bruce, *Acts* (New International Commentary on the New Testament; rev. ed., Grand Rapids: Eerdmans, 1988), 466: "The 'goads' against which he was now told it was fruitless for him to kick were not the prickings of a disturbed conscience but the new forces which were now impelling him in the opposite direction to that which he had hitherto pursued, the new 'necessity' which was henceforth laid upon him (1 Cor. 9:16)."

Chapter Three

1. Debra Bouey, "Accusers of the Brethren or Good Bereans?" circulated via the Internet. Relevant here are the cautions and warnings of the nineteenth century leader William Sprague, cited in B.J. Oropeza, *A Time to Laugh* (Peabody, MA: Hendrickson, 1995), 181-82.

2. The American Standard Version translates here that the Berean Jews "were more open-minded..."; cf. also the comments of Bruce, *Acts*, 327: "With admirable freedom from prejudice, they brought the missionaries' claims to the touchstone of Holy Writ. Their procedure is worthy of imitation by all who have some new form of religious teaching pressed on their acceptance....As might be expected from those who welcomed the gospel so eagerly, many of them believed." For detailed discussion of the Greek word *eugenes*, "noble minded," cf. Celsas Spicq, O.P., *Theological Lexicon of the New Testament* (trans. and ed. by James D. Ernest; Peabody, MA: Hendrickson, 1994), 2:93-96.

3. See Andrew Strom's New Zealand Revival Bulletin, "Eyewitness Warnings of Brownsville, Pensacola." For a good example of a detailed eyewitness response to Pensacola sent to Strom but ignored by him, see Ruth Seydel Hebert, "Is Pensacola Making a Positive Difference?" (available through Larry Hebert, 72764.3432@compuserve.com).

4. After writing this section of the book, I came across a similar use of both Proverbs 6:16-18 and Matthew 11:16-19 in James R. Spencer, *Heresy Hunters* (Lafayette, LA: Huntington House, 1993). Although readers might differ at some points with Spencer's defense of various doctrinal points attacked by the "heresy hunters," it is difficult to discount his insightful—and often cutting—exposé of the faulty methodology of the critics.

5. I refer here to P. Yesupadam, founder and president of Love-N-Care Ministries based in the city of Vishakapatnam in Andhra Pradesh, India. We have worked with him closely in India since 1993.

6. It is possible, of course, for all these leaders to be wrong and for some individual congregants to be right. However, it is important for all those who strongly oppose the current revival to ask themselves: "Am I really open to hear from the other side? Am I willing to give any credence to weighty, serious testimonies? Is it prideful to think that my discernment is right [perhaps without ever even spending a week in the meetings!] whereas the discernment of so many other godly leaders is completely off?"

7. This is taken from Moody's letter to the members of the Chicago Avenue Church; see W.R. Moody, *The Life of Dwight L. Moody*, 130.

8. G. Campbell Morgan, *The Letters of Our Lord* (London: Pickering & Inglis, n.d.), 27.

9. Charles Hodge, *An Exposition of 1 & 2 Corinthians* (repr., Wilmington, DE: Sovereign Grace, 1972), 293, explains the phrase "believes all things" in 1 Corinthians 13:7 to mean, "is not suspicious, but readily credits what men say in their own defense." This quality is sadly lacking among many critics.

10. See the *Florida Baptist News*, January 23, 1997, 4.

11. Erich Bridges, ibid.

12. For discussion of the biblical imagery of the river of God, cf. A.A. Anderson, *Psalms (1–72)* (New Century Bible; Grand Rapids: Eerdmans, 1972), 357, commenting on Psalm 46:4, "As a river flowed out of Eden (Gen. 2:10), so a similar river would give joy and blessing to the city of God, and from here to the whole world (cf. 65:9...87:7; Isa. 33:21; Ezek. 47:1ff.; Jl. 3:18; Zech. 14:8)." Apparently unaware of this rich biblical language, some critics have recently categorized the popular revival song, "The River of God" as New Age (*sic*). The fact is, there is a holy river of refreshing flowing *from the throne of God to His thirsty people*, creating in them a fresh appreciation for and deep devotion to their Lord and Savior, Jesus Christ. Other recent "river of God" songs also reflect this scriptural truth, which is hardly New Age (obviously!).

Chapter Four

1. For excellent insights on this passage, cf. Charles Bridges, *Proverbs* (repr., Carlisle, PA: Banner of Truth, 1987), 27-31. Note also, more concisely, Derek Kidner, *Proverbs* (Tyndale Old Testament Commentaries; Downers Grove, IL: InterVarsity, 1964), to the respective verses cited.

2. Note, however, that the Hebrew is subject to several possible interpretations; cf., e.g., the Psalms commentaries of J.A. Alexander, F. Delitzsch, H.J. Kraus, A.A. Anderson, and L.C. Allen, and note also the variety among different English translations. Still, the overall sense of the positive value of godly rebuke is clear.

3. For discussion of the Hebrew text, see Robert Gordis, *The Book of Job: Commentary, New Translation, and Special Studies* (New York: Jewish Theological Seminary, 1978), 58-60; for the larger interpretive issues, cf. David J.A. Clines, *Job 1–20* (Word Biblical Commentary; Dallas: Word, 1989), 147-54.

4. Professor John Woodbridge, a noted Church historian at Trinity Evangelical Divinity School in Deerfield, Illinois, reminded me that in the opinion of Jonathan Edwards, the ultimate cause of the decline of the Great Awakening was pride; cf. on this Oropeza, *A Time to Laugh*, 150, n. 24. For further thoughts on Edwards and the decline of the Awakening, see the Appendix.

5. Taken from the public Internet recantation of Bobby Ripp, a former critic of the Brownsville Revival.

6. Brown, *From Holy Laughter to Holy Fire*, 40-61; see also Frank Damazio, *Seasons of Revival: Understanding the Appointed Times of Spiritual Refreshing* (Portland: BT Publishing, 1996), 247-73.

7. Although for the most part, my comments here are meant as an obviously sarcastic caricature, all too often, the "holy remnant" mentality prevails among the critics to the point that they consider the spiritual condition of the great majority of born-again believers to be highly suspect. Illustrative of this mentality among some critics is the *complete* rejection of the validity of a movement such as Promise Keepers, writing it off as a conspiracy of compromise and false ecumenism.

8. For these quotes, see Albert M. Wells, Jr., *Inspiring Quotations: Contemporary and Classical* (Nashville: Thomas Nelson, 1988), 19-21. Note also the

words of Paul Billheimer in ibid., 19: "The average critic has more confidence in criticism than in prayer to remedy the situation."

9. I have been amazed to see just how many critics of the current revival have freely circulated ugly *opinions* about fine Christian leaders (such as, "his eyes were glazed with a demonic appearance"—really!) or unfounded *judgments* about a particular spiritual phenomena (such as, "she works herself into an altered state of consciousness by shaking her head violently until she loses touch with reality") without getting firsthand knowledge of the facts. Yet they disseminate their views as widely as possible, through all the means at their disposal. This is highly displeasing to the Lord Jesus, the Head of the Church.

10. For discussion of Jeremiah 1:10, cf. Michael L. Brown, *Israel's Divine Healer* (Studies in Old Testament Biblical Theology; Grand Rapids: Zondervan, 1995), 183 and 379, n. 4, with references to further literature.

11. G. Richard Fisher and M. Kurt Goedelman, "The Murky River of Brownsville: The Strange Doctrine and Practice of the Pensacola Revival," *The Quarterly Journal* (The Newsletter Publication of Personal Freedom Outreach), Vol. 17, No. 2 (April-June 1997), 19. They characterize the whole service as "a journey into emotion and imagination gone riot" (ibid.).

12. Having been in the very meeting vilified by Fisher and Goedelman, and having subsequently viewed the video of that meeting with friends, I was absolutely shocked to read their description of that same service (which they too viewed by video). In fact, I vividly remember making eye contact with one of the last people to respond to the altar call that night, a large, sinful-looking young man with tears streaming down his cheeks. His name was Patrick Waters, and he was a drug-dealing, violence-loving bouncer at a bar, who was finally "flushed out" when Steve Hill, by the leading of the Lord, pointed to the area in the balcony where Patrick was sitting and exclaimed, "God knows all about your drug problem, young man," shortly after which his mother encouraged him that it was time for him to give his life to the Lord. And God met him that night! As of this writing (May, 1997), Patrick, who is a transformed man, has just completed his first semester in our School of Ministry and serves as an usher in the revival. For his testimony, see the *Destiny Image Digest*, Vol. 5, No. 1 (Winter, 1997), 30-33.

13. I would be more specific and give the details of this quote if not for the fact that to do so would be to spread someone's filthy, totally untrue judgment about a fine Christian individual whose identity I will not disclose. I'm sure you understand!

14. For a listing of important works on New Testament prophecy, cf. M. Eugene Boring, "Prophecy (Early Christian)," in David Noel Freedman, ed., *The Anchor Bible Dictionary* (New York: Doubleday, 1992), 5:501-02 (the entire article is on 495-502).

15. For some examples of this, cf. the transcript of my weekly Internet chat (chat.reapernet.com) dated May 6, 1997.

16. For further discussion on "the fear of the Lord," cf. H.F. Fuhs, "*yārē'*," in G. Johannes Botterweck and Helmer Ringgren, eds., *Theological Dictionary of the Old Testament* (Eng. tr., David E. Green; Grand Rapids: Eerdmans, 1990), 6:291-315.

17. This is taken from one of the "testimonies" posted in Strom's "Eyewitness Warnings of Brownsville, Pensacola." Her full-blown concerns about "river worship" reflect her continued study of the subject.

18. Cf. George R. Beasley Murray, *John* (Word Biblical Commentary; Waco, TX: 1987), 120, with reference to Exodus Rabbah 21:3.

19. Cf. Raymond E. Brown, *The Epistles of John* (Anchor Bible: Garden City, NY: Doubleday, 1982), 530-32, for discussion of 1 John 4:18 in context (and with Brown's particular reconstruction of the background).

20. Cf. E.E. Ellis, "Pastoral Letters," in Gerald F. Hawthorne and Ralph P. Martin, eds., *Dictionary of Paul and His Letters* (Downers Grove, IL: InterVarsity, 1993), 659-66 (esp. 661) for the general background to these verses.

Chapter Five

1. Derek Prince, *Protection From Deception: Navigating through the Minefield of Signs and Wonders* (rev. ed., Charlotte, NC: Derek Prince Ministries, 1996), 47-60, lists four safeguards against deception: We must humble ourselves, receive the love of the truth, cultivate the fear of the Lord, and make and keep the cross central. Although the subtitle of his book speaks of the "minefield of signs and wonders," my point in this chapter is that faithfully following Jesus is not like navigating one's way through a minefield. On these varied points of emphasis we fully agree.

2. For references to the key scholarly literature on the biblical imagery of the Lord as Shepherd, cf. Brown, *Israel's Divine Healer*, 394-95, nn. 131, 136.

3. Oropeza, *A Time to Laugh*, 147-56, provides a convenient summary of the views of Jonathan Edwards relative to discerning revival phenomena, a subject of considerable interest in the current outpouring; for more on this, see the Appendix. For Edwards, outward responses like shaking, crying out, or falling neither proved nor disproved that the work was of God and therefore served as no criteria for passing judgment on the work (pro or con). Rather, the determining issue was the conformity of the life to the character of Christ and the Word of God. See also Brown, *Holy Fire*, 167-232.

4. As Edwards so forcefully noted, "Those ministers of Christ and overseers of souls, that busy themselves, and are full of concern about the involuntary motions of the fluids and solids of men's bodies, and from thence full of doubts and suspicions of the cause, when nothing appears but that the state and frame of their minds, and their voluntary behaviour is good, and agreeable to God's word; I say, such ministers go out of the place that Christ has set them in, and leave their proper business, as much as if they should undertake to tell who are under the influence of the Spirit by their looks, or their gait. I cannot see which way we are in danger, or how the devil is likely to get any notable advantage against us, if we do but thoroughly do our duty with respect to those two things, viz. The state of persons' minds, and their moral conduct, seeing to it that they be maintained in an agreeableness to the rules that Christ has given us. *If things are but kept right in these respects, our fears and suspicions arising from extraordinary bodily effects seem wholly groundless*" (my emphasis; see *Edwards on Revival* [Worchester:

Moses W. Grout, 1832], 96). How these wise words need to be heeded by the critics today!

5. For the main issues of interpretation and application, cf. D.A. Carson, *Matthew 13–28* (Expositor's Bible Commentary; Grand Rapids: Zondervan, 1995), 488-95. Derek Morphew, *Renewal Apologetics* (n.p.: n.p., n.d.), 11-12, points out how critics have misused texts such as Mark 13:22 and Matthew 24:3, 23-25, with 2 Thessalonians 2:1-15. See further, below, n. 14.

6. For a sampling of teachings of "the Rebbe," cf. Menachem Mendel Schneerson, *Toward a Meaningful Life*, adopted by Simon Jacobson (New York: William Morrow, 1995).

7. Cf. David Allen Lewis, *Smashing the Gates of Hell in the Last Days* (Green Forest, AR: New Leaf Press, 1987), 62-63.

8. Cf. Ralph P. Martin, *2 Corinthians* (Word Biblical Commentary; Waco, TX: Word, 1986), 326-42.

9. More than 70 years ago, Pentecostal leader Smith Wigglesworth said, "If you want to manifest natural discernment, focus the same on yourself for at least twelve months and you will see so many faults in yourself that you will never want to fuss about the faults of other." See *Smith Wigglesworth: The Complete Collection of His Life and Teachings*, compiled by Roberts Liardon (Tulsa, OK: Albury, 1996), 365, from the message "The Discerning of Spirits," preached December 8, 1923.

10. Taking the Brownsville Revival as an example, every single sermon preached in the revival is on audiotape or videotape (in fact, every revival service has been captured on video), while every teaching session in the daytime and every class in the School of Ministry has been recorded on audiotape. It is easy enough for an honest inquirer to listen to dozens of messages by Evangelist Steve Hill, Pastor John Kilpatrick, Youth Pastor Richard Crisco, or myself, and find out exactly what is taught (in context, and not as selectively excerpted by the critics). In addition to this, there are several books that have recently been published by the leaders of the revival, with several more about to be released. For books by Stephen Hill published since the revival began, cf. *Time to Weep* (Orlando, FL: Creation House, 1997); *White Cane Religion and Other Messages From the Brownsville Revival* (Shippensburg, PA: Destiny Image, 1997); *The God Mockers and Other Messages From the Brownsville Revival* (Shippensburg, PA: Destiny Image, 1997); *The Pursuit of Revival* (Orlando, FL: Creation House, 1997); for books by John Kilpatrick, see *Feast of Fire: The Father's Day of Outpouring* (Pensacola, FL:, n.p., 1995); *When the Heavens Are Brass: Keys to Genuine Revival* (Shippensburg, PA: Destiny Image, 1997). Books by Pastor Richard Crisco and worship leader Lindell Cooley are also scheduled for immediate publication. A careful and thorough examination of these books will indicate that there is no other Jesus being preached and no other spirit being received. In fact, if anything, one could argue that, as the revival deepens in intensity and effect, the messages are becoming more and more simple and Christ-centered. For an "authorized" eyewitness account of the first year of the Brownsville Revival, cf. Renee DeLoriea, *Portal in Pensacola* (Shippensburg, PA: Destiny Image, 1997).

11. Unfortunately, even since these words were written, some critics are beginning to raise such ugly and slanderous charges. For an example of an outspo-
ken critic who clearly goes too far, cf. the Appendix.

12. Cf. Brown, *Israel's Divine Healer*, 63-66, with extensive references on
291-95, nn. 215-244.

13. Cf. Michael L. Brown, *It's Time to Rock the Boat* (Shippensburg, PA:
Destiny Image, 1993), 85-96, and note the comments of Archibald Thomas
Robertson, *Word Pictures in the New Testament* (repr., Grand Rapids: Baker, n.d.),
4:119, to 1 Corinthians 6:9-11, "All these will fall short of the kingdom of God.
This was plain talk to a city like Corinth. It is needed today. It is a solemn roll call
of the damned, even if some of their names are on the church roll in Corinth
whether officers or ordinary members."

14. For discussion of 2 Thessalonians 2:13-14, cf. F.F. Bruce, *1 & 2 Thessalonians* (Word Biblical Commentary; Waco, TX: Word, 1982), 189-92, with insights also into the biblical concept of God's electing grace. Cf. also the insightful
remarks of Wayne Grudem, "Should Christians Expect Miracles Today? Objections and Answers from the Bible," in Gary Grieg and Kevin Springer, eds., *The
Kingdom and the Power* (Ventura, CA: Regal, 1993), 56-57, cited in Morphew,
Renewal Apologetics, 11. Grudem exposes the faulty logic which reasons that:
"False Christs work miracles; Miracles are occurring in church A; Therefore I will
stay away from church A just to be safe (I really couldn't discern the falsehood
anyway)," finding such thinking to be contrary to the New Testament mentality
(with reference to Matthew 7:16; John 10:27). Rather, Grudem emphasizes, it is
better to teach Christians to utilize the biblical guidelines for recognizing error
(cf. 2 Pet. 2:1-22; 1 John 4:1-6) than to give "a bare warning about miracles that
will make people think they have no way of telling false Christs from the true"
(ibid., 57; his whole article is found on 55-110). Morphew also notes (re: 2 Thess.
2:1-15) that, "The anti-Christ is not going to be difficult for Christians to
spot....Someone who exalts himself over everything that is called God and sets
himself up as an object of worship is not difficult to spot (2:4)....Paul is confident
that the Christians will not be deceived" (11-12).

15. For background and commentary to 2 Corinthians 11:13-15, cf. Martin,
2 Corinthians, 349-56, with literature on 326-27.

16. This theme is treated at length in Chapter Thirteen, "Is Good News Bad
News for the Gloomers and Doomers? Exposing the Laodicean Lie."

Chapter Six

1. For an insightful contrast of false prophetism and true prophetism in Israel, cf. Willem A. VanGemeren, *Interpreting the Prophetic Word* (Grand Rapids:
Zondervan, 1990), 59-69, with reference to the important recent literature.

2. For general discussion of this passage, cf. Peter C. Craigie, *The Book of
Deuteronomy* (New International Commentary on the Old Testament; Grand Rapids: Eerdmans, 1976), 220-25.

3. Orthodox Jewish author Michoel Drazin entitles one chapter of his
book, *Their Hollow Inheritance: A Comprehensive Refutation of the New Testament and Its Missionaries* (Jerusalem: Gefen, 1990), "Pious Fraud" (see 15-24).

4. E.g., Fisher and Goedelman, "Murky River," 20, ridicule the idea that some Pentecostal believers have actually seen a "blue haze" during meetings, attributing such visions to lack of sleep (*sic*). Such a phenomenon, the authors emphasize, is found nowhere in the Bible. However, the authors are cessationists and do not believe that the experiences of, e.g., the apostles or prophets are in any way paradigmatic for believers today! (This was explicitly confirmed to me by Rev. Fisher in a private conversation on April 7, 1997.) So, if the Bible *did* talk about Ezekiel or Isaiah seeing a blue haze (which, quite frankly, would hardly have been worth recording in light of the other things they saw!), it would not serve as a precedent or possible validation for such a vision by a believer today. In any case, I know of no current revival or renewal movement that emphasizes blue haze visions.

5. For discussion of the formation of the canon of Scripture, cf. F.F. Bruce, *The Canon of Scripture* (Downers Grove, IL: InterVarsity, 1988).

6. As stated by George Whitefield, "Watch, therefore, I pray you, O believers, the motions of God's blessed Spirit in your souls, and always try the suggestions or impressions that you may at any time feel, by the unerring rule of God's most Holy Word. And if they are not found to be agreeable to that, reject them as diabolical and delusive! By observing this caution, you will steer a middle course between the two dangerous extremes many of this generation are in danger of running into; I mean, Enthusiasm, on the one hand, and Deism, and downright infidelity, on the other" (cited in Murray, *Jonathan Edwards*, 248). Again, the question regarding spiritual experiences and phenomena is, "Is this agreeable to the Word?" as opposed to, "Is this explicitly described in the Word?"

7. Interestingly, the pieces of material that were taken from Paul and used for healing were, according to Bruce, *Acts* (367-68), "presumably those which Paul used in his tentmaking or leather-working—the sweat rags for tying around his head and the aprons for tying around his waist." All the more then would it be clear that the healing efficacy proceeded from Jesus and not the rags!

8. See conveniently *Jonathan Edwards on Revival* (Carlisle, PA: Banner of Truth, 1987), 89.

9. In addition to *Holy Fire* and *Whatever Happened to the Power of God*, some earlier titles of mine are also relevant here; cf. *The End of the American Gospel Enterprise* (Shippensburg, PA: Destiny Image, 1989); *How Saved Are We?* (Shippensburg, PA: Destiny Image, 1990); cf. further *It's Time to Rock the Boat*, 75-82.

10. For summaries of recent revivals around the world, cf. Colin Whitaker, *Great Revivals* (Springfield, MO: Gospel Publishing House, 1984); Wesley L. Deuwel, *Revival Fire* (Grand Rapids: Zondervan, 1995).

11. See Carson, *Matthew 13–28*, 503, to Matthew 24:23-25.

12. See P.H. Alexander, "Slain in the Spirit," in Stanley M. Burgess and Gary B. McGee, eds., *Dictionary of Pentecostal and Charismatic Movements* (Grand Rapids: Zondervan, 1988), 789-91.

13. See the Appendix for examples of such slanted treatment.

14. For miracles as a verification of Jesus' ministry, cf. the literature cited in Brown, *Israel's Divine Healer*, 225-27, with nn. 89-98 on 414-16.

15. Representative of many recent works on the Jewishness of Jesus is James H. Charlesworth, ed., *Jesus' Jewishness: Exploring the Place of Jesus within Early Judaism* (New York: Crossroad, 1991). For further bibliography, cf. Michael L. Brown, *Our Hands Are Stained With Blood: The Tragic Story of the "Church" and the Jewish People* (Shippensburg, PA: Destiny Image, 1992), 35-41, 233-34.

16. For a typical example of Jewish, anti-missionary mocking of Paul (i.e., by Jewish leaders who endeavor to pull their fellow Jews away from Jesus), cf. Drazin, *Hollow Inheritance*, 18: "The authors of the New Testament had a powerful personality to emulate in Saul of Tarsus (Paul), who openly advocated 'pious fraud'," with quotes following from Romans 3:7-8; 1 Corinthians 9:20-23; 2 Corinthians 12:16 ("...I was crafty, you say, and got the better of you by guile"); and Philippians 1:18. (Drazin quotes each verse in full, and they should be looked up by the reader so as to feel the full force of his claims.) This should serve as a warning to all critics of revival (as well as to those swayed by them): It is easy to make someone look deceptive and foolish—even Paul!—if that person's material is quoted in a non-contextual or non-sympathetic way. Just because a quote of a revival leader or a snippet of a revival video is played, does *not* mean that an accurate picture has been painted.

17. In my review of Hank Hanegraaff's *Counterfeit Revival* (Dallas: Word, 1997; see the Appendix, "Counterfeit Criticism"), I have *not* sought to do this. Rather, I have addressed some of the book's most serious and obvious shortcomings. One could practically go on *ad infinitum* exposing every flaw, inaccuracy, and infelicity in the book.

18. I have dealt with this similar problem in the context of my dialogue with Jewish rabbis anti-missionaries. See "Unequal Weights and Measures: A Critique of the Methodology of the Anti-Missionaries," published in the 1993 issue of *Messianic Literature Outreach*.

19. The literature on Jesus, Jewish law, and the Sabbath is vast. For a concise survey (with basic literature), see S. Westerholm, "Sabbath," in *Dictionary of Jesus and the Gospels*, 716-19; for specific discussion of Jesus' Sabbath healings, cf. Brown, *Israel's Divine Healer*, 220-22, with further literature.

20. Note, e.g., D.A. Carson, *Exegetical Fallacies* (Grand Rapids: Baker, 1984), 137, where, in critiquing some of the interpretations of Zane Hodges, Carson states: "To the best of my knowledge not one significant interpreter of Scripture in the entire history of the church has held to Hodge's interpretation of the passages he treats," concluding, "That does not necessarily mean Hodges is wrong; but it certainly means he is probably wrong, and it probably means he has not reflected seriously enough on the array of fallacies connected with distanciation."

21. Cf. Oropeza, *Time to Laugh*, 151, who notes that, for Jonathan Edwards, "if the fruits produced include a saint such as David Brainerd, evangelist to the American Indians, the critics can call 'true experiential religion' whatever they will."

Chapter Seven

1. In *Counterfeit Revival*, Hanegraaff, while not making reference to *any* positive fruit taking place in any current renewal movement, does attribute some

unusual phenomena (which, basically, he discounts as bogus) to the devil; see the Appendix.

2. For discussion of this passage, cf. D.A. Carson, *Matthew 1–12* (Expositor's Bible Commentary; Grand Rapids: Zondervan, 1995), 288-89, and note the quotation from John Broadus there (288): "For the prince of demons to cast out his subjects would be virtually casting out himself, since they were doing his work."

3. For John's unique usage of *sarx*, cf. A. Sand, "*sarx*, flesh," in Horst Balz and Gerhard Schneider, eds., *Exegetical Dictionary of the New Testament* (Grand Rapids: Eerdmans, 1993), 3:232.

4. For discussion of Paul's understanding of *sarx*, cf. C.E.B. Cranfield, *The Epistle to the Romans, Volume I* (International Critical Commentary; Edinburgh: T & T Clark, 1974), especially 379ff.

5. Cited in *The Prayers That Avail Much Daily Planner* (Tulsa, OK: Harrison House, n.d.), no original sources given.

6. Quoted in Leonard Ravenhill, *Why Revival Tarries* (Minneapolis: Bethany, 1962), 35.

7. Professor Doug Oss has emphasized to me the importance of verses such as John 6:44 and 12:32, indicating that people come to Jesus because God—not the devil—draws them. This underscores the completely unscriptural (not to mention absurd) nature of the argument of some critics that it is Satan who is actually drawing people to Jesus in the current revival and counterfeiting holiness in their lives (really!), only to lead them into the great deception. (It was a professor of Bible who actually made this claim. I kid you not!)

8. For discussion of this verse, cf. Stephen S. Smalley, *1, 2, 3 John* (Word Biblical Commentary; Waco, TX: 1984), 265-67.

9. Ibid., n. 7.

10. For representative testimonies, cf. *The Pentecostal Evangel* (Nov. 10, 1996; cf. also the follow-up report in the June 8, 1997, edition), and the *Destiny Image Digest*, Vol. 5, No. 1 (Winter, 1997).

11. We can attest firsthand to the exceptionally high keeping rate of teen converts who enter the youth discipleship program at Brownsville Assembly of God under Pastor Richard Crisco.

12. *The Works of John Wesley* (from the Sage Digital Library CD-ROM, Albany, OR: Sage Software), 8:490.

13. Cf. n. 1, above.

14. This claim is made extensively in Hanegraaff, *Counterfeit Revival*; see the Appendix.

15. See the refutation of this notion in Patrick Dixon, *Signs of Revival* (Eastbourne: Kingsway, 1994), 247 (cited below in the Appendix).

16. Cited in Harvey Cox, *Fire from Heaven* (Reading, MA: Addison-Wesley, 1995), 61. For Parham's full report, see Mrs. Charles Parham, *The Life of Charles F. Parham* (Birmingham, AL: Commercial Printing, 1930), 163-70.

17. For a sympathetic overview of William J. Seymour's life and work, cf. Roberts Liardon, *God's Generals* (Tulsa, OK: Albury, 1996), 137-66.

18. Moody, *The Life of Dwight L. Moody*, 426.

19. Among those most powerfully impacted by Moody's ministry were young men such as C.T. Studd and Wilfred Grenfell, both of whom became missionaries of almost legendary stature; for short sketches, cf. Ruth A. Tucker, *From Jerusalem to Irian Jaya* (Grand Rapids: Zondervan, 1983), 261-68, 328-32. Note also that an entire Christian student movement arose on university campuses in England and America as a fruit of Moody's work.

20. See Bonamy Dobreé, *John Wesley* (New York: Macmillan, 1933), 48. Although this is hardly a notable biography of Wesley, it does serve to underscore just how much others can read their own ideas into the subjects that they analyze and discuss.

21. Morphew, *Renewal Apologetics*, 1-2.

22. Cheong, *Deceiving the Elect*, 60.

Chapter Eight

1. Some cessationists point to Jesus' words to Thomas in John 20:29, "Because you have seen Me, you have believed; blessed are those who have not seen and yet have believed," in an effort to discount the importance of signs and wonders confirming the Word. Of course, the argument is off base: Signs and wonders point to the invisible God, strengthening our faith in Him. And so we believe in Him, even though we have never seen Him. Thus, Paul could emphasize the importance of preaching the gospel with miraculous signs following (1 Cor. 2:1-5) as well as state that we walk by faith and not by sight (2 Cor. 5:7). Moreover, unless the cessationist would want to argue that the Book of Acts represents a step *backwards* from John 20:29 (seeing that there was often miraculous confirmation of the preaching), then he would have to admit that powerful miracles that back up the preaching of the gospel are a help to, not a hindrance of, true faith.

2. For the cosmic dimensions of the plagues on Egypt, see Terrence E. Fretheim, "The Plagues as Ecological Signs of Historical Disaster," *Journal of Biblical Literature* 110 (1991), 385-96, and cf. further Brown, *Israel's Divine Healer*, 67-69.

3. The most common answer of the critics would be, of course, "The Bible speaks of a great apostasy at the end of the age, marked by counterfeit miracles of every kind." This objection is addressed several times throughout this book; in addition to the discussion in the end of this chapter, note also the relevant sections of Chapter Five and Chapter Thirteen.

4. Cf., e.g., Oropeza, *Time to Laugh*, 63-65, who overstates the case here, and cf. n. 5, immediately below.

5. Cf. C.K. Barrett, *The Acts of the Apostles, Volume One* (International Critical Commentary; Edinburgh: T & T Clark, 1994), 137-38. Barrett sees the signs here primarily as signs of salvation, also stating that the "celestial portents" spoken of by Luke "will form the immediate prelude to the coming of Christ."

6. For brief discussion of *dunamis* with reference to the key literature, cf. Brown, *Israel's Divine Healer*, 212, with n. 20 and 219, with n. 63.

7. For discussion of the Old Testament background to the usage of the Greek word *enduō* "to clothe, put on, wear," along with rabbinic parallels, cf.

Hermann L. Strack and Paul Billerbeck, *Kommentar zum Neuen Testament aus Talmud und Midrasch* (München: C.H. Beck, 1924), 2:301.

8. In the last ten years, there has been a marked increase in sound, anti-cessationist literature; for extensive references to recent discussion, cf. Brown, ibid., 225-27, with nn. 89-98 on 414-416; for an excellent cross-section of differing views, cf. Wayne Grudem, ed., *Are Miraculous Gifts for Today? Four Views* (Grand Rapids: Zondervan, 1996); for a strong restatement of the cessationist view, cf. Thomas R. Edgar, *Satisfied by the Promise of the Spirit: Affirming the Fullness of God's Provision for Spiritual Living* (Grand Rapids: Kregel, 1996). Also to be included in recent anti-cessationist literature (although not by primary design as much as by nature of the treatment of the relevant material) are Fee, *First Corinthians*, and Brown, *Israel's Divine Healer*.

9. Contrast the treatment of this verse by Richard Gaffin in Grudem, ibid., 37-38. Gaffin sees Acts 1:8 as completely fulfilled in Acts itself.

10. Cf. Jon Ruthven, *On the Cessation of the Charismata* (Journal of Pentecostal Theology, Supp3; Sheffield: Sheffield Academic Press, 1993), 119, on the reception of the charismata in terms of overall salvation history.

11. Cf. Grieg and Springer, *The Kingdom and the Power*, 393-97 ("Appendix 2—John 14:12—The Commission to All Believers to Do the Works of Jesus"). Note also W.R. Bodine, "Power Ministry in the Epistles: A Reply to the Cessasionist Position," in ibid., 203-04, n. 8, and cf. C. Dietzfelbinger, "Die grösseren Werke (Joh 14. 12f.)," *New Testament Studies* (1989), 27-47.

12. Cf. n. 8, for references, and see the discussion in Grudem, *Miraculous Gifts*.

13. Fee, *First Corinthians*, 644-46 rightly (and quite decisively) dismisses 1 Corinthians 13:10, "but when perfection comes, the imperfect disappears," as having any possible reference to the cessation of the gifts of the Spirit with the closing of the canon of Scripture. Note also D.A. Carson, *Showing the Spirit* (Grand Rapids: Baker, 1987), for an example of an important treatment of 1 Corinthians 12–14 by a non-charismatic New Testament scholar wherein it is recognized that there is no explicit scriptural support for the view that the New Testament *charismata* ceased with the close of the canon.

14. As Jonathan Edwards wrote, "...If we look back into the history of the church of God in past ages, we may observe that it has been a common device of the devil to overset a revival of religion; when he finds he can keep men quiet and secure no longer, then he drives them to excesses and extravagances. He holds them back as long as he can; but when he can do it no longer, then he will push them on, and, if possible, run them upon their heads," cited in Murray, *Jonathan Edwards*, 235; cf. also the words of D. Martyn Lloyd-Jones, cited above, 92.

15. In his attempt to discredit Jesus and His followers as impostors and frauds, Drazin, *Their Hollow Inheritance*, 25-41 (the chapter entitled "The Ancient 'God-Men' "), provides detailed lists paralleling Jesus' life and teaching with that of Krishna and Buddha. In all candor, it must be said that Drazin's negative arguments based on pagan parallels and precedents—arguments which Christians would find either pathetic or laughable—are far more persuasive than the

similar, anti-revival arguments of the critics. This should say something about the weakness of the critics' approach!

16. Cf. Morton Smith, *Jesus the Magician* (London: Gollancz, 1978). Note that much of *A Survey of Old Testament Introduction* (rev. ed., Chicago: Moody, 1974) by Gleason L. Archer, Jr., is devoted to refuting critical reconstructions of the Old Testament.

17. For a historical perspective, cf. the literature cited in Brown, *Israel's Divine Healer*, 63-66, with nn. 214-44 on 291-95. On a more popular level, cf. the 1933 volume of George Jeffreys, *Pentecostal Rays: The Baptism and Gifts of the Spirit*, excerpted extensively in Dixon, *Signs of Revival*.

18. See n. 17, immediately above.

19. For an assortment of twentieth century miracle testimonies, cf. Ralph W. Harris, *Acts Today: Signs & Wonders of the Holy Spirit* (Springfield, MO: Gospel Publishing House, 1995); for a medical assessment of recent healing claims, cf. David Lewis, *Healing: Fiction, Fantasy or Fact? A Comprehensive Analysis of the Healings and Associated Phenomena at John Wimber's Harrogate Conference* (London: Hodder & Stoughton, 1989).

20. As noted above, n. 4 to Chapter Two, I have often addressed these issues as a Pentecostal/charismatic insider; cf. also my "Theological and Practical Reflections," in *Israel's Divine Healer*, 243-47.

21. This information was supplied to me in April, 1997, by Pentecostal historian Vinson Synan. For a detailed statement through 1988, cf. David B. Barrett, "Global Statistics," in *Dictionary of Pentecostal and Charismatic Movements*, 810-30. See also below, n. 4 to Chapter Thirteen.

22. For a solid treatment of 1 Corinthians 2:1-5, cf. Fee, *First Corinthians*, 88-97.

23. For discussion of these verses, cf. Smalley, *1, 2, 3, John*, 214-31.

24. On the two witnesses in Revelation 11:3-14, cf. Robert H. Mounce, *The Book of Revelation* (New International Commentary on the New Testament; Grand Rapids: Eerdmans, 1977), 221-29.

25. This is not to deny the importance of giving proper pastoral oversight to revival meetings and revival "phenomena"; this is only to state the obvious, viz., that the verses under discussion are completely unrelated to a possible excess or extreme. In a different vein, cf. Jonathan Edwards' caustic comments to those who wait for a revival without any blemishes, cited in part on 180, above. He further cautioned those who were slow in acknowledging the divine origin of the Great Awakening, saying, "This pretended prudence, in persons waiting so long before they acknowledged this work, will probably in the end prove the greatest imprudence. Hereby they will fail of any share of so great a blessing, and will miss the most precious opportunity of obtaining divine light, grace, and comfort, heavenly and eternal benefits that God ever gave in New England. While the glorious fountain is set open in so wonderful a manner, and multitudes flock to it and receive a rich supply for the wants of their souls, they stand at a distance, doubting, wondering, and receiving nothing, and are like to continue thus till the precious season is past" (*Jonathan Edwards on Revival*, 134, from the *Distinguishing Marks*). How appropriate these words are for today!

26. Cf. Bruce, *1 & 2 Thessalonians*, 179-88, "Excursus on Antichrist."

27. For thorough discussion of the main interpretative issues, cf. Carson, *Matthew 13–28*, and Donald A. Hagner, *Matthew 14–28* (Word Biblical Commentary; Dallas: Word, 1995), *ad loc.*

Chapter Nine

1. For the eschatological/charismatic dimensions of these verses, cf. Oss, in *Are Miraculous Gifts for Today?*, 249-57.

2. On the New Testament concept of "the last days," cf. the discussions on eschatology throughout George Eldon Ladd, *A Theology of the New Testament* (rev. by Donald A. Hagner; Grand Rapids: Eerdmans, 1993).

3. For the "last hour" concept, cf. Brown, *The Epistles of John*, 330-34; on James 5:3, cf. Peter H. Davids, *The Epistle of James* (New International Greek Testament Commentary; Grand Rapids: Eerdmans, 1982), 177, who notes, "The phrase 'last days' refers to the NT conviction that the end times, the age of consummation, had already broken in upon the world in Jesus (e.g., Hos. 3:5; Is. 2:2; Je. 23:20; Ezk. 38:16; Da. 2:28; 'the kingdom of God is near' in the synoptics; Acts 2:17; Heb. 1:2; 2 Tim. 3:1; cf. Cullman [*Christ and Time*])."

4. John Calvin, *Institutes of the Christian Religion*, ed., John T. McNeill (Philadelphia: Westminster, 1977), 2:1155.

5. Cf. the comments of A.T. Hanson, *The Pastoral Epistles* (New Century Bible; Grand Rapids: Eerdmans, 1982), 87, "It is very probable...that the **later times** to which he refers are intended to be the period at which the author was actually writing....The **later times** of this verse are no doubt to be identified with the **last days** of 2 Tim. 3:1. Thus this is nor really a strong eschatological prophecy and it does not suggest that the author had a vivid sense of the imminence of the parousia." Note that Hanson's rejection of the Pauline authorship of the pastoral epistles actually underscores the non-eschatological dimensions of his comments.

6. See immediately above, n. 5.

7. For the issue of heresy in the early Church, cf. Hans Dieter Betz, "Heresy and Orthodoxy in the New Testament," *Anchor Bible Dictionary*, 3:144-47.

8. Cf. above, n. 14 to Chapter Five.

9. Cf. above, n. 1 to Chapter Five, for Derek Prince's suggested safeguards to deception.

10. This e-mail was from my earlier interaction with Bobby Ripp before he recanted of his previous views; see above, n. 5 to Chapter Four.

11. This mentality was effectively addressed by Arthur Wallis, *In the Day of Thy Power* (repr., Columbia, MO/Fort Washington, PA: Cityhill/Christian Literature Crusade, 1988), 34-42.

12. Strom, "Brownsville, Pensacola: 'Toronto' or Not?"

13. To speak again from the context of my personal experience, I cannot begin to count the number of leaders who have attended meetings in the Brownsville Revival—having been warned that they would see the weird and the wild and being just a little unsure about what they were stepping into—who turned to us after a day or two and said, "What in the world are people talking about? I am amazed

to see how orderly the services are and how the whole emphasis is on salvation and holiness." Of course, these leaders had an unfair advantage on some of their critical friends. They checked things out for themselves! Note also that although I take time in this book to deal with issues such as shaking and "falling under the power," it is by no means a given that any of these phenomena will be seen in revival services today. In fact, it is virtually certain that these phenomena will not be the *focus* of the meeting.

14. Of course, when the Scriptures speak of "bowing down" before the Lord (or, a superior) they speak of prostrations (Hebrew *hishtāḥăvāh*), a common expression of veneration in the ancient Near East, and still customary today in, e.g., Islamic prayer. No doubt, Strom is claiming that a "manifestation" of bowing is not scriptural; my response to him here—which is slightly sarcastic in light of the triviality of his objection—is that the *principle* of bowing low before the Lord is quite scriptural, and, therefore, for someone to be moved on by the Spirit to bow before Him can hardly be deemed *un*scriptural. In any case, such "manifestations" are hardly the norm in the current revival.

15. Note these comments by Charles H. Spurgeon to Matthew 24:4-5, *A Popular Exposition to the Gospel According to Matthew* (repr., Pasadena, TX: Pilgrim, 1996), 417: "They were to beware lest any of the pretended Messiahs should lead them astray, as they would pervert many others. A large number of impostors came forward before the destruction of Jerusalem, giving out that they were the anointed of God; almost every page of history is blotted with the names of such deceivers; and in our own day we have seen some come in Christ's name, saying that they are Christs. Such men seduce many; but they who heed their Lord's warning will not be deluded by them." Note that this was written well over 100 years ago.

16. See Alexander Roberts and James Donaldson, eds., *The Anti-Nicene Fathers* (repr., Grand Rapids: Eerdmans, 1975), 7:932.

17. For discussion of Matthew 16:18 against the backdrop of early Jewish thought (especially Qumran), cf. David Hill, *The Gospel of Matthew* (New Century Bible; Grand Rapids: Eerdmans, 1972), 260-62; for a hortatory treatment, cf. Spurgeon, *Popular Exposition*, 268.

18. Commenting on Matthew 24:14, Hill, ibid., 320-21, rejects the more unlikely interpretations of this passage, instead stating the obvious: "The idea concerns the plan of God that all nations shall have an opportunity of hearing the Gospel before the end." Cf. further J.W. Thompson, "The Gentile Mission as an Eschatological Necessity," *Restoration Quarterly* 14 (1971), 18-27.

19. On Romans 13:11-14, cf. James D.G. Dunn, *Romans 9–16* (Word Biblical Commentary; Dallas: Word, 1988), 783-94; on 1 John 2:8, cf. Smalley, *1, 2, 3 John*, 57-58. Although the words of Jesus in John 9:4b, "Night is coming, when no one can work," are sometimes cited from pulpits with reference to a coming period of darkness in the world (viz., *the* "tribulation" period), the context is clearly against such a view, since Jesus would not have been urging His disciples to work for God while they yet had the opportunity because 2,000 years later "darkness" would come! Cf. also John 8:12; 9:5; 11:9-10.

Chapter Ten

1. Cf. Oropeza, *Time to Laugh*, 147; for the actual anecdote from which the term "Quaker" is said to have derived, cf. Stanley M. Burgess, "Quakers (Society of Friends)," who recounts that when George Fox was brought to trial "for his attacks on the ordained clergy, he told the judge that the latter should tremble at the Word of God, and the justice then called Fox 'a Quaker'—a name that has remained," *Dictionary of Pentecostal and Charismatic Movements*, 752. The Quakers, of course, were not without numerous idiosyncracies and irregularities, even in their formative years.

2. *Joy Unspeakable*, cited in Dixon, *Signs of Revival*, 211-12.

3. Commenting on Acts 4:31, Oropeza, *Time to Laugh*, 118, notes that "the 'place' was shaking, not the people!" It would seem, however, that if the building shook then the people inside shook too. In any case, Oropeza is not hostile to the concept of Christians being shaken through an encounter with God's powerful presence; see ibid., 119.

4. See immediately above, n. 3.

5. Cf. the similar line of reasoning in Edwards, *Distinguishing Marks*, in *Jonathan Edwards on Revival*, 91-94.

6. How would the critics have responded to Jacob's encounter with the angel of the Lord in Genesis 32, resulting in his lifelong limp? And how would they have viewed Ezekiel? It is interesting that William Sanford LaSor, David Allan Hubbard, and Frederic William Bush, *Old Testament Survey* (2nd ed., Grand Rapids: Eerdmans, 1996), 357, after noting that "Ezekiel has sometimes been called psychotic, and schizophrenic," find it necessary to cite the German study of B. Brun, a psychiatrist who "has judged that, while Ezekiel had ecstatic experiences, the way he is described in the book shows no psychotic or schizophrenic symptoms" (796, n. 2)! Even more interesting is the fact that this second edition of this important Old Testament survey has altered the original text (from the earlier, 1982 edition), which apparently has not been carefully edited here, resulting in the superfluous comma after the word "psychotic" above. The 1982 edition (462) read: "Ezekiel has been called ecstatic, visionary, neurotic, psychotic, and schizophrenic. Indeed, his behavior was 'abnormal'—but what is 'normal' with regard to a prophet on whom the Spirit of God has fallen?"

7. As a good example of the critics' tendency to devote much of their attention to things like shaking or being "slain in the Spirit," cf. the relevant references to Hanegraaff's *Counterfeit Revival* in the Appendix.

8. For a detailed philological discussion of this verse, cf. my paper delivered at the 1988 national meeting of the Society of Biblical Literature, "*gîlû birᵉadâ* and *naššequ bar* (Psa. 2:11b-12a): Toward a Satisfactory Solution." Cf. also the rendering of the New Jewish Version.

9. Note that the Hebrew word *hārēdîm* (literally, "those who tremble") has become the colloquial name for ultra-Orthodox Jews, especially in Israel; cf. above, n. 1, with reference to George Fox and the Quakers. For recent studies on the ultra-Orthodox movement, cf. Samuel Heilman, *Defenders of the Faith* (New York: Schocken, 1992); David Landau, *Piety and Power* (New York: Hill and Wang, 1993).

10. *Religious Affections*, cited in Oropeza, 152.

11. *Holy Fire*, 121-40; for fascinating reading of the early days of Azusa Street (straight out of the participants' own mouths), see *The Azusa Street Papers: A Reprint of the Apostolic Faith Mission Publications, Los Angeles (1906–1908), William J. Seymour, Editor* (Foley, AL: Together in the Harvest Publications, 1997).

12. Some of these are discussed in *"gîlû bir^eadâ* and *naššeqû bar* (Psa. 2:11b-12a)," cited above, n. 8. Biblical Hebrew verbs for shake and tremble include *ḥyl, rā'ad, rāgaz,* and *ḥārad*.

13. For discussion of the broader context of the restoration promise in Jeremiah 33:1-9, cf. Walter Brueggemann, *To Build, To Plant: A Commentary on Jeremiah 26–52* (International Theological Commentary; Grand Rapids: Eerdmans), 91-95.

14. Cf. Brown, *Holy Fire*, 16-25.

15. Cited in Elfion Evans, *The Welsh Revival of 1904* (Wales: Evangelical Press of Wales, 1969), 137.

16. For general discussion on these chapters, cf. Fee, *1 Corinthians* and Carson, *Showing the Spirit, ad loc.*

17. Since hearing about this particular incident early in 1997, I have heard a number of other striking testimonies—some far more amazing and inexplicable—where God literally shook up lost sinners in (or, out of) a public service, and transformed their lives.

18. See above, n. 16.

19. Cited in Dixon, *Signs of Revival*, 1.

20. There is no finer treatment of the overwhelming nature of the prophet's encounter with God and His Word than that of Abraham Joshua Heschel, *The Prophets* (2 vol. edition; New York: Harper & Row, 1962), especially his opening chapter, "What Manner of Man Is the Prophet?" (1:3-26) Cf. also William McKane, *Jeremiah 1–25* (International Critical Commentary; Edinburgh: T & T Clark, 1985), 567-79, to Jeremiah 23:9.

21. It is interesting that Ronald Y. K. Fung, *The Epistle to the Galatians* (New International Commentary on the New Testament; Grand Rapids: Eerdmans, 1988), 202-03, misses all reference to prayer and intercession in his (otherwise insightful) discussion of Galatians 4:19.

22. See Garth M. Rosell and Richard A.G. Dupuis, eds., *The Memoirs of Charles G. Finney* (Grand Rapids: Zondervan, 1989), 316-17, for the full, unedited text.

23. On the experience of the prohets, cf. above, n. 20.

24. On Daniel's visionary experience, cf. H.C. Leupold, *Exposition of Daniel* (repr., Grand Rapids: Baker, 1969), 446-64. Perhaps an ancient critic would have suggested that Daniel's vision was not real, atttributing it instead to fasting-induced hallucination. See above, n. 6 to Chapter Four.

Chapter Eleven

1. For some thoughts on hype and the flesh in contemporary services, cf. Michael L. Brown, *The End of the American Gospel Enterprise* (Shippensburg,

PA: Destiny Image, 1989), 75-79; idem., *How Saved Are We?* (Shippensburg, PA: Destiny Image, 1990), 43-50; *Whatever Happened to the Power of God?*, 33-44, 95-100. See also, more broadly, Michael Horton, ed., *The Agony of Deceit* (Chicago: Moody, 1990); Douglas D. Webster, *Selling Jesus: What's Wrong with Marketing the Church* (Downers Grove, IL: InterVarsity, 1992).

2. Cf. H.J. Fabry, *"lēb,"* in *Theological Dictionary of the Old Testament*, 7:399-437; Hans Walter Wolff, *Anthropology of the Old Testament* (Eng. tr., Margaret Kohl; Philadelphia: Fortress, 1974), 40-44.

3. For typical scenes, cf. Ezra 3:10-13; Nehemiah 8; cf. also above, n. 11 to Chapter Ten.

4. See *The Works of John Wesley*, 8:25.

5. For this quote (along with other choice selections), cf. I.D.E. Thomas, ed., *The Golden Treasury of Puritan Quotations* (repr., Carlisle, PA: Banner of Truth, 1989), 215 (see also 209-21).

6. Cf. Fee, *First Corinthians*, 645, n. 23: "It is perhaps an indictment of Western Christianity that we should consider 'mature' our rather totally cerebral and domesticated—but bland—brand of faith, with the concomitant absence of the Spirit in terms of supernatural gifts! The Spirit, not Western rationalism, marks the turning of the ages, after all; and to deny the Spirit's manifestations is to deny our present existence to be eschatological, as belonging to the beginning of the time of the End."

7. For cultural background and commentary, cf. William L. Holladay, *Jeremiah 1* (Heremenia; Philadelphia: Fortress, 1986), 309-15.

8. Brown, *It's Time to Rock the Boat*, 41-47 (the chapter entitled "Connoisseur Christians and a Gourmet Gospel").

9. For a serious presentation of such a position, cf. John MacArthur, Jr., *Our Sufficiency in Christ* (Dallas: Word, 1991).

10. Discernment Ministries, from their Website.

11. Cited in William DeArteaga, *Quenching the Spirit: Discover the REAL Spirit Behind the Charismatic Controversy* (2nd ed., Orlando, FL: Creation House, 1996), 51.

12. *The Works of Wesley*, 8:124-25.

13. Ibid., 8:242.

14. Cf. DeArteaga, *Quenching the Spirit*, 49.

15. For relevant discussion of Matthew 22:32, cf. Carson, *Matthew 13–28*, 462.

16. Brown, *The End of the American Gospel Enterprise*, 7-8.

17. I heard this maxim often in my times alone with Ravenhill; on Paul's "Damascus Road" experience as the formative foundation of his theology, cf. Seyoon Kim, *The Origin of Paul's Gospel* (Grand Rapids: Eerdmans, 1982).

18. For discussion of 2 Peter 1:16-19 (with special reference to *bebaioterov*, "more certain, more reliable"), cf. Richard Bauckham, *Jude, 2 Peter* (Word Biblical Commentary; Waco, TX: Word, 1983), 204-27. He notes (223) that "the majority opinion of scholars takes this verse to be saying that the Transfiguration has confirmed OT prophecy."

19. Cf. my forthcoming book, *Will the Real Messiah Please Rise: Answering Jewish Objections to Jesus* (Baltimore, MD: Lederer, 1997). In my capacity as a specialist in this field, I have served as Visiting Professor of Jewish Apologetics at Fuller Theological Seminary School of World Mission. Thus it should be clear to all that I in no way denigrate the value of apologetics!

20. A number of famous conversion accounts are included in *Eerdman's Book of Christian Classics*, compiled by Veronica Zundel (Grand Rapids: Eerdmans, 1985).

21. Cf. Arnold Dallimore, *Spurgeon: A New Biography* (Carlisle, PA: Banner of Truth, 1988), 15-20; cf. further Brown, *Holy Fire*, 91-103.

22. Cf. James Houston, ed., *The Mind on Fire: An Anthology of the Writings of Blaise Pascal* (Portland, OR: Multnomah, 1989).

23. For a wide-ranging (and, sometimes, controversial) treatment of these verses (and the Song of Solomon in general), cf. Marvin H. Pope, *The Song of Songs* (Anchor Bible; Garden City, NY: Doubleday, 1977). Note that Cheong, *Deceiving the Elect*, 3-4, refers to David Ruis' song, "True Love," with its Song of Solomon-like references to Jesus (speaking of the kisses of His mouth and His warm embrace, etc.) as "blasphemous" and making "a mockery of the spiritual relationship between Christ and His bride."

24. William Law, *A Humble, Earnest, and Affectionate Address to the Clergy* (from the Sage Digital Library CD-ROM), 26.

25. Charles H. Spurgeon, *The Spurgeon Sermon Collection: 55 Selected Expositions* (from the Sage Digital Library CD-ROM), 32-33, from his sermon, "The Personality of the Holy Ghost."

Chapter Twelve

1. Most recently, Joseph Chambers, "The End Times and Victorious Living," Vol. 11, No. 2 (March/April, 1997), 1, states, "After an incredible amount of research, I am convinced beyond doubt that the Pensacola event is one of the first main 'apparition' type revivals to invade the modern evangelistic/charismatic churches," claiming that the revival is driven by "emotions or experiences that have appeared in the past but [were] usually rejected by the leaders and revivalists as Satanic and disruptive."

2. Cf. above, n. 13 to Chapter Nine.

3. Cf. the relevant portions of my testimony as briefly stated in *Whatever Happened to the Power of God?*, vii-xi.

4. Cf. William Lane, *Hebrews 1–8* (Word Biblical Commentary; Dallas: Word, 1991), 139-40; Lane (140) believes that each of the six articles listed here "is related to the high priestly christology developed in the subsequent chapters [in Hebrews]...." His overall treatment, however, is somewhat cursory.

5. Cf. David P. Wright and Robert F. O'Toole, "Hands, Laying on of," in *Anchor Bible Dictionary*, 3:47-49, with reference to the important secondary literature.

6. For discussion of Leviticus 16:21-23 (representing some varied perspectives), cf. John E. Hartley, *Leviticus* (Word Biblical Commentary; Dallas: Word, 1992); Baruch A. Levine, *Leviticus* (The JPS Torah Commentary; Philadelphia, Jewish Pub. Society, 1989); and Jacob Milgrom, *Leviticus 1–16* (Anchor Bible; New York: Doubleday, 1991), *ad loc.*

7. For discussion on the canonical status of this portion of Scripture, cf. Bruce M. Metzger, *A Textual Commentary on the Greek New Testament* (New York: United Bible Societies, 1971), 122-28.

8. This interpretation to 1 Timothy 5:22 is, of course, standard in the commentaries, although Hanson, *Pastoral Epistles*, 103, also cites as a possibility the view that the laying on of hands spoken of in the text has to do with "the reconciliation of the excommunicated," based on the (later attested) custom of reconciliation which "was effected by the bishop laying hands on the penitent sinner."

9. On Romans 1:11, cf. Cranfield, *Romans, Volume 1*, 78-79.

10. For discussion on *metadidomai*, cf. James D.G. Dunn, *Romans 1–8* (Word Biblical Commentary; Dallas: Word, 1988), 30-31.

11. The following statement from an individual concerned about the Brownsville Revival is typical: "The 'spirit' came from Argentina and from Holy Trinity Brompton (in England), both of which are directly linked to the 'spirit' of Toronto....As it is the same spirit, I fail to see how, as some Brownsville proponents try to do, you can separate the two...." Thus if someone discounts the "Toronto Blessing"—even based on hearsay—they will immediately discount Brownsville as well.

12. See, however, n. 22 to Chapter Fourteen, below.

13. Hank Hanegraaff has been especially critical of the phenomenon of being "slain in the Spirit"; cf. the Appendix for references.

14. *Works of Wesley*, 8:74. Elsewhere, as is correctly (and commonly) noted by the critics, Wesley had a problem with spiritual "laughter" (cf., e.g., Oropeza, *Time to Laugh*, 156-59, for references). However, the anti-manifestation picture of Wesley painted by the critics seriously misses the mark, and, in stark contrast, other historians have sometimes faulted him for actually *looking* for outcries and faintings in his meetings as signs and tokens of God's presence (at least in his earlier years of ministry). For a recent scholarly biography that is not in awe of Wesley, cf. Henry D. Rack, *A Reasonable Enthusiast: John Wesley and the Rise of Methodism* (Philadelphia, PA: Trinity, 1989).

15. Cf. Morphew, *Renewal Apologetics*, 12-13, who actually seeks to interact with the critics over the issue of falling forward or backward from a biblical perspective. For the prevalence of "prostrations" in the 1859 Ireland revival, see Deuwel, *Revival Fire*, 151-60, where both the importance of the phenomenon, along with the controversy surrounding it, are discussed. It is also interesting to note that, while the Ireland prostrations were different in many ways than the "slain in the Spirit" phenomenon, the critics still found fault with the extreme and disruptive nature of these intense responses to the convicting presence of God. According to Professor William Gibson, a leader in the 1859 revival, the prostrations "roused the slumbering mass; they startled whole streets; they called special attention to the deep conviction of the person affected; they awed and awakened the minds of many whom curiosity had brought to 'come and see'; and they were overruled to send many back to their homes and churches to think of their own lives, to cry to God for their own souls, and to look to Christ for pardon and acceptance as they had never looked before" (cited by Deuwel, 160).

16. For a scholarly study of the unusual phenomena (especially visionary) associated with some early American piety, cf. David D. Hall, *Worlds of Wonder, Days of Judgment* (Cambridge: Harvard, 1989); see also Jon Butler, *Awash in a Sea of Faith* (Cambridge: Harvard, 1990); Michael J. Crawford, *Seasons of Grace* (New York: Oxford, 1991). For Iain Murray's comments on Edwards' famous sermon, cf. idem, *Jonathan Edwards*, 217.

17. Once again, this underscores why it is so important for the preaching and teaching of the Word of God to always have a prominent, central role in renewal and revival movements. Cf. also Matthew's summary of Jesus' ministry: "Jesus went throughout Galilee, teaching in their synagogues, preaching the good news of the kingdom, and healing every disease and sickness among the people" (Matt. 4:23; cf. also 9:35), and see again Brown, *Holy Fire*, 235-49.

18. At Brownsville, we receive floods of similar testimonies from leaders who have visited the revival and who have had wonderful moves of the Spirit break out in their churches and ministries.

19. One of the most notable testimonies of this kind is that of Robert Lowell, summarized in *The Pentecostal Evangel* (Nov. 8, 1996), 14. His actual video testimony—when only one week old in the Lord—can be viewed on the videotape entitled "Awesome God," available through the Brownsville Assembly of God.

20. For an insightful statement, cf. Richard Lovelace, *Dynamics of Spiritual Life*, as cited in *Holy Fire*, 216.

21. Relevant here are the comments of Edwards, "How unreasonable is it that we should be backward to acknowledge the glory of what God has done, because the devil, and we in hearkening to him, have done a great deal of mischief!", cited in Murray, *Jonathan Edwards*, 235.

22. For an extreme example of the destructive aspects of negative criticism, cf. the Appendix.

23. Brown, *Holy Fire*, 197-232.

24. I have suggested some practical ministry guidelines relative to revival throughout *Holy Fire*.

25. I heard this directly on an (undated) audiotape message from Duncan Campbell. (Although Campbell died in 1972, there are a number of his tapes on the Hebrides Revival available, along with some short written works, primarily sermon transcripts.)

26. Cited in Murray, *Jonathan Edwards*, 211.

27. Cf. John Wesley, *Works*, 8:25: "You are on the brink of the pit, ready to be plunged into everlasting perdition. Indeed you have a zeal for God; but not according to knowledge. O how terribly have you been deceived! posting to hell, and fancying it was heaven. See, at length, that outward religion, without inward, is nothing; is far worse than nothing, being, indeed, no other than a solemn mockery of God. And inward religion you have not."

28. See the reference to Margaret Poloma's survey in the Appendix. Although there are a relatively small number of vocal and aggressive critics who make a lot of noise in the anti-revival cause, they are completely outnumbered by those being touched by the current revival at the grass roots level.

29. For discussion of John 4:22-24, cf. Barnabas Lindars, *The Gospel of John* (New Century Bible; Grand Rapids: Eerdmans, 1981), 188-90.

30. For references to the principal literature on Azusa Street, cf. C.M. Robeck, Jr., "Azusa Street Revival," in *Dictionary of Pentecostal and Charismatic Movements*, 36 (for the whole article, cf. 31-36).

31. For the full, unedited text, cf. Rosell and Dupuis, *Memoirs*, 323-24.

32. See Evans, *The Welsh Revival of 1904*, 170-71. Interestingly, these remarks of Cynddylan Jones date to December 22, 1904, less than two months into the Welsh Revival.

Chapter Thirteen

1. For a classic study on the letters to the seven churches, cf. Sir William M. Ramsay, *The Letters to the Seven Churches of Asia* (repr., Grand Rapids: Baker, 1963).

2. This interpretation is commonly found among dispensational teachers and scholars; cf. Mounce, *Revelation*, 83-84.

3. Representing the view that the chapters fit well with Church history is John Walvoord, who claims that, "The order of the messages to the churches seems to be divinely selected to give prophetically the movement of history" (cited in Mounce, ibid., 84). In contrast with this, Donald W. Richardson finds such a reading to be "based on pure fancy" (ibid.).

4. Cf. David B. Barrett, "Annual Statistical Table on Global Mission: 1997," *International Bulletin of Missionary Research* 22 (January, 1997), 24-25, in particular the chart on 25, and see below, n. 13. Cf. also James and Marti Hefley, *By Their Blood* (Grand Rapids: Baker, 1979), for the stories of numerous twentieth century martyrs (a second, updated edition has recently been printed).

5. I have addressed this especially in *How Saved Are We?*

6. Such a scenario is also difficult with texts such as Psalms 2 and 110.

7. See above, n. 17 to Chapter Nine.

8. See Clarence Larkin, *Dispensational Truth or God's Plan and Purpose in the Ages* (Philadelphia: Larkin, 1918), the two-page chart entitled, "The Failure of Christianity," located between 77-78.

9. According to Hagner, *Matthew 14–28*, 695, "The failure of love [i.e., in Matt. 24:12] refers more likely to love for others (hence, canceled by the treachery and hatred mentioned in the preceding verses) rather than a failure of love in relation to the truth (as in 2 Thess. 2:10) or God (as in 2 Tim. 3:4; cf. Rev. 2:4), although these contexts too refer to the increase of iniquity. One must remember that love, for Matthew, is the summary of the law (cf. 22:36-40)."

10. For discussion of the broader context, cf. ibid., 692-96, entitled by him, "Persecution and Proclamation before the End."

11. There are some teachers who would point out that 2 Thessalonians 2:3 also predicts an end-time apostasy (cf. Bruce, *1 & 2 Thessalonians*, 162-68, for comments, although his emphasis on political rebellion will not satisfy all); regardless, however, of the exact interpretation of the text, the *application* of the text is perfectly clear: This "falling away" will center in on the worship of a man who claims to be God; cf. above, n. 14 to Chapter Five.

12. For some of the current pretenders, cf. Lewis, *Smashing the Gates of Hell*, cited above, n. 7 to Chapter Five. One of the most influential "divine incarnations" in India today is Sai Baba, himself an alleged reincarnation of an even more famous Sai Baba, prominent earlier this century, whose picture can be seen throughout the nation (i.e., on signs hanging in front of stores and businesses, on the backs of trucks, and on pendants and good luck charms).

13. The Voice of the Martyrs, which has chronicled the atrocities in Sudan for some years now, has a short documentary video available, "Mission Sudan," along with an audiotape, "Testimonies from Sudan." They can be contacted at: P.O. Box 443, Bartlesville, OK 74005. For the inspiring (and shattering) story of the suffering Church in China, cf. now Danyun, *Lilies Amongst Thorns* (Eng. tr., Brother Dennis [Balcombe]; Kent, England: Sovereign World, 1991).

14. For commentary and discussion on Revelation 7:9-14, cf. again Mounce, *Revelation*, 170-76.

15. According to Carson, *Matthew 13–28*, 503, " 'If that were possible' clearly suggests that 'deceive' is not ecbatic (i.e., 'with the result that')," noting however, that the verse does not offer "any comment on how ultimately successful such attacks will be." According to Hagner, *Matthew 14–28*, 706, "The implication of *ei dunaton*, 'if possible,' is that the *elektoi*, 'elect' or 'chosen' (elsewhere in Matt. 22:14; 24:22, 31), are in the care of their Father (cf. 10:29-31) and that it is therefore not within the power of these enemies to accomplish their purpose." Still, one must wonder why earlier in His discourse Jesus specifically said to His disciples, "Take heed that no one deceive you ..."—if deception were, in fact, impossible for the elect.

16. See above, n. 18 to Chapter Nine. On the prospects of evangelizing the entire world by the year 2000, cf. David B. Barrett, *Our Globe and How to Reach It: Seeing the world evangelized by AD 2000 & Beyond* (Birmingham, AL: New Hope, 1990).

17. Exact lists of translations are readily available through the major Bible societies (especially the United Bible Society).

18. I first heard this oft-quoted information from David Shibley at a missions conference held in Rockville, Maryland, in 1992, which is statistically confirmed in works such as the *World Christian Encyclopedia*, ed. by David W. Barrett. See also, more broadly, Frank Kaleb Jansen, ed., *Target Earth* (Global Mapping International/University of the Nations, 1989).

19. These statistics, prepared by the Lausanne Action Committee (headed by Barrett), were amplified and distributed by *Mission Frontiers* (US Center for World Mission) and circulated via Internet.

20. These statistics from Barrett date back several years now and, hence, could be somewhat outdated. For Barrett's most recent figures and projections—with some sobering data on the job yet to be done—cf. his "Annual Statistical Table," 24-25.

21. For an edifying treatment of Zechariach 10:1, cf. David Baron, *The Visions and Prophecies of Zechariah* (repr., Grand Rapids: Kregel, 1972), 337-41.

22. See concisely Frank S. Frick, "Rain," in *Anchor Bible Dictionary*, 5:612.

23. Note the remarks of C.F. Keil, in idem and F. Delitzsch, *Commentary on the Old Testament* (repr., Grand Rapids: Eerdmans, 1973), 2:44-47.

24. Ravenhill made this comment to Steve Hill just weeks before his stroke in September, 1994, a stroke from which he never regained consciousness, going to be with the Lord in November, 1994. When the Spirit of God fell suddenly at Brownsville Assembly of God after Steve preached there on Father's Day, 1995 (the beginning, of course, of the Brownsville Revival), Steve remembered these words, which helped him to decide to cancel all his other engagements (including some overseas church-planting work) in order to seize this "opportunity of a life-time" for the glory of God.

25. Cited in Wallis, *In the Day of Thy Power*, 18.

26. Relevant here are the commentaries to passages such as Matthew 7:13-14 and Luke 13:23-30.

27. See above, n. 12.

28. For a good example of a modern post-millennial interpretation of Matthew 24, cf. J. Marcelus Kik, *Matthew Twenty-Four: An Eschatology of Victory* (repr., Philadelphia: Presbyterian & Reformed, 1961).

29. Brown, *How Saved Are We?*, 119-20.

Chapter Fourteen

1. From his sermon, "Gratitude for Deliverance from the Grave," in *55 Selected Expositions*, 457.

2. Ibid.

3. See Joseph Tracy, *The Great Awakening* (repr., Carlisle, PA: Banner of Truth, 1989), 79.

4. See Murray, *Jonathan Edwards*, 247.

5. From his sermon, "A Warning to Believers," in *55 Selected Expositions*, 785.

6. Cited in Ravenhill, *Why Revival Tarries*, 68; see also Brown, *How Saved Are We?*, 105.

7. See above, n. 19 to Chapter Six, for relevant literature.

8. To this day, one of the most common Jewish objections to the Messiahship of Jesus is that He died without establishing the visible, earthly kingdom of God on the earth (as per the classical statement of Maimonides, Mishneh Torah, Sepher Shophetim, Hilkhot Melakhim, Chapter 11). For responses to this, see my forthcoming study, *Will the Real Messiah Please Rise*.

9. From his sermon "Fragrant Graces," in *55 Selected Expositions*, 813.

10. There is, of course, a time to offer strong rebuke to critics, especially when: 1) they misrepresent a work of God; 2) they slander other believers, groups, and leaders; 3) they misuse the Word; 4) they distort the truth (or even lie!); 5) they bring serious divisions to the Body. Unfortunately, as mentioned briefly in the Preface, some critics of the current revival have been guilty of all of the above, either cumulatively or individually. For New Testament exhortations (especially to leadership) on the importance of rebuke, cf., e.g., Luke 17:3; 1 Timothy 5:20; 2 Timothy 4:1-4; Titus 1:10-13; 2:15; 3:10-11; Revelation 3:19.

11. Cf. Murray, *Jonathan Edwards*, 475-80, for a chronological listing of his writings.

12. In point of fact, I am not aware of any current revival critic who is fostering anything that can be called "revival," and, in general, the critics have been so destructive and, often, judgmental that any valid concerns they might raise are lost in their sea of negativity; cf. my closing remarks in the Appendix.

13. As noted by the secular media in its coverage of the Brownsville Revival, as of this writing (May, 1997), this revival is now the longest and most influential religious phenomenon of its kind in America in 90 years! Cf. Rick Bragg, writing in the *New York Times*, May 27, 1997, A1, who called it "apparently the largest and longest-running Pentecostal revival in more than a century," while Peter Carlson in the *Washington Post*, April 27, 1997, F4, noted that, "The Pensacola Outpouring is easily the longest-running revival in America since the famous Azusa Street Revival that began in Los Angeles in 1906 and lasted for nearly three years...."

14. This quote is from Wesley's sermon on Mark 9:38-39 entitled, "A Caution Against Bigotry." To cite him more fully—and in the context of his Scripture text from Mark, dealing with a man who drove out demons in Jesus' name but whom the disciples wanted to stop because he was not "one of us"—Wesley stated: "...if we either directly or indirectly forbid him, 'because he followeth not us,' then we are bigots. This is the inference I draw from what has been said. But the term bigotry, I fear, as frequently as it is used, is almost as little understood as enthusiasm. It is, too strong an attachment to, or fondness for, our own party, opinion, Church, and religion. Therefore he is a bigot who is so fond of any of these, so strongly attached to them, as to forbid any who casts out devils because he differs from himself in any or all these particulars....Do you beware of this. Take care, (1.) That you do not convict yourself of bigotry, by your unreadiness to believe that any man does cast out devils, who differs from you. And if you are clear thus far, if you acknowledge the fact, then examine yourself, (2.) Am I not convicted of bigotry in this, in forbidding him directly or indirectly? Do I not directly forbid him on this ground, because he is not of my party?—because he does not fall in with my opinions?—or, because he does not worship God according to that scheme of religion which I have received from my fathers?" See *The Works of Wesley*, 5:592. How applicable these words are today!

15. In all candor, this book would never have been completed if I had taken the time to reply to every such critical query, nor would other revival leaders be able to give themselves to the lost and backslidden if they tried to respond to similar questions or charges.

16. Although the critics often disdain the popular comment that "God offends the mind to reveal the heart," Jonathan Edwards actually made a similar comment: "It is with Christ's works as it was with his parables; things that are difficult to men's dark minds are ordered of purpose, for the trial of their dispositions and spiritual sense; and that those of corrupt minds and of an unbelieving, perverse, cavilling spirit, 'seeing might see and not understand.'" (From the *Distinguishing Marks*; see *Jonathan Edwards on Revival*, 133). These principles apply, by extension, to *believers* with unbelieving or "cavilling" attitudes.

17. Cited in Murray, *Jonathan Edwards*, 202.

18. Charles G. Finney, *Revivals of Religion* (repr., Old Tappan, NJ: Revell, n.d.), 124-25.

19. Ibid., 125.

20. See, briefly, my relevant comments in the Appendix. By the way, it should also be noted that those who are allegedly being worked into an "altered state of consciousness" (ASC) in a revival service should presumably enter into some such state during or after the meeting. In other words, they should experience at least *some* alteration in their emotional or mental condition that becomes evident at a certain point. (Forgive me for stating the obvious!) Unfortunately for the critics, some of the very people whom they claim work themselves into an "ASC" are perfect examples of level-headed, sound Christianity—singing, worshiping, taking notes on sermons, praying, casually conversing, etc.—the whole time they are supposedly "losing touch with reality." So because the critics have a problem with a certain kind of worship music or preaching, or because they are troubled by a particular manifestation or phenomena, or because they find no way of denying the reality of the fruit produced, they resort to using sophisticated-sounding—but factually untrue and inappropriate—terms like "shamanism" and "ASCs," as mentioned often throughout this book. Aside from their analysis being almost always incorrect, it is highly opinionated, speaking sometimes of things of which it has no right to speak. Cf. above, n. 9 to Chapter Four. Furthermore, many psychologists would point out that the concept of "ASCs" is quite nebulous, since one's conscious state is generally altered numerous times through a given day with nothing dangerous or ominous implied. Finally, in the words of one of my students, some people need to have their state of consciousness altered!

21. Finney, *Revivals of Religion*, 133.

22. There are, however, exceptions to this! Cf. the actual words of one critic cited above, n. 9 to Chapter Four, as well as even uglier, sicker things (really!) that are now being written and spoken. For example, the very moment that I finished compiling the notes to this chapter, a colleague alerted me to what can only be called a perverse Website (it actually features an audio download of someone vomiting) with almost unbelievable references to Brownsville: "a most terrifying display of Satanic devil possession"; "this filth from Hell"; "the Brownsville Mafia." Accordingly, it supplies a picture of one Brownsville leader whom it describes as "devil possessed," also stating that any churches listed on www.brownsville-revival.org/churches.html (a list of churches and ministries favorable to the Brownsville Revival) are "part of God's vomit" (Rev. 3:16; this text, of course, explains the tasteful audio download). Of course, unmitigated trash like this is the exception, not the rule, and it would be unfair to the majority of critics to associate them with this kind of junk. However, as the revival increases and intensifies, more and more critics are becoming increasingly vile and hostile in their attacks, and the Internet provides an uncensored and unaccountable medium through which the more unknown scoffers can disseminate their views. But none of this fazes the Lord, nor should it faze us!

23. Speaking of the terrible sufferings of our Savior, Melito of Sardis wrote (late second century): "He who hung the earth [in its place] hangs there, he who fixed the heavens is fixed there, he who made all things fast is made fast upon the

tree, the Master has been insulted, God has been murdered, the King of Israel has been slain by an Israelite hand. O strange murder, strange crime! The Master has been treated in unseemly fashion, his body naked, and not even deemed worthy of a covering that [his nakedness] might not be seen. Therefore the lights [of heaven] turned away, and the day darkened, that it might hide him who was stripped upon the cross" (cited in Gerald G. O'Collins, "Crucifixion," *Anchor Bible Dictionary*, 1:1210; for the entire article, see 1207-10). In light of what *He* has done for *us* (and remember Romans 5:6-10!), how can we do any less for Him? Cf. also the words of missionary Amy Carmichael: "To any whom the Hand Divine is beckoning: count the cost, for He tells us to, *but take your slate to the foot of the Cross and add up the figures there*"; see Elizabeth Elliot, *A Chance to Die* (Old Tappan, NJ: Fleming H. Revell, 1987), 99. Some of her other comments are no less stinging. She wrote, "I don't wonder apostolic miracles have died. Apostolic living certainly has" (ibid., 85), observing that, "Satan is so much more in earnest than we are—he buys up the opportunity while we are wondering how much it will cost" (ibid.). Formative in the thinking of Amy Carmichael were the words of Francois Coillard, missionary of the Zambesi: "The evangelization of the world is a desperate struggle with the Prince of Darkness and with everything his rage can stir up in the shape of obstacles, vexations, oppositions, and hatred, whether by circumstances or by the hand of man. It is a serious task. Oh, it should mean a life of consecration" (ibid., 117). Does it?

Appendix

1. In keeping with a commitment I made to the author during an extended phone conversation on March 20, 1997, I have made only selective reference to *Counterfeit Revival* in the main body of endnotes in this book, instead devoting this special appendix to its review. In any case, the bulk of *Let No One Deceive You* was already completed before my copy of *Counterfeit Revival* was sent to me, and its arguments have little bearing on the issues I treat here. However, because Hanegraaff has made it clear that he wants *Counterfeit Revival* to be taken seriously, I have subjected it to a careful review. Nonetheless, I have resisted the temptation to exhaustively critique his study, since objections could have been raised and clarifications offered on almost every page of the book.

2. Other leading Word authors include Max Lucado and Pat Robertson. One of their most recent projects was the *Everyday Study Bible*, to which I was one of the contributing Old Testament scholars.

3. In point of fact, I am not a spokesman for any of the movements which Hanegraaff attacks throughout his book and cannot evaluate in each and every case whether they have been accurately represented. My only official relationship is with the Brownsville Revival, which Hanegraaff mentions just once on 244, again, in an imprecise context: "While pastors and parishioners are traveling to 'power centers' like Toronto, Canada, and Pensacola, Florida, looking for a quick fix, the solution is found in the fundamentals." Although I am not qualified to speak for Toronto, having never attended a meeting there, I can say that the emphasis in Pensacola is on the fundamentals: "Get the sin out of your life, get right with God, walk in intimacy with Jesus, and reach out to the lost. We, on our part,

will pray for you that the Lord would give you a fresh touch of His Spirit." Is this "a quick fix"?

4. Notwithstanding Hanegraaff's conciliatory comment on 157. Interestingly, Hanegraaff has a background with the Church of God, one of the largest Pentecostal denominations, and would not classify himself as anti-charismatic.

5. Those specifically singled out are A.A. Allen, William Branham, and Jack Coe, either because they have at times been referred to in positive terms by some renewal leaders (see, e.g., 131), or because they, among all the prominent healing evangelists, had the most debatable and/or scandalous practices or doctrines. In any case, Hanegraaff's broad-stroked brush also manages to smear the ministries of Maria Woodworth-Etter, Aimee Semple MacPherson, and Kathryn Kuhlman (165-70). In contrast with this totally negative assessment is the important scholarly work of David Edwin Harrell, Jr., *All Things Are Possible: The Healing and Charismatic Revivals in Modern America* (Bloomington: Indiana University Press, 1975). For Hanegraaff, Harrell, whom he cited, served only as a documentor of "the bad and the ugly," since in *Counterfeit Revival*, "the good" was simply left out. See also idem, *Oral Roberts: An American Life* (Bloomington: Indiana University Press, 1985).

6. The fact that men such as Word of Faith teacher Kenneth Hagin and Vineyard founder John Wimber are both fashioned to be "Counterfeit Revival" leaders—when in fact, they have certainly never ministered together, have probably never even met, and are involved in very different spiritual camps and flows—indicates just how broadly (and imprecisely) Hanegraaff has cast his net.

7. On 61, his assessment, again without any documentation, is slightly more moderate in tone: "Followers who at first crowded through the front doors of [the renewal] churches often become disillusioned and fall out the back door, *some* even into the kingdom of the cults" (my emphasis).

8. Cf., e.g., 22-29, with reference to Rodney Howard-Browne, and note especially 28: "[Karl] Strader [at Carpenter's Home Church in Lakeland, Florida] provided Howard-Browne with the opportunity to finally capture his claims on camera. As thousands looked on, however, Howard-Browne's claims of the miraculous did not materialize." Note also the following descriptions of John Wimber's alleged duplicity: "Wimber uses what appears to be an elaborate deception to fool followers...Wimber again uses his term switching tactic to fool followers...it appears that Wimber uses socio-psychological manipulation tactics to work his devotees into altered states of consciousness. Not only that, but as we have seen, seekers are seduced through a variety of Scripture-twisting tactics as well" (184, 186, 190). In point of fact, what Hanegraaff labels willful deception on Wimber's part (in terms of interpretation of Scripture) is better explained as misunderstanding of the Hebrew or Greek, an all too common occurrence in many pulpits across the land today, but hardly a matter of intentional duplicity.

9. It is ironic at best and hypocritical at worst for Hanegraaff to quote the famous "unity, liberty, charity" maxim, a motto of Richard Baxter, in a completely non-charitable book such as *Counterfeit Revival*.

10. Jack Deere, *Surprised by the Power of God* (Grand Rapids: Zondervan, 1993); idem, *Surprised by the Voice of God* (Grand Rapids: Zondervan, 1996). In

these books, Deere also presents a very different picture of Paul Cain than does Hanegraaff.

11. Similarly, Hanegraaff chooses only to quote Mike Bickle's audiotapes, ignoring his recent book *Passion for Jesus* (Orlando: Creation House, 1993), which clearly communicates Bickle's heart and gives us a more complete picture of what this so-called "Counterfeit Revival leader" believes. Likewise, some of Wimber's more extreme audio comments are extracted by Hanegraaff, while his important, written works are not cited at all. (Only one such work, *Power Evangelism*, is included in the bibliography, but it is not incorporated into any of Hanegraaff's discussion.)

12. Ruthven was kind enough to supply me with a transcript summarizing his discussion with Mrs. Lilliman. After his 45-minute phone interview, he called her back and restated the material to her for confirmation. Thus he has assured me of the accuracy of his discussion with her.

13. Mrs. Lilliman continued, "In the hospital she was blind but she's not blind now. [In the hospital before prayer] you could put your hand suddenly right in front of her eyes and she couldn't see anything." Ruthven notes that, "At another point in the interview responding to the same question" (viz., that of Sarah's alleged legal blindness), Mrs. Lilliman said, "Oh no, no. She can see...she has videos she watches; she does cursive writing...she goes for walks ["without a cane!"—said Mrs. Lilliman, a joking reference to the claim she is blind], does cooking, etc." Furthermore, Ruthven states, "Mrs. Lilliman stressed that the healing consisted of the restoration of a paralyzed and blind girl back to her original state [which does not mean perfect health or sight, but rather a return to her prior condition, which included some mental and physical disabilities from birth] before she became almost fatally ill. She has no question that what happened to her daughter was 'a miracle.' "

14. See his *Thoughts on Stewardship I* and *II* (n.p.: n.p., n.d.).

15. Note also the following inaccuracies from the index on 310-15 (and this list is certainly not exhaustive): Mike Bickle is described as a "Kansas City prophet" (instead of pastor); Jack Deere is a "revivalist" (instead of Vineyard teacher or pastor); Patrick Dixon is also a "revivalist" (instead of an author and medical scholar [specializing in genetics]). Interestingly, it is the revival critic Nick Needham who is called "Dr." The impression this gives, of course, is obvious. Whoever Nick Needham is, he carries authority! (By the way, this is certainly not meant as a dig against Dr. Needham, whose points as quoted by Hanegraaff are sometimes well taken. It is with Hanegraaff's selective use of the term "Dr." that I take issue.)

16. In private correspondence between Ravenhill and Hanegraaff, initiated by the former, Hanegraaff reaffirmed that he felt he had accurately represented Ravenhill, claiming, however, that his description of him as a "prophet" was not meant to be pejorative.

17. *Quenching the Spirit: Discover the REAL Spirit Behind the Charismatic Controversy* (2nd ed., Orlando, FL: Creation House, 1996). This edition has a new chapter entitled "The Tragedy of Hank Hanegraaff and the CRI"),

along with additional notes. In *Counterfeit Revival*, only the first edition (1992) is cited.

18. Please note that I have carefully avoided taking cheap shots at *Counterfeit Revival*. The issues treated here are substantive and revealing.

19. As a Jewish believer in Jesus, as well as a contributor to the *Oxford Dictionary of Jewish Religion* (New York: Oxford University Press, 1997), I am painfully aware of both sides of the debate, on the one hand holding to the conviction that the Pharisees of old, just like the rabbis of today, needed to receive Jesus as their promised Messiah, while on the other hand recognizing that Jewish leaders have been demonized through the years by various Church leaders. For more on the former, see my forthcoming book, *Will the Real Messiah Please Rise: Answering Jewish Objections to Jesus* (Baltimore, MD: Lederer, 1997); for more on the latter, see *Our Hands Are Stained With Blood: The Tragic Story of the "Church" and the Jewish People*. In Chapter Four of this present book, I characterized as "blind guides" those leaders whom Jesus specifically rebuked as such, as opposed to applying this to all Pharisees, which is similar to the rest of Hanegraaff's statement on 269, n. 66, where he notes that the Pharisees, "for the most part, rejected Christ and attributed Christ's works to Beelzebub or Satan." It is, however, the first part of Hanegraaff's description that is so distasteful.

20. Note also that Hanegraaff frequently cites the *Dictionary of Pentecostal and Charismatic Movements* as a final authority, failing to deal with primary sources and documents, and failing to realize that the rather short articles in the *Dictionary* (which is, of course, a valuable reference tool) can hardly be expected to provide comprehensive coverage of the subjects treated. For example, he casts aspersion on the claim of Kenneth Hagin and Benny Hinn (among others) that healing evangelist Maria Woodworth-Etter once went into a 24-hour (or, three-day) trance while preaching, because the *Dictionary* only asserts that she "often went into trances during services and would stand 'like a statue for an hour or more with her hands raised while the services continued' " (165-66). So, because the *Dictionary* only gives general, corroborating information and not the specific, detailed report, Hinn and Hagin are deceivers. (By the way, Woodworth-Etter is also dismissed by Hanegraaff as a false prophet and false teacher, who, "Like leaders of today's Counterfeit Revival...was a master at taking Scripture out of context and using it as a pretext to support endtime restorationism as well as the practice of slaying subjects in the spirit." See 166-67.)

21. Cf. David E. Aune, *Prophecy in Early Christianity and the Early Mediterranean World* (Grand Rapids: Eerdmans, 1983) for comprehensive discussion up to the early 1980's. For further references to key works on New Testament prophecy, see n. 14 to Chapter Four, above. Suffice it to say here that there are several differences between Old Testament and New Testament prophets that are quite obvious. For example: 1) there was no binding, earthly, spiritual authority over Old Testament prophets, whereas New Testament prophets are part of an (accountable) leadership structure; 2) the audience of the Old Testament prophets was often apostate and, even when godly, was limited in its ability to discern apart from the written Word, whereas the audience of New Testament prophets is essentially the Church, hence consisting of believers (even if somewhat compromised),

all of whom have the Spirit within and the (potential) ability to discern by that indwelling Spirit, as well as by the Word; 3) Old Testament prophets spoke during the period of canonization of Scripture, whereas New Testament prophets continued to speak after the canon was closed (a distinction noted in the very article in the *New Bible Dictionary* cited by Hanegraaff). Note further that Old Testament prophecy was limited to select individuals or groups, whereas in the New Testament the Spirit is poured out on all flesh, hence calling for more discernment and judging by the other (prophetic?) leaders in the Body. Cf. also Wayne A. Grudem, *The Gift of Prophecy* (Westchester, IL: Crossway, 1988).

22. Cf. these remarks on 220: "Like Gnostics in the second and third centuries, *many* who claim the name of Christ are taking a trip beyond Christianity into the world of the *occult*. They are being convinced by leaders of the Counterfeit Revival that reality can be reduced to a personal experience of enlightenment—a transformation of consciousness that will initiate them into 'true spirituality'" (my emphasis). Note again that nothing that has been stated before or after these pages substantiates these extraordinary claims.

23. For details of the survey of Margaret Poloma, a University of Akron sociologist, see Jon Ruthven's forthcoming review of *Counterfeit Revival* in *Charisma* ("The reports of 850 people surveyed contradicted Hank Hanegraaff's book at the significant points.") Hanegraaff has scorned *Charisma* as "the *National Enquirer* of Christian magazines" and he twice accuses leaders of the "Counterfeit Revival" of using *National Enquirer* type tactics. However, readers of *Counterfeit Revival* might find Hanegraaff's sensationalistic, bombastic attacks reminiscent of the very publication he refers to as the epitome of yellow journalism.

24. Dr. Patrick Dixon, *Signs of Revival* (Eastbourne: Kingsway, 1994), 247, part of his chapter entitled "Medical Perspectives on Manifestations" (233-79). Dixon is a highly qualified medical researcher and Christian author whose chapter referred to here provides important data. Although certain points can be disputed (including his usage of certain texts), his scientific explanations are highly valuable.

25. On 227, Hanegraaff notes, "As has been well documented from studies of the world of the occult, the dangerous effects [achieved through working people into altered states of consciousness] may involve depression, detachment, depersonalization, disillusionment, and many equally serious disorders." However, although Hanegraaff may be able to point to some Christians whose experience in recent renewal meetings left them depressed and disillusioned, multiplied thousands of Christians from around the world would attest to the exact *opposite* experience in their own lives—short term and long term. (Such testimonies are readily available.) See again the results of Poloma's survey, cited in Ruthven's review (see n. 23 above).

26. In typical fashion, Hanegraaff recounts the tragic death of a woman in a Benny Hinn meeting caused by someone falling on her after being "slain in the Spirit" (173-74), but makes no reference to the fact that a number of attendees at Hinn rallies attest to being *healed* of terminal illnesses after prayer. (If I am correct, Hanegraaff does not believe that anyone has truly been healed of such illnesses through Hinn's ministry.)

27. To give one case in point of just how undermining to pastoral authority Hanegraaff's show can be, on August 16, 1996, a caller asked whether he should leave a church in which the pastor had begun to show videos from one particular revival. Hanegraaff's answer was that this was a "no brainer" and that by staying he was putting his children "in harm's way." To add fuel to this caller's fire, Hanegraaff then played a highly selective portion of one audiotape from this revival, further exacerbated by his painting a thoroughly misleading picture of what the corresponding videotape actually portrayed.

28. Predictably, Hanegraaff offers a totally extreme example as if it were typical, describing a service in which a song was sung for over three hours in a Rick Joyner conference (221), almost giving the impression that such an occurrence was not completely extraordinary and highly unusual.

29. A typical example of such "non-proving" proofs can be found on 222. First, Hanegraaff claims that the "Counterfeit Revival" leaders, "like Eastern gurus...work their devotees into altered states of consciousness," quoting Rick Joyner in alleged support of this: "Joyner, in fact, says that 'experience is a much better teacher than words'." However, Joyner's fairly innocuous statement hardly proves Hanegraaff's point. Nonetheless, he proceeds, as if his quotes and dogmatic statements have somehow demonstrated his point, declaring, "In stark contrast, Dr. Elizabeth Hillstrom warns that altered states of consciousness can be an open invitation for demonic deception" (a quote from Dr. Hillstrom then follows). Even to the mildly discerning reader, it is clear that Hanegraaff has demonstrated nothing here except: 1) he has a very negative opinion of current renewal services; and 2) altered states of consciousness can be dangerous. But nothing has been proven. Reminiscent of this is the comment of John Wesley to one of his critics: "You have brought five accusations against me; and have not been able to make one good. However, you are resolved to throw dirt enough, that some may stick."

30. Ibid., 247.

31. I am not referring here to the acronyms FLESH and APES, which, of course, are overt acronyms.

32. See also above, Chapter Four, characteristic five of a destructive, critical spirit (viz., it feeds on negativity and fosters unbelief, suspicion, and fear).

33. Other important works, such as Edith L. Blumhofer and Randall Balmer, eds., *Modern Christian Revivals* (Urbana and Chicago: University of Illinois Press, 1993), and Richard M. Riss, *20th-Century Revival Movements in North America* (Peabody, MA: Hendrickson, 1988), that give a far more balanced perspective on recent revival movements are not cited at all. Note also John Avant, Malcom McDow, and Alvin Reid, eds., *Revival!* (Nashville: Broadman & Holman, 1996), documenting the college awakenings "in Brownwood, Ft. Worth, Wheaton, and Beyond" (from the subtitle). Undoubtedly, these awakenings must be viewed as just another part of the worldwide awakening to which I have frequently referred in this book. God *is* moving around the world today!

34. Richard F. Lovelace, *Dynamics of Spiritual Life: An Evangelical Theology of Renewal* (Downers Grove, IL: InterVarsity, 1979).

35. Oropeza, a former researcher for the Christian Research Institute, recently informed me that his overall perspective on current renewal and revival is now somewhat more positive than it was at the time of writing *Time to Laugh*. This change in perspective, of course, does not in any way detract from the charitable and analytical style of his book, since what has changed is *not* historical revival phenomena but rather current revival movements, which are clearly deepening and maturing.

36. Interestingly, the current repentance-based revival bears all the main characteristics of a true visitation as outlined in *Counterfeit Revival*, 103-116 (although here too, Hanegraaff has used Edwards for his own purposes, for which see immediately below).

37. For those who are unfamiliar with the term "historical revisionism," it is most commonly used today to describe those who deny that the Holocaust occurred. Thus historical revisionists rewrite the past so as to make it suit their own agenda and beliefs.

38. *Catch the Fire: The Toronto Blessing—an experience of renewal and revival* (London: Marshall Pickering, 1994).

39. Iain H. Murray, *The Banner of Truth* (1995), 28. Murray's review is a fine example of gracious Christian scholarship (in stark contrast with *Counterfeit Revival*), although his anti-Pentecostal convictions certainly underlie much of his critique: "We do not believe that the way forward for the church today is to take up the distinctives of Pentecostalism in the hope of revival....there is too much in Pentecostalism which positively encourages the temporary and the illusory" (29). Pentecostals, no doubt, would suggest that there is too much in *non*-Pentecostalism that positively encourages formalism and staid traditionalism! Further dialogue on such issues would certainly be profitable and mutually enlightening.

40. Chevreau privately communicated to me that the issue for him was one of pastoral treatment of the physical phenomena, thus attention needed to be given to these unusual things.

41. Whether or not someone accepts Dixon's views on the charismatic renewal is not the issue here; rather, I only point out that he is fully aware that services today—even without "revival" phenomena—are often quite different than eighteenth and nineteenth century services were. Thus Dixon cites an example of Wesley's problem with the laughter phenomenon in 1740 ("he was clearly convinced that laughter was so unhelpful that presumably it was demonic") yet adds, "I have no doubt that if he had been alive in 1994 he might well have seen it differently" (*Signs of Revival*, 126). Obviously, some readers would take strong exception to this statement. However, it shows Dixon's awareness of some of the larger problems of cultural and church experience that must be addressed, and he is quite candid with the evidence he treats: "It was clearly just as confusing then as it is today" (ibid., 132).

42. Although Hanegraaff's errors with regard to Edwards were very apparent to me, I consulted with three different Edwards' scholars, two of whom are engaged in the production of Yale University's multi-volume project *The Works of Jonathan Edwards*. They confirmed to me the accuracy of my understanding. Once again, the lack of interaction with serious Edwards scholarship in *Counterfeit Revival* is striking (and there exists quite an extensive bibliography on the

writings and thought of Edwards), the two primary sources cited being Murray's fine biography and Needham's self-published work, *Was Jonathan Edwards the Founding Father of the Toronto Blessing?* (Welling, Kent, England: Nick Needham, 1995).

43. All these caveats, which I have previously made (cf. most recently *Holy Fire*, 16-25 and 234-49), hardly apply to the current repentance-based revival in which the piercing preaching of the Word plays a pivotal role and in which sobs, wails, prostrations, and even loss of strength and collapsing are commonly the result of the ministry of the Word.

44. A more full picture of even Iain Murray's position can be gained by reading his entire chapter, "Division and Disorder," *Jonathan Edwards: A New Biography*, 203-29; see further ibid., 233-67.

45. Oropeza, *Time to Laugh*, 150-51. In *Holy Fire*, 216-32, I also present this material in somewhat fuller form, making practical application of Edwards' signs to help us in evaluating current revival movements.

46. See conveniently *Jonathan Edwards on Revival* (Carlisle, PA: Banner of Truth, 1984), 91-94.

47. See *Edwards on Revival* (Worchester: Moses W. Grout, 1832), 95-96; for the conclusion to this quote, which is even stronger, see n. 4 to Chapter Five.

48. It should be noted here that Edwards is saying that the principle of *sola Scriptura* militates *against* making any judgments as to the genuineness of a spiritual work based on bodily responses. Thus, while the critics often raise the cry of, "The Scriptures alone are our all-sufficient guide," they actually *go beyond* the Scriptures and *outside* the Scriptures in disclaiming the validity of a move of the Spirit because of unusual physical manifestations or emotional responses.

49. Oropeza, *Time to Laugh*, 151.

50. I believe that Oropeza's concise summary of Edwards' views on the Awakening (*Time to Laugh*, 147-56) is quite fair, and, in the few pages devoted to the subject, evidences far more interaction with relevant Edwards scholarship than does Hanegraaff in all of *Counterfeit Revival*.

51. In the case of James Davenport, he was actually pronounced mentally unfit and brought under Church discipline. Thankfully Edwards and others were successful in restoring him to fruitful pastoral ministry.

52. Oropeza, *Time to Laugh*, 151-53.

53. Cf. also *Counterfeit Revival*, 14: "The lying signs and wonders [Jonathan] Edwards and [Peter] Cartwright denounced have taken center stage in today's Counterfeit Revival."

54. The primary source cited by Hanegraaff to back this up, *Religion in America*, by George C. Bedell, Leo Sandon, Jr., and Charles T. Wellborn (New York: Macmillan, 1975), 153, was also dismissed by this Edwards scholar as hardly authoritative.

55. Although Hanegraaff makes reference to the "extemporaneous [preaching] manner of men like [Presbyterian minister] James McGready" (117), anyone reading McGready's sermons today would be struck by their penetrating, convicting, and systematic content. Though he may well have preached extemporaneously, he certainly did not preach out of any empty head and heart.

56. For references, cf. again Oropeza, *Time to Laugh*, 163; note that Earle E. Cairns, *An Endless Line of Splendor: Revivals and Their Leaders from the Great Awakening to the Present* (Wheaton, IL: Tyndale, 1986), 85-116, dates the "Second Awakening" from 1776 to 1810, labelling the period from 1813–46 the "Protestant Transatlantic Revival" (116-46). In doing so, he does not follow the general scholarly consensus, since, he observes, "Most scholar writing on revival combine movements of 1776–1810 with those of 1813–46, referring to the movements as the Second Awakening" (117).

57. In this light, it is altogether appropriate that this lengthy review should close out the present volume.

58. I would remind readers that the subtitle of one of my books asks the question "Is the Charismatic Church Slain in the Spirit or Down for the Count?", reflecting my burden to see those of us who call ourselves "Spirit-filled" believers really live the Spirit-filled, Heaven-empowered life. Moreover, one of my (still unpublished) poems, written in September, 1995, is entitled "Slobbering in the Spirit," sarcastically critiquing the excesses that often accompany experience-based, superficial, "bless-me" meetings; see also the selection from my poem, "We All Fall Down," in *Holy Fire*, 22-23. Thus, it is fair to say that I am anything but a proponent of "anything goes" renewal.

59. Other parts of the world, of course, have been experiencing seasons of true revival for decades now. In fact, one interesting proof of the universal nature of the current outpouring is the fact that many similar songs and choruses—with precious revival themes—have been written independently around the world. Although Hanegraaff's assessment of current renewal/revival songs is totally negative ("today's Counterfeit Revival has spawned songs that can only be classified as superficial, shallow, and shameful"; 245), the fact is that many of these songs speak of intimacy with the Lord, reveal deep spiritual hunger, convey a longing to see the glory of God fill the earth, express an ardent desire to see the lost saved, and cry for holiness and purity. In fact, it was some of these very songs that helped me to realize just how wonderfully the Spirit *was* moving throughout the Church around the world.

60. See, conveniently *The Oxford Dictionary of Quotations* (3rd ed., New York: Oxford University Press, 1980), 169-70.

61. For those who were hoping that Hanegraaff would have embraced the current repentance-based visitation as epitomized in the Brownsville Revival—since the emphasis in Brownsville is clearly on holiness and the harvest—the fact is that he has singled out this revival for regular attack in his radio broadcasts, grouping its practices with those of cults such as Jonestown, Waco, and Heaven's Gate, and accusing its leaders of preaching false and dangerous doctrines. History will record just how tragically he has missed the mark here.

Destiny Image
Revival Books
by Dr. Michael L. Brown

THE END OF THE AMERICAN GOSPEL ENTERPRISE
In this important and confrontational book, Dr. Michael Brown identifies the sore spots of American Christianity and points out the prerequisites for revival.
Paperback Book, 112p. ISBN 1-56043-002-8 Retail $7.99

FROM HOLY LAUGHTER TO HOLY FIRE
America is on the edge of a national awakening—God is responding to the cries of His people! This stirring book passionately calls us to remove the roadblocks to revival. If you're looking for the "real thing" in God, this book is must reading!
Paperback Book, 294p. ISBN 1-56043-181-4 Retail $9.99

HOW SAVED ARE WE?
This volume clearly challenges us to question our born-again experience if we feel no call to personal sacrifice, separation from the world, and the hatred of sin. It will create in you the desire to live a life truly dedicated to God.
Paperback Book, 144p. ISBN 1-56043-055-9 Retail $7.99

IT'S TIME TO ROCK THE BOAT
Here is a book whose time has come. It is a radical, noncompromising, no-excuse call to genuine Christian activism: intercessory prayer and the action that one must take as a result of that prayer.
Paperback Book, 210p. ISBN 1-56043-106-7 Retail $8.99

WHATEVER HAPPENED TO THE POWER OF GOD
Why are the seriously ill seldom healed? Why do people fall in the Spirit yet remain unchanged? Why can believers speak in tongues and wage spiritual warfare without impacting society? This book confronts you with its life-changing answers.
Paperback Book, 210p. ISBN 1-56043-042-7 Retail $8.99

Available at your local Christian bookstore.

Internet: http://www.reapernet.com

Prices subject to change without notice.

Destiny Image
Revival Books

IT'S TIME
by Richard Crisco.
"We say that 'Generation X' does not know what they are searching for in life. But we are wrong. They know what they desire. We, as the Church, are the ones without a revelation of what they need." It is time to stop entertaining our youth with pizza parties and start training an army for God. Find out in this dynamic book how the Brownsville youth have exploded with revival power...affecting the surrounding schools and communities!
Paperback Book, 182p. ISBN 1-56043-690-5 Retail $8.99

A TOUCH OF GLORY
by Lindell Cooley.
This book was written for the countless "unknowns" who, like Lindell Cooley, are being plucked from obscurity for a divine work of destiny. Here Lindell, the worship leader of the Brownsville Revival, tells of his own journey from knowing God's hand was upon him to trusting Him. The key to personal revival is a life-changing encounter with the living God. There is no substitute for a touch of His glory.
Paperback Book, 182p. ISBN 1-56043-689-1 Retail $8.99

THE GOD MOCKERS
And Other Messages From the Brownsville Revival
by Stephen Hill.
Hear the truth of God as few men have dared to tell it! In his usual passionate and direct manner, Evangelist Steve Hill directs people to an uncompromised Christian life of holiness. The messages in this book will burn through every hindrance that keeps you from going further in God!
Paperback Book, 182p. ISBN 1-56043-691-3 Retail $8.99

THE POWER OF BROKENNESS
by Don Nori.
Accepting Brokenness is a must for becoming a true vessel of the Lord, and is a stepping-stone to revival in our hearts, our homes, and our churches. Brokenness alone brings us to the wonderful revelation of how deep and great our Lord's mercy really is. Join this companion who leads us through the darkest of nights. Discover the *Power of Brokenness*.
Paperback Book, 168p. ISBN 1-56043-178-4 Retail $8.99

Available at your local Christian bookstore.

Internet: http://www.reapernet.com

Prices subject to change without notice.

Destiny Image
Revival Books

WHEN THE HEAVENS ARE BRASS
by John Kilpatrick.
Pastor John Kilpatrick wanted something more. He began to pray, but it seemed like the heavens were brass. The lessons he learned over the next seven years helped birth a mighty revival in Brownsville Assembly of God that is sweeping through this nation and the world. The dynamic truths in this book could birth life-changing revival in your own life and ministry!
Paperback Book, 168p. ISBN 1-56043-190-3 (6" X 9") Retail $9.99

WHITE CANE RELIGION
And Other Messages From the Brownsville Revival
by Stephen Hill.
In less than two years, Evangelist Stephen Hill has won nearly 100,000 to Christ while preaching repentance, forgiveness, and the power of the blood in what has been called "The Brownsville Revival" in Pensacola, Florida. Experience the anointing of the best of this evangelist's life-changing revival messages in this dynamic book!
Paperback Book, 182p. ISBN 1-56043-186-5 Retail $8.99

PORTAL IN PENSACOLA
by Renee DeLoriea.
What is happening in Pensacola, Florida? Why are people from all over the world streaming to one church in this city? The answer is simple: *Revival!* For more than a year, Renee DeLoriea has lived in the midst of the revival at Brownsville Assembly of God. *Portal in Pensacola* is her firsthand account of this powerful move of the Spirit that is illuminating and transforming the lives of thousands!
Paperback Book, 182p. ISBN 1-56043-189-X Retail $8.99

Available at your local Christian bookstore.

Internet: http://www.reapernet.com

Prices subject to change without notice.